Climate Consciousness and Environmental Activism in Composition

ECOCRITICAL THEORY AND PRACTICE

Series Editor: Douglas A. Vakoch, METI

Advisory Board:
Sinan Akilli, Cappadocia University, Turkey; Bruce Allen, Seisen University, Japan; Zélia Bora, Federal University of Paraíba, Brazil; Izabel Brandão, Federal University of Alagoas, Brazil; Byron Caminero-Santangelo, University of Kansas, USA; Chia-ju Chang, Brooklyn College, The City College of New York, USA; H. Louise Davis, Miami University, USA; Simão Farias Almeida, Federal University of Roraima, Brazil; George Handley, Brigham Young University, USA; Steven Hartman, Mälardalen University, Sweden; Isabel Hoving, Leiden University, The Netherlands; Idom Thomas Inyabri, University of Calabar, Nigeria; Serenella Iovino, University of Turin, Italy; Daniela Kato, Kyoto Institute of Technology, Japan; Petr Kopecký, University of Ostrava, Czech Republic; Bei Liu, Shandong Normal University, People's Republic of China; Serpil Oppermann, Cappadocia University, Turkey; John Ryan, University of New England, Australia; Christian Schmitt-Kilb, University of Rostock, Germany; Joshua Schuster, Western University, Canada; Heike Schwarz, University of Augsburg, Germany; Murali Sivaramakrishnan, Pondicherry University, India; Scott Slovic, University of Idaho, USA; Heather Sullivan, Trinity University, USA; David Taylor, Stony Brook University, USA; J. Etienne Terblanche, North-West University, South Africa; Julia Tofantšuk, Tallinn University, Estonia; Cheng Xiangzhan, Shandong University, China; Hubert Zapf, University of Augsburg, Germany

Ecocritical Theory and Practice highlights innovative scholarship at the interface of literary/cultural studies and the environment, seeking to foster an ongoing dialogue between academics and environmental activists.

Recent Titles
Climate Consciousness and Environmental Activism in Composition: Writing to Save the World edited by Joseph R. Lease
Rethinking Nathaniel Hawthorne and Nature: Ecocriticism and the Tangled Landscape of American Romance by Steven Petersheim
Ecocritical Concerns and the Australian Continent edited by Beate Neumeier and Helen Tiffin
The Poetics and Politics of Gardening in Hard Times edited by Naomi Milthorpe
Masculinity and Place in American Literature since 1950 by Vidya Ravi
The Way the Earth Writes: How the Great East Japan Earthquake Intervened in Conventional Literary Practice and Produced the Post 3.11 Novels by Koichi Haga
Ecomasculinities: Negotiating Male Gender Identity in U.S. Fiction by Rubén Cenamor and Stefan Brandt
Ecopoetics and the Global Landscape: Critical Essays by Isabel Sobral Campos
The Human-Animal Boundary: Exploring the line in Philosophy and Fiction edited by Mario Wenning and Nandita Batra
Towards the River's Mouth (Verso la foce), Gianni Celati, A Critical Edition edited, translated, and introduced by Patrick Barron
Gender and Environment in Science Fiction edited by Bridgitte Barclay and Christy Tidwell
Ecological Crisis and Cultural Representation in Latin America: Ecocritical Perspectives on Art, Film, and Literature edited by Mark Anderson and Zelia M. Bora
Confronting Climate Crises through Education: Reading Our Way Forward by Rebecca Young
Environment and Pedagogy in Higher Education edited by Lucie Viakinnou-Brinson

Climate Consciousness and Environmental Activism in Composition

Writing to Save the World

Edited by Joseph R. Lease

LEXINGTON BOOKS
Lanham • Boulder • New York • London

Published by Lexington Books
An imprint of The Rowman & Littlefield Publishing Group, Inc.
4501 Forbes Boulevard, Suite 200, Lanham, Maryland 20706
www.rowman.com

Unit A, Whitacre Mews, 26-34 Stannary Street, London SE11 4AB

Copyright © 2020 The Rowman & Littlefield Publishing Group, Inc.

All rights reserved. No part of this book may be reproduced in any form or by any electronic or mechanical means, including information storage and retrieval systems, without written permission from the publisher, except by a reviewer who may quote passages in a review.

British Library Cataloguing in Publication Information Available

Library of Congress Cataloging-in-Publication Data

Names: Lease, Joseph R., 1977- editor.
Title: Climate consciousness and environmental activism in composition : writing to save the world / edited by Joseph R. Lease.
Description: Lanham : Lexington Books, 2020. | Series: Ecocritical theory and practice | Includes bibliographical references and index. | Summary: "This volume addresses the pressing need to continue the work of bringing sustainability into the college classroom. It provides accounts from a variety of instructors' experiences with and best practices for incorporating climate change issues into writing-intensive courses"— Provided by publisher.
Identifiers: LCCN 2019057303 (print) | LCCN 2019057304 (ebook) | ISBN 9781498528825 (cloth) | ISBN 9781498528849 (paper) | ISBN 9781498528832 (epub)
Subjects: LCSH: English language—Rhetoric—Study and teaching. | Natural history—Authorship—Study and teaching. | Environmental literature—Authorship—Study and teaching. | Ecology—Authorship—Study and teaching. | Interdisciplinary approach in education. | Academic writing—Study and teaching. | Nature study.
Classification: LCC PE1404 .C5455 2020 (print) | LCC PE1404 (ebook) | DDC 808/.042071—dc23
LC record available at https://lccn.loc.gov/2019057303
LC ebook record available at https://lccn.loc.gov/2019057304

Contents

Introduction: Now More than Ever   1
Joseph R. Lease

1   Sustainability and Writing: Radishes, Scythes, Thoreau, and Students   7
Ron Balthazor

2   Ecotopia Revisited in Image: The Imagined (and Enacted) Peril and Promise of Portland   29
Hill Taylor

3   "meanderings to the river": A Sustainable Approach to Teaching Sustainability in First-Year Composition   51
Deborah Church Miller, Lindsay Tigue, and Kim Waters

4   Reflecting on Action and Acting on Reflection: High-Impact Practices for Transformative Learning in Sustainability   89
Justin Rademaekers and Cheryl Wanko

5   Design Thinking and Sustainability Problem Solving: Reconceptualizing a First-Year Writing-Intensive Seminar   115
Joseph R. Lease, Matthew R. Martin, and Joanne Chu

6   Creating Sustainability through Creativity: Using Creative Writing to Reframe and Build Connections   129
Lesley Hawkes

7   East to West: The Interconnectedness of All Things Created   151
Pamela Herron

| 8 | "Against Sustainability": And Other Provocations for a First-Year Writing-Intensive Seminar
Abby L. Goode | 175 |

Bibliography	197
Index	211
About the Contributors	215

Introduction
Now More than Ever
Joseph R. Lease

It has been nearly twenty years since Christian Weisser and Sidney Dobrin released their highly influential *Ecocomposition: Theoretical and Pedagogical Approaches*, initiating a surge in interest in bringing environmental issues into the classroom.[1] In spite of these efforts to raise awareness and encourage students toward action, somehow, incredibly, the United States is going backward in its efforts to lessen its contributions toward human-influenced climate change. Perhaps even worse is the evidence that most Americans still do not understand either the full urgency of the situation or the consensus with which the world's scientific community agrees about climate change. According to the Yale Program on Climate Change Communication, even those Americans who are most concerned about the issue fall "well short" in their estimates of the percentage of scientists who agree that "human-caused global warming is happening," a gap they attribute in part to "misinformation campaigns that have spread doubt about climate change."[2] Of course, this problem is global and does not belong to just one country, but, if the United States will not do its part to combat human caused climate change, then the whole world will suffer.

    The hows and whys of these circumstances are important, but, for educators the most critical question is: *What can we do to help*? One viable thing we can do is to continue to seek out best practices for bringing sustainability issues into our classes in order to keep challenging students to develop empathy for our planet and all who live on it. In this volume, instructors from all over the United States, and one from Australia, have contributed works describing their best efforts to build a sense of urgency and responsibility around climate change and sustainability practices in their writing classrooms. But "Why writing classrooms?" you may ask. Well, why not? There is no more important issue in our world today than human-caused climate change, and getting students to think, discuss, and *write* about these problems can be a powerful catalyst for change, not only in their lives but also in the life and health of our planet.

In chapter 1, "Sustainability and Writing: Radishes, Scythes, Thoreau, and Students," Ron Balthazor starts the discussion off with a reminder of the importance of place and how it should be considered in all actions. His chapter aims to dig down to the root of connections between sustainability and composition through an extended metaphor comparing gardening to writing. Then, he provides a description of an assignment that helps students bring that metaphor into real life and practice by getting out into nature to write about what happens to them, what they observe, and why it matters.

Next, Hill Taylor's "Ecotopia Revisited in Image: The Imagined (and Enacted) Peril and Promise of Portland" continues this place-based emphasis on sustainability. He opens by arguing that overcoming complacency and exhaustion in students who have been bombarded with messaging about environmental crises all their lives is an extremely challenging task. However, by offering students opportunities to argue both from a situated rhetorical position and with particular focus, Taylor has found a way to reengage his students in sustainability-themed courses. The key is getting students to envision a utopic environment clearly enough that they become emotionally invested in working toward it. Beginning with Ernest Callenbahk's *Ecotopia* as a shared text, his class allows students studying in Portland, Oregan, to focus on their immediate surroundings as they seek out connections between their city and the novel. These observations are then shared with the class via student-captured photographs of things and places in their daily lives that either strongly align or contrast with *Ecotopia*. This action-oriented course work has led to increased student engagement, through writing, with local environmental issues that they see as both laudable and lamentable.

Chapter 3 is "'meanderings to the river': A Sustainable Approach to Teaching Sustainability in First-Year Composition," by Deborah Church Miller, Lindsay Tigue, and Kim Waters. These coauthors offer the perspectives of a writing program administrator, a creative writer, and a linguist, respectively, on how they have incorporated sustainability into the University of Georgia's (UGA) First-year Composition (FYC) program. Inspired by the UGA Office of Sustainability's syllabus workshop, which included a tour of areas on campus where the university is confronting issues of sustainability, Church Miller discusses how she set out to develop a sustainability-themed sample syllabus for a program that employs nearly one hundred composition instructors. She explains how she learned along the way, however, that helping instructors envision and develop their own syllabi and assignments, via a similar tour and resource workshop, was much more effective than providing the syllabus herself. Tigue and Waters then follow with their own accounts of how the sustainability workshop helped them develop their own eco-themed FYC courses at UGA. Ultimately, Church Miller's vision has been realized, and there is now a clear path for FYC instructors to create sustainability-themed courses with consistency across the UGA program.

Next is "Reflecting on Action and Acting on Reflection: High-Impact Practices for Transformative Learning in Sustainability," by Justin Rademaekers and Cheryl Wanko, who discuss an experiential learning assignment in which they ask students to live a "no impact" lifestyle for one week, modeled on an experiment developed by Colin Beavan. Students document the experience through reflective writing, hopefully meeting Rademaekers's and Wanko's goal of having a transformative learning experience. The authors note, though, that assessing transformative change is difficult, and creating pedagogical practices that can lead to higher levels of transformational learning is even more challenging. In response, they finish their chapter with a series of suggestions to help facilitate a deeply meaningful experience for students in a sustainability-themed, writing-intensive course.

In Chapter 5, "Design Thinking and Sustainability Problem Solving: Reconceptualizing a First-Year, Writing-Intensive Seminar," Joseph R. Lease, Matthew R. Martin, and Joanne Chu recount the redesign of a first-year, writing-intensive seminar that was already tasked with developing students' research writing skills to include a sustainability component in response to a campus-wide goal for environmental education. In order to facilitate this merging of student learning outcomes, they chose to incorporate design Thinking (DT) into the course both to help students avoid the phenomenon of compassion fade by building empathy for an individual in need and to give them problem solving skills for local and global sustainability issues. Merging the iterative, creative nature of DT with writing assignments that would not steal momentum from the students' projects proved a challenging task. However, the teaching team settled on a pair of papers and a reflective portfolio, detailed in the chapter, that could be used as shared assignments across all sections of the course in order to ensure that students were getting similar instruction and skill-building opportunities throughout the semester. Ultimately, the composition work students undertook in the course proved an effective means of getting them to think deeply about the sustainability-themed issues of their individual course section while maintaining focus on the user they were solving for in their DT work.

Lesley Hawkes takes things in a different direction in chapter 6, "Creating Sustainability through Creativity: Using Creative Writing to Reframe and Build Connections," by discussing how she has brought sustainability issues into a creative writing course. Hawkes introduces an approach she uses at Australia's Queensland University of Technology that asks students to combine a focus on place and theory in order to apply what they have learned about ecocriticism in a practical way. This emphasis on bioregion among her creative writing students helps them challenge anthropocentric assumptions they may have had when starting the class. Through a series of reading and writing exercises, students learn to challenge the binary thinking that leads so many to dismiss Nature as less important than human concerns because of its nonhuman status. While her students do struggle to create nonhuman voices and perspectives in their writing, Hawkes concludes that this methodology is worthy of further study.

In chapter 7, "East to West—The Interconnectedness of All Things Created," Pamela Herron recounts her efforts to create a course called "Dao De Jing and the Environment at the University of Texas at El Paso," which at the time of the class's inception had no environmentally themed courses outside of those in environmental science. Drawing on her extensive background teaching classes related to Chinese and Asian literatures and cultures, Herron discusses building on the Eastern emphasis on the interconnectedness of all things in order to heighten awareness in her students about looming environmental disaster. Writing in the course combines low-stakes assignments, such as student wikis and discussion board posts, with more formal paper assignments, and all elements merge to create an atmosphere that can reorient her students' thinking toward meaningful, sustainability-centered change.

Finally, Abby Goode closes out the volume with a challenge to all instructors who want to bring sustainability issues into their classrooms. In "'Against Sustainability': And Other Provocations for a First-Year Writing-Intensive Seminar," Goode provides ways for teachers to test, with our students, the notion that many of the daily things we do to be sustainable help at all, noting that other fields have moved ahead of Composition when it comes to providing honest yet tough critiques of sustainability so that students can move toward more meaningful engagement with environmental action. Following an extensive review of the scholarship of ecocomposition, Goode recounts her experience designing and piloting a writing-intensive seminar in which she catered writing assignments to help her students begin to critique sustainability, culminating in proposals for sustainability initiatives to make real, meaningful change on their campus.

My sincere hope is that the ideas and instructional practices in this volume will inspire our colleagues to reenvision how they incorporate sustainability into their courses. If not, I urge readers to keep searching until they find something that will work for them. The stakes are too high to do otherwise. Now, more than ever, we must encourage our students to think, talk, and write about the problems they see in the world around them, and we must convince them that they can do something to make those problems better. In twenty-first-century composition, we are writing to save the world, and we must not fail, else we risk losing everything.

NOTES

1. Christian R. Weisser and Sidney I. Dobrin, eds., *Ecocomposition: Theoretical and Pedagogical Approaches* (Albany: State University Press of New York, 2001).

2. "Even Americans Highly Concerned about Climate Change Dramatically Underestimate the Scientific Consensus," Yale Program on Climate Change Communication, accessed July 29, 2019, https://climatecommunication.yale.edu/publications/even-americans-highly-concerned-about-climate-change-dramatically-underestimate-the-scientific-consensus/.

Chapter One

Sustainability and Writing
Radishes, Scythes, Thoreau, and Students

Ron Balthazor

PART 1: FROM COMPOSE TO COMPOST

To build, to plant, whatever you intend,
To rear the column, or the arch to bend,
To swell the terrace, or to sink the grot;
In all, let Nature never be forgot.
But treat the goddess like a modest fair,
Nor overdress, nor leave her wholly bare;
Let not each beauty ev'rywhere be spied,
Where half the skill is decently to hide.
He gains all points, who pleasingly confounds,
Surprises, varies, and conceals the bounds.
Consult the genius of the place in all;
That tells the waters or to rise, or fall;
Or helps th' ambitious hill the heav'ns to scale,
Or scoops in circling theatres the vale;
Calls in the country, catches opening glades,
Joins willing woods, and varies shades from shades,
Now breaks, or now directs, th' intending lines;
Paints as you plant, and, as you work, designs.

—Alexander Pope[1]

It is an old idea, though perhaps often forgotten, that we should "let Nature never be forgot" and "Consult the genius of the place in all." Pope's *Epistle* is as much about taste as gardening, though we should take him at his word that we should seek nature's genius through a deep awareness of processes of place in all that we do. In fact, nature has served as guide to much of the human experience, from the Pentateuch to *Pilgrim at Tinker Creek*.

Many years ago a friend and colleague asked why I hadn't pursued a tenure track position. I told him it would get in the way of my gardening. I have, over the years, discovered that gardening and scholarship needn't be mutually exclusive; indeed, in so many ways, books are ecologies, you might say gardens themselves, literally and metaphorically. Seen contrapose, I have found much in my life, letters, and teaching by returning almost daily to what Wendell Berry calls "the dumb life of roots."[2] At the very roots of my thinking, our words, our texts, and our books have always been bound to the soil. To begin to imagine the relationship of sustainability to composition, to imagine a fruitful composition for ourselves or for our students, perhaps we should start by digging about in the soil of composing, exploring the roots of writing by looking at the tangled bank of etymologies. So I'll begin with a most playful etymology, that of the radish.

> Etymology: Originally < classical Latin *rādīc-*, *rādīx*, with palatalization of the final plosive in English. Subsequently reinforced by Anglo-Norman *radich*, Anglo-Norman and Middle French *radice* (13th cent. in Anglo-Norman; an assumption of currency in Old French in the late 12th cent. appears to be unfounded; French *radis*) < classical Latin *rādīc-*, *rādīx*.[3]

The radish is a root word in every way; its etymology points to *radix,* the Latin for "root." The root word for "radish" is "root," as if when vegetables were first named, radish was first in line and was simply named what it is. Fundamentally, the definition of "radish" or "root" includes its relation to the soil; a root is, by definition, underground. In its second definition of "root," the *Oxford English Dictionary* (OED) makes the systemic interconnection explicit: "The part of a plant or tree, normally underground, which attaches it to the ground (or other supporting medium) and conveys water and nutrients from the ground to the body of the plant or tree; an individual branch of a system of such parts." Not only is the root in the ground, but it is deeply connected to the ground. "Root," as you might expect, has an old and complex etymology, which leads, albeit circuitously, to "wyrt" and an all too appropriate OED twist: "for the history of the spelling and pronunciation, see the note to WORM n."[4]

Like the nearly infinite interconnection of words offered by the OED to craft linguistic context for the word "root," the soil (including its rich web of the roots of other plants often working in concert, fungi extending the reach and relations of those roots, and bacteria, worms, and a near infinite catalogue of organisms) is in rich relationship with roots; it is the stuff of ecology. Over the years in the garden, my own focus, my own sense of the use of soil, has shifted. Standard garden culture has for generations considered soil the canvas for the garden's painting of plants. I have come to learn, though, that the soil is no more flat than the web of words that envelop "radish" or "root." Soil scientists and microbiologists are only now scratching the surface of what is called the "soil food web," the most complex community of organisms and interactions that facilitate the life of plants. Healthy soil is a community in conversation, a true ecosystem, with all the basic requirements of life generally: water, air, and food. We would be wise to feed the soil, not merely the plants that live in it.

In his *Fundamentals of Ecology,* as Betty Jean Craige notes, Eugene Odum defines an ecosystem as "a system composed of biotic communities and their abiotic environment interacting with each other."[5] Odum himself often called upon the metaphor of the theater to explain it, noting that is it not merely the players we are interested in, but the relationships of players with each other, the relationship of players and the sets, the music, and even the audience. Most often considered the father of modern ecology, Odum was fond of reminding us that at the root of "ecology" is the Greek *oikos* for "household," and its sister "economy" is you might say the management of the household. The shift from biology to ecology is one of relationships; we as ecologists (in research somewhat analogous to that of linguists) no longer simply investigate the radish, but rather the radish in context, in the soil system that surrounds it. The radish is no less a part of the ecology of the soil than "radish" is in this sentence (until it is removed from the soil and begins to die). This root is fundamentally a node of complex interactions and part of a larger set of complex interactions (even as sentences are essentially part of the larger complex interaction of the paragraph, the essay, etc.).

We have long known that an ecosystem of words lives in our books. The root of "book" nods, in a way, to the origin of writing, at least the household of such an origin:

> Etymology: Cognate with Old Frisian *bōk* book, Old Dutch *buok* large written document, book (Middle Dutch *boec* book, document, Dutch *boek*), Old Saxon *bōk* book, writing tablet (Middle Low German *bōk*, *būk*), Old High German *buoh* book, written text, scripture, (in an isolated attestation) letter of the alphabet (Middle High German *buoch*, German *Buch*), Old Icelandic *bók* book, story, history, Old Swedish *bok* book (Swedish *bok*), Old Danish *bok* book (Danish *bog*), and also (in a different declension: feminine ō -stem) Gothic *bōka* letter (of the alphabet), in plural *bōkōs* also in the sense "(legal) document, book" (perhaps also in singular in this sense, as indicated by the compound *frabauhtabōka* document of sale), probably < the same Germanic base as beech n.[6]

The etymology itself shows the underlying ecology of letters, lines, documents, collections, and even the very source of the page. Of course the book has special and spiritual possibilities, but I like best the very end of the etymology, the simple and perfectly logical root in the beech tree. In a turn analogous with our humble radish beginnings, the beech is a fruitful tree.

The following may well be a rhizome too far, but one book whose roots depend upon a tree with edible fruit is Genesis. The Pentateuch is one of the first stories of a people's connection to the soil, and much of the text works to establish a people's right relation to the land. Duke theologian Ellen Davis writes in *Scripture, Culture, and Agriculture* that "God formed the human being ['adam], from dust from the fertile soil ['adama]."[7] She notes that the wordplay is "captured surprisingly well by the English pun 'humans from humus.'" Davis emphasizes, as the Hebrew suggests, a comparable color of skin and soil. She notes that the language "evokes the specific relationship between a people and their particular place," perhaps the very first "ecology." To be human, like the radish, is to be of the soil, to be in a rich relationship with the soil, to recognize of what we are composed.

The roots of "compose" ultimately suggest "to put together," the very act of crafting ecology (for do not our words once placed begin to interact with each other). "Compose" itself has a tangled bank of etymology:

> Etymology: < French *compose-r* (12th cent. in Littré), < *com-* together + *poser* to place, put down < Romanic *posare* = late Latin *pausāre* to cease, lie down, lay down, etc.: see pose n.1, repose n. Through form-association with inflections of Latin *pōněre*, *posui*, past participle *positum*, *postum*, Italian *posto*, Old French *post*, *pos*, and contact of sense, this *-poser* came to be treated as a synonym of Old French *-pondre*, and finally took its place in the compounds, so that *composer* to *compose* is now used instead of *compondre* to *compone*, *compound*, and naturally associated with *compositor*, *composition*, *compost*.[8]

As writers, to follow the most apparent etymological thread, we place words together, though we probably prefer to imagine the action of "placing" rather than the Latin suggestion of "reposing," unless we embrace the notion of composing as ceasing to wrestle with ideas or finding the words on the page as completion. The definitions are more satisfying: "To make by putting together parts or elements: to make up, form, frame, fashion, construct, produce" and "To fashion, frame (the human body, etc.)." The analogy between composing and gardening becomes more powerful, the more you know about the nature of gardening and the soil.

A good compost is quite literally the best food for the whole community of souls residing in the soil, cycling nutrients and crafting pathways for other organisms. A compost, as the OED defines it, is first "a composition, combination, compound," second, "a stew of various ingredients," and third, "a mixture of various ingredients for fertilizing or enriching land, a prepared manure or mould." Jed Rasula, in his introduction to *This Compost*, begins with Thoreau. His book is an ecological meditation on poetry, a literary compost itself. Rasula writes (and in true composting fashion, my quotation quotes and recycles other quotes):

> "All our literatures are leavings," writes Gary Snider (Practice of the Wild, 112) recycling Thoreau's remark "Decayed literature makes the richest of all soils" ... *Walden*, that prospectus of wild moods, is a compost of rhetorical jubilation Thoreau prepared with geophysical patience. The years he spent writing *Walden* are testimony to a composting sensibility.... Thoreau's palpable delight in the Homeric battle of the ants is not just pleasure in the rhetorical inversion, but reverence for microcosms rendered visible in the scale of human prejudice, revisiting old paradigms of what Melville called our mortal inter-indebtedness.[9]

Citing Thoreau's battle of the ants may seem a curious beginning for a text fundamentally about poetry, but Rasula, I suspect, is intent on drawing (or intends to draw) insight from the residents of the soil itself and the remarkable chemistry of mortal interindebtedness: the life and death of ants cast in classical attire for a particularly moral purpose. Thoreau in "Brute Neighbors" writes:

> They fought with more pertinacity than bulldogs. Neither manifested the least disposition to retreat. It was evident that their battle-cry was "Conquer or die." In the meanwhile there came along a single red ant on the hillside of this valley, evidently full of excitement, who either had despatched his foe, or had not yet taken part in the battle; probably the latter, for he had lost none of his limbs; whose mother had charged him to return with his shield or upon it. Or perchance he was some Achilles, who had nourished his wrath apart, and had now come to avenge or rescue his Patroclus. He saw this unequal combat from afar—for the blacks were nearly twice the size of the red—he drew near with rapid pace till he stood on his guard within half an inch of the combatants; then, watching his opportunity, he sprang upon the black warrior, and commenced his operations near the root of his right fore leg, leaving the foe to select among his own members; and so there were three united for life, as if a new kind of attraction had been invented which put all other locks and cements to shame. I should not have wondered by this time to find that they had their respective musical bands stationed on some eminent chip, and playing their national airs the while, to excite the slow and cheer the dying combatants. I was myself excited somewhat even as if they had been men. The more you think of it, the less the difference.[10]

E. O. Wilson, in the extended apostrophe that introduces this text *The Future of Life*, offers correction to Thoreau's Homeric observation:

> May I presume to tell you what you saw? It was a slave raid. The slavers were the red ants, most likely *Formica subintegra*, and the victims were the black ants, probably *Formica subsericea*. The red ants capture the infants of their

victims, or more precisely, their cocoon-clad pupae. Back in the red-ant nest the kidnapped pupae complete their development and emerge from their cocoons as adult workers. Then, because they instinctively accept the first workers they meet as nestmates, they enter into voluntary servitude to their captors. Imagine that! A slave raid at the doorstep of one of America's most ardent abolitionists. For millions of years this harsh Darwinian strategy has prevailed, and so will it ever be, with no hope that a Lincoln, a Thoreau, or an Underground Railroad might arise in the formicid world to save the victim colonies.[11]

Mortal interindebtedness indeed. Rasula's nimble mind turns a playful collection of texts into a fruitful medium for thought, a complex mixture that in a heat, transforms into the stuff of new life, or here, new poetry, new truth. As an environmental text, Rasula's description of *Walden* seems perfect: "a compost of rhetorical jubilation prepared with geophysical patience."

The title of Rasula's work recycles Whitman as he celebrates the earth in his poem "This Compost," a strange verse on death . . . and life. Whitman's poem, like a vulture, seeks fundamentally to transform death into new life literally, to discover and present a curious transcendence (vultures are of the family Cathartidae and are thus etymologically related to cartharsis (which of course comes from the Greek to cleanse or purge)). Whitman sings,

> SOMETHING startles me where I thought I was safest;
> I withdraw from the still woods I loved;
> I will not go now on the pastures to walk;
> I will not strip the clothes from my body to meet my lover the sea;
> I will not touch my flesh to the earth, as to other flesh, to renew me.
> O how can it be that the ground does not sicken?
> How can you be alive, you growths of spring?
> How can you furnish health, you blood of herbs, roots, orchards, grain?
> Are they not continually putting distemper'd corpses within you?
> Is not every continent work'd over and over with sour dead?
> Where have you disposed of their carcasses?
> Those drunkards and gluttons of so many generations;
> Where have you drawn off all the foul liquid and meat;
> I do not see any of it upon you to-day—or perhaps I am deceiv'd;
> I will run a furrow with my plough—I will press my spade through the sod, and turn it up underneath;
> I am sure I shall expose some of the foul meat.[12]

In these opening lines, Whitman's nature is not the stuff of sunsets, is far from romantic facade; rather nature seems only a repository of decay. It is as if he woke from a dream in which nature seemed a grocery store chicken breast, carefully packaged on styrofoam and wrapped in plastic, a kind of nature that wants to forget that blood ever ran through its veins. The poor poet no longer has our culture's infinite ability to deny ugliness. He has, you might say, lost his ability to eat processed food.

    Whitman was born on Long Island, and he was a great lover of the city. By the 1830s, nearly 250,000 people lived in New York, and municipal sanitation was extremely limited. In 1832, 3,500 people died of cholera.[13] Certainly Whitman's poem responds in some ways to the ugly side of city life. Life in the early nineteenth century was not so very sanitized. Moreover, he revised and expanded his collection *Leaves of Grass* throughout his life, and though "This Compost!" is written prior to the Civil War, it seems to me perfectly appropriate to imagine this poem as a response to the horrors of the war as well. Whitman knew of the bodily carnage intimately as he volunteered as a nurse during the war. At the close of the war, I can only imagine the line "How can you be alive, you growths of spring?" taking on profound new meaning. The transcendental vultures are at work. Cleansing is at hand.

> Behold this compost! behold it well!
> Perhaps every mite has once form'd part of a sick person—Yet behold!
> The grass of spring covers the prairies,
> The bean bursts noiselessly through the mould in the garden,
> The delicate spear of the onion pierces upward,
> The apple-buds cluster together on the apple-branches,
> The resurrection of the wheat appears with pale visage out of its graves,
> The tinge awakes over the willow-tree and the mulberry-tree,
> The he-birds carol mornings and evenings, while the birds sit on their nests,
> The young of poultry break through the hatch'd eggs,
> The new-born of animals appear—the calf is dropt from the cow, the colt from the mare,
> Out of its little hill faithfully rise the potato's dark green leaves,
> Out of its hill rises the yellow maize-stalk—the lilacs bloom in the door-yards;
> The summer growth is innocent and disdainful above all those strata of sour dead.
> What chemistry!
> That the winds are really not infectious,
> That this is no cheat, this transparent green-wash of the sea, which is so amorous after me,
> That it is safe to allow it to lick my naked body all over with its tongues,
> That it will not endanger me with the fevers that have deposited themselves in it,
> That all is clean forever and forever,
> That the cool drink from the well tastes so good,
> That blackberries are so flavorous and juicy,
> That the fruits of the apple-orchard, and of the orange-orchard—that melons, grapes, peaches, plums, will none of them poison me,
> That when I recline on the grass I do not catch any disease,
> Though probably every spear of grass rises out of what was once a catching disease.

The Christian sacraments raise the pedestrian to the sacred. Shared bread becomes the Eucharist, a bath is baptism. When Ash Wednesday returns we will hear "to dust you shall return." Yet, how can we see death as holy? How is death transformed save in resurrection? These theological musings are of a mind with Whitman, though he might be offering faith for the coming age of Darwin. His "Behold" has biblical weight even as the miracle is purely ecological. Death is transformed in the soil, in compost. The encomium to Lincoln, "the lilacs bloom in the door-yards," isn't added until the 1871 edition and draws even the carnage of the Civil War into Whitman's universe of death transformed. We have manured our fields for six thousand years. We eat the fruit of death daily, or we eat not at all. In this poetic figure, every field is cemetery. The remarkable Whitman carries us over in a metaphoric and literal resurrection with the miracle of soil.

> Now I am terrified at the Earth! it is that calm and patient,
> It grows such sweet things out of such corruptions,
> It turns harmless and stainless on its axis, with such endless successions of diseas'd corpses,
> It distils such exquisite winds out of such infused fetor,
> It renews with such unwitting looks, its prodigal, annual, sumptuous crops,
> It gives such divine materials to men, and accepts such leavings from them at last.

The fruit of summer is liminal, the very "divine material" Whitman speaks of. When we pick fruit of any kind, when we remove it from its ecosystem, we stop its source of life and it begins to die. Fruit perfectly ripe calls to us to be picked that we might spread its seed; all our gardening is symbiosis. I am completely seduced by blueberries, cantaloupe, and tomatoes. Once picked, all the works of death begin, not the least of which happens in my stomach. For we most local of locavores, life and death meet intensely when we eat in the garden: the most life, the most death. The best fruit has no shelf life (now there's a pun worthy of Thoreau, no?). We must embrace the seasons, celebrate the slant of the planet, the collision of life and death in a perfectly picked tomato, and the promise of next year in the mound of death we call compost. And in the most simple miracle of spring, we will plant radishes.

PART 2: MYSTIC, TRANSCENDENTALIST, AND NATURAL PHILOSOPHER

> There was never a sound beside the wood but one,
> And that was my long scythe whispering to the ground.

> What was it it whispered? I knew not well myself;
> Perhaps it was something about the heat of the sun,
> Something, perhaps, about the lack of sound—
> And that was why it whispered and did not speak.
> It was no dream of the gift of idle hours,
> Or easy gold at the hand of fay or elf:
> Anything more than the truth would have seemed too weak
> To the earnest love that laid the swale in rows,
> Not without feeble-pointed spikes of flowers
> (Pale orchises), and scared a bright green snake.
> The fact is the sweetest dream that labor knows.
> My long scythe whispered and left the hay to make. —Robert Frost[14]

In the fall of 2013, I went to a gardening workshop in which the instructor brought his scythe. He let me pretend to mow the linoleum of the botanical garden's education room. It was more than just my silly desire to spend Halloween as the Grim Reaper; I was intrigued by a technology probably as old as agriculture itself that still had widespread use into the twentieth century and that had so quickly become so foreign. I had never held a scythe, never seen one save in the movies. In short order, my scythe arrived, custom crafted to my height, hip to ground length, and my cubit, the length of the arm from elbow downward. That fall I heard for the first time the whispering of the blade when I mowed my buckwheat.

Sometime after, a colleague who knew of my fascination, invited me to lead a discussion for an environmental ethics seminar on an essay by Paul Kingsnorth entitled "Dark Ecology." Kingsnorth opens the essay discussing his scythe:

> Etymology can be interesting. Scythe, originally rendered sithe, is an Old English word, indicating that the tool has been in use in these islands for at least a thousand years. But archaeology pushes that date much further out; Roman scythes have been found with blades nearly two meters long. Basic, curved cutting tools for use on grass date back at least ten thousand years, to the dawn of agriculture and thus to the dawn of civilizations. Like the tool, the word, too, has older origins. The Proto-Indo-European root of scythe is the word sek, meaning to cut, or to divide. Sek is also the root word of sickle, saw, schism, sex, and science.[15]

The essay by Kingsnorth then goes on to present a provocative posture, ostensibly offering that he has been persuaded by the writings of Theodore Kaczynski, better remembered as the Unibomber. In sum, Kingsnorth uses his scythe to front a fact: namely that the environmental movement is deeply divided. On the one hand are traditional conservationists, those for whom the preservation of wildness is essential, in the most extreme way represented by Ted Kaczynski. On the other hand are the neo-environmentalists, represented by Peter Kareiva, the chief scientist of the Nature Conservancy, who embraces the spirit of the Anthropocene, that there is no wildness per se, and that we should pragmatically use the ecosystem services (as they are now named) nature offers to the fullest. Kareiva means to be as provocative as Kingsnorth, if less elegant in his analogies. In his article "Conservation in the Anthropocene" he writes:

> Scientists have coined a name for our era—the Anthropocene—to emphasize that we have entered a new geological era in which humans dominate every flux and cycle of the planet's ecology and geochemistry. . . . At the same time, the global scale of this transformation has reinforced conservation's intense nostalgia for wilderness and a past of pristine nature. But conservation's continuing focus upon preserving islands of Holocene ecosystems in the age of the Anthropocene is both anachronistic and counterproductive.[16]

All of the above is really an extravagant introduction to a piece in the *Huffington Post* by Jedediah Purdy, a professor at Duke Law school, titled "In the Shit with Thoreau: A *Walden* for the Anthropocene."

Purdy's playful and provocative, if less than family-friendly, title points to the wonders of Thoreau's sandflows at the end of "Spring" in *Walden*. He writes:

> In the ecological mysticism of these passages, there is no essential difference between the earth's bowels and its "living poetry like the leaves of a tree." This vital, filthy, gorgeous unity persuades him that that the earth is alive at every point, and only beginning its passage into future forms. This, in turn, persuades him that the same is true of human lives and institutions—"plastic like clay in the hands of the potter."
>
> Now consider where all this takes place. It is on the cut of a railroad bank, a quarter-mile gash in the earth.[17]

Purdy's essay essentially demythologizes an environmental Thoreau, the poster child for wilderness, the Thoreau of the Sierra Club coffee table book ("In Wildness is the Preservation of the World"), the Thoreau we know more from John Muir than *Walden* and "Walking." He instead offers a Thoreau that is keenly aware of how humanity has disturbed nature, how we have "ruptured" it and "profaned" it. He writes that *Walden*'s key passages, like the sandflow, actually begin with and essentially depend upon rupture:

> It may be that even to think of nature, let alone act on it, is to make it a joint product of human and natural activity, so that even to come to the pond is to

profane it, but profanation is simply the condition of the world. It is redeemed, if at all, by our understanding that condition more clearly.

Seen through this Thoreauvian lens, Purdy reminds us that we are living on a planet that is remarkably and irrevocably changed by our activity on it, and we carry the weight of responsibility for understanding the rupture we have created if we hope in any way to redeem it for our children and grandchildren. On our little farm, we are constantly reminded of a humble truth: nothing organic is waste for someone will eat it. Perhaps the truth that Frost's scythe speaks ("anything more than the truth would have seemed too weak") is that we must remain close, even intimate, with the death our deeds instantiate, regardless of how much life it brings. It is Whitman's great truth in "This Compost!" In a way, Purdy is offering a more complex and thoughtful response to the divide cut by Kingsnorth's scythe, between traditional conservation and environmental pragmatism, between the Anthropocene and the Ecozoic (Thomas Berry's positing of an era marked by the reintegration of human endeavors into a larger ecological consciousness). He is saying that Thoreau is a prototypical advocate for sustainability.

What might sustainability mean to Thoreau? Though this text is meant to focus on a more particular and current awareness of "sustainability," "sustain" itself has a rather long and complex history that richly prefigures its current manifestations:

> Etymology: < Anglo-Norman *susteiner, susteigner, sustener, sustigner, sostener*, Anglo-Norman and Old French *sustenir*, Anglo-Norman and Old French, Middle French *soustenir,sostenir*, Old French, Middle French *soutenir* (French *soutenir*) to bear, withstand, endure (c880), to provide food for (c1050), to strengthen (c1100), to bear the weight of, hold up (c1140), (of a person) to stand up, remain standing (c1165), to provide the means of subsistence (for someone) (c1170), to provide moral or psychological support for (someone) (13th cent.), to keep in existence, to perpetuate (early 13th cent.), to continue, to defend, support (an opinion, belief, statement, cause, etc.) (both 1269–1278; compare *soutenir un thèse* (1649)), to bear a charge or expense (1297), to uphold (a person's reputation, honour, etc.) (1340) < classical Latin *sustinēre* to hold up, support, to maintain, preserve, to uphold, to keep from failing or giving way, to support with food or resources, to withstand, to bear the weight of, shoulder, to play the part of, to submit to, endure, to tolerate, to hold back, to put off, defer, in post-classical Latin also to wait for (Vetus Latina) < *sus-* SUB- *prefix* + *tenēre* to hold, keep (see TENANT *n.*).[18]

The Latin roots prefigure nicely any of the various venn diagrams used now to visualize definitions of sustainability (e.g., the intersection of social, economic, and ecological spheres): "to hold up, support, to maintain, preserve, to uphold, to keep from failing or giving way, to support with food or resources, to withstand, to bear the weight of, shoulder, to play the part of, to submit to, endure, to tolerate, to hold back, to put off, defer." It would not be lost on Thoreau that the etymology of "sustain" leads to "tenant" even as the root of "ecology" points to "household." Thoreau, lover of language that he was, often explored the complex interactions of words, of ideas, of lives. The "sandflows" to which Purdy refers offer a remarkable example:

> It is wonderful how rapidly yet perfectly the sand organizes itself as it flows, using the best material its mass affords to form the sharp edges of its channel. Such are the sources of rivers. In the silicious matter which the water deposits is perhaps the bony system, and in the still finer soil and organic matter the fleshy fibre or cellular tissue. What is man but a mass of thawing clay? The ball of the human finger is but a drop congealed. The fingers and toes flow to their extent from the thawing mass of the body. Who knows what the human body would expand and flow out to under a more genial heaven? Is not the hand a spreading palm leaf with its lobes and veins? The ear may be regarded, fancifully, as a lichen, *umbilicaria*, on the side of the head, with its lobe or drop. The lip—*labium*, from *labor* (?)—laps or lapses from the sides of the cavernous mouth. The nose is a manifest congealed drop or stalactite. The chin is a still larger drop, the confluent dripping of the face. The cheeks are a slide from the brows into the valley of the face, opposed and diffused by the cheek bones. Each rounded lobe of the vegetable leaf, too, is a thick and now loitering drop, larger or smaller; the lobes are the fingers of the leaf; and as many lobes as it has, in so many directions it tends to flow, and more heat or other genial influences would have caused it to flow yet farther.[19]

What a remarkable tutorial in integrative thinking. Based on careful and constant observation of nature (though ruptured nature, nature in the wake of the most transformative technology of day, the railroad that passed his humble Walden home), Thoreau fluently moves from physics to physiology, from lips to letters to leaves.

One possible path for exploring the nature of this prototype for contemporary sustainability is the Venn diagram that Thoreau once playfully deployed to describe himself: a Mystic, a Transcendentalist, and a Natural Philosopher to boot. In her book *World as Lover, World as Self*, Joanna Macy unravels deep connections between Buddhism and ecology. She works to construct an integrated and holistic environmentalism. Central to her work is "the greening of the self":

> What Alan Watts called "the skin-encapsulated ego" and Gregory Bateson referred to as "the epistemological error of Occidental civilization" is being unhinged, peeled off. It is being replaced by wider constructs of identity and

self-interest—by what you might call the ecological self or the eco-self, coextensive with other beings and the life of our planet. It is what I will call "the greening of the self."[20]

Her "green self" has many past lives, not the least of which is Henry Thoreau. Thoreau's investment in and affection for "other beings and the life of our planet," albeit primarily the life around Concord, is well-known, from "A Winter Walk" to "Brute Neighbors" to *The Dispersion of Seeds*.

Similarly, William Wolf quotes Bronson Alcott to define the nature of Thoreau's turn of mind: "He is less thinker than observer; a naturalist in tendency but of a mystic habit, and a genius for detecting the essence in form and giving forth the soul of things seen. . . . His mysticism is alike solid and organic, animal and ideal."[21] Wolf goes on to declare that "Thoreau is 'the nature mystic' par excellence." His contemplative practice, no doubt, is to linger in nature where he finds a kind of mystical union with and deep affection for Nature. Thoreau writes: "Nature must be viewed humanly to be viewed at all; that is, her scenes must be associated with humane affections, such as are associated with one's native place, for instance. She is most significant to a lover. A lover of Nature is preeminently a lover of man."[22] Macy's "green self," a holistic and integrated self, a self with permeable boundaries, seems to me perfectly akin to Alcott's mystic, an organic mysticism that grows out of awareness born of great affection. In *The Dispersion of Seeds*, Thoreau lingers over the willow with a kind of care that comes only with great investment, unravelling the mysteries of propagation. He concludes this investigation with the voice of a lover: "Ah willow, willow, would that I always possessed thy good spirits; would that I were as tenacious of life."[23] The detailed investigation leads to what E. O. Wilson would call "biophilia," our deep love of life as seen in the bios.[24] How could such of lover of life not long to sustain it? How could we not long to sustain this home?

Richard Schneider, focusing on ecological succession in Thoreau's *A Week on the Concord and Merrimack Rivers*, shows that Thoreau engaged in integrated ecological thinking throughout his writings. Noting that Thoreau draws a connection between succession in nature and in humans, Schneider quotes Thoreau's *Journal* from October 1837 titled "The Mould our Deeds Leave":

> Every part of nature teaches that the passing away of one life is the making room for another. The oak dies down to the ground, leaving within its rind a rich virgin mould, which will impart a vigorous life to an infant forest—The pine leaves a sandy and sterile soil—the harder woods a strong and fruitful mould.—So this constant abrasion and decay makes the soil of my future growth. As I live now so shall I reap. If I grow pines and birches, my virgin mould will not sustain the

oak, but pines and birches, or, perchance, weeds and bramble, will constitute my second growth.[25]

Schneider goes on to argue that "Our goal, Thoreau suggests, should be to use our successive selves to strive toward a higher consciousness, 'a *purely* sensuous life'" (Thoreau's emphasis). The *Journal* passage, with its model of self-predicated on nature (more particularly, predicated on earth mould) names a particularly Thoreauvian thread of transcendentalism, a transcendentalism less bathed in blithe air than rooted in compost, a transcendentalism with a distinctly green self at the center. The organic mystic above, the great lover of life, now more than analogous to the earth mould, sees a higher order of life, of thought, of consciousness, through a kind of biological transmigration.

Though the late writings of Thoreau are now widely recognized for the value of their natural observations and for his work as a natural philosopher, they proceed from a deeply integrated turn of mind and from his affection for Nature. The mind of Thoreau as natural philosopher is no doubt the product of the earth-mould self above, now home to the seeds of pitch pines. The maturing of his philosophy reveals itself most clearly in *The Dispersion of Seeds*. It is a hybrid self, you might say, or the evolution of a species, the mutation of Thoreau's mind brought about by Darwin; it is a child of the organic mystic, of the earthy transcendentalist, of the environmental theorist. As such, Thoreau indeed speaks in a voice prescient, a voice that resonates with contemporary ecological and sustainability thinking. Thoreau's focus on seeds seems a delightful collision of humility and extravagance. As introduction to his text, with a bit of a prophetic turn, Thoreau notes, "As time elapses and the resources from which our forests have been supplied fail, we too shall of necessity be more and more convinced of the significance of the seed."[26] Here again is Purdy's rupture; here is Whitman's sour dead. Of course the purpose of Thoreau's text generally is to explore the dispersion of seeds, but we see a hint of a larger metonymic move here as the "seed" carries more rhetorical weight, as it suggests rich arrays of metaphoric possibilities even as it becomes the center of natural observation. The seed carries with it the promise of new life, it bares the source of next year's food, it is real hope, practically observed. It is the metaphor of sustainability.

At the very heart of sustainability is a cross-disciplinary wholeness, most often defined as the integration of the ecological, economic, and social spheres; such holistic, integrated thinking runs contrary to our current pedagogical practice, namely our discipline-specific approach to higher education. In sum, we in higher education would do well to learn from Henry Thoreau how to imagine a more integrated and holistic view of education generally, one that would inspire a deeper affection for our world, one that would enliven our discussions of crafting sustainable solutions. Perhaps our curriculum should be reimagined by a mystic, a transcendentalist, and a natural philosopher. For those of us lucky enough to teach composition and literature (particularly writers like Thoreau), it is, when we are at our best, what we have been doing all along.

PART 3: ECOLOGIES IN THE CLASSROOM: OBSERVATION, CONVERSATION, INSIGHT

> In summer, I stalk. Summer leaves obscure, heat dazzles, and creatures hide from the red-eyed sun, and me. I have to seek things out. —Annie Dillard[27]

There is now a twenty-year history of defining sustainability, from the Brudtland Commission to the Earth Charter to the UN's Sustainable Development Goals. Perhaps no definition speaks to me more clearly than my own desire to plant beans with my grandson. A 1997 UNESCO report summarizes a key curricular component of sustainability: "A basic premise of education for sustainability is that just as there is a wholeness and interdependence to life in all its forms, so must there be a unity and wholeness to efforts to understand it and ensure its continuation."[28] "A Call to Action," published by the Association for the Advancement of Sustainability in Higher Education, outlines part of the challenge we face as we work to imagine such a wholeness: "Sustainability is inherently interdisciplinary and the organization of our institutions around departments and disciplines does not always support the kind of curriculum innovation that is needed."[29] In the fall 2012 *Liberal Education Journal of the Association of American Colleges and Universities*, Weisman points out the overlap between education for sustainability and the liberal arts:

> Writing in the *Chronicle of Higher Education* in 2006, then Cornell University President Frank Rhodes proposed that "the concept of sustainability could provide a new foundation for the liberal arts and sciences." While there have been many calls for curricular commitment to sustainability in the past, Rhodes singularly argued for the integral connection between education for sustainability (EfS) and liberal learning. Indeed, he labeled sustainability "the ultimate liberal art."[30]

Weisman further highlights the connection between education for sustainability and the Essential Learning Outcomes identified by the Association of American Colleges and Universities, which includes knowledge of human cultures and of the physical and natural world, skills ranging from critical thinking to problem solving, and the development of personal and social responsibility. Much of the literature about sustainability in the curriculum points to creative pedagogical approaches for reaching the larger programmatic objectives of sustainability.

So practically speaking, how do we meet these objectives in the writing classroom? I have for some years now had the good fortune to teach environmental literature each spring. The course as I have taught it remains rooted in American writers that have a keen eye for nature. The texts are most often a curious kind of hybrid that defies categorization, that perhaps best might be described as Thoreauvian; we indeed linger over several of Thoreau's works. Nature observation is a constant theme. In order to apply or, to a degree, experience this type of nature observation, I require the class periodically to go outside, observe, and then write. As Thoreau notes in his essay "Walking":

> Of course, it is of no use to direct our steps to the woods, if they do not carry us thither. I am alarmed when it happens that I have walked a mile into the woods bodily, without getting there in spirit. In my afternoon walk I would fain forget all my morning occupations, and my obligations to society. But it sometimes happens that I cannot easily shake off the village. The thought of some work will run in my head, and I am not where my body is; I am out of my senses. In my walks I would fain return to my senses. What business have I in the woods, if I am thinking of something out of the woods?[31]

The assignment is quite simple:

> Spend some time in nature. I would prefer that you choose the same place each time as it will be different each time you visit through the term. . . . Any place that would allow you to focus on the natural environment is fine. You should spend at least thirty minutes; some of the time, you should be still, though walking is good as well. . . . Then, write about your time.

The task, however, is incredibly challenging: the students must return to their senses, literally. Good English majors all too easily look for metaphors under every stone. I encourage them to look first, observe, and record what they see, lest they see only metaphor. They need to seek things out; they need to forget all their morning occupations.

Laura Kelly beautifully reflects more than I hoped for in this assignment. She, naturally, begins her first post of the assignment with a detailed observation:

> As I sat in silence, enjoying the juxtaposition of the cool earth with the warm sunshine, I noticed I was joined in my arbor by a variety of birds. To my left

a blue jay hopped busily through the leaves, while a robin poked around the trunk of one of the fallen trees with gusto. I heard the feathery whisper of wings and caught a brief glimpse of brilliant plumage as a cardinal flitted through the tangled bracken. A pleasant variety of birdsong filled the air, and in the distance a woodpecker drummed his steady rhythm into the bark of some tree. As I peered through the canopy above I saw a vulture gliding through the air currents, and even his accustomed gloom seemed cheerful and benign. As these various activities took place around me I felt a strange mixture of significance and insignificance. Life was taking place around me and inside of me; I was both observer and partaker of the simple life-flow that seemed to surround me.

The class must compose a summary reflection of the nature observations for their final portfolio. Here is a portion of Kelly's:

> I learned a lot from these nature observations, more than I can articulate. Through them I reconnected with nature and with myself and grew from the experience. Without this class I would never have spent an evening on the forest floor behind loop ten observing the lichen flakes that littered the ground, or listened to the birdsong in the wooded bracken in the Botanical gardens. I would not have taken the time necessary to reflect on my feelings about the roots of a certain oak sapling and would have instead bottled them up inside where they could offer no comforting insight. This assignment has given me the priceless lesson that nature holds more comfort and wisdom than anything I could watch on TV or even find in a novel, reminding me to step out of my door and open my heart and my eyes to the beauty and wonder outside.

I fundamentally believe that our first source for sustainable solutions, even for clarity on the nature of sustainability problems, is careful observation of nature. The practice of lingering in nature over the practices of nature that natural selection has refined for millennia is powerfully instructive about the beauty and strength of natural systems, what Kelly calls "the simple life-flow." Such lingering is analogous to the work done in the explication of a poem or the exploration of a novel through a variety of theoretical lenses. It takes knowledge and experience, but essentially it takes attention.

In my class, the focus on observing nature hopefully leads to the insights of nature and nature observation as writing exercise. Laura George offers a wonderful reflection of the practice of writing that the nature observations taught her, a practice that ostensibly aligns to entangle natural and textual observations:

> The nature journal was also a writing workshop in that it was a chance to try and mimic our favorite author and thus better our ability to put into words the natural beauty that lay all around us. As I worked on the assignments, both while observing nature and while writing, I felt myself trying to find what Haskell, Leopold

or Dillard might have found and trying to express what I found like those same authors would likely have expressed it. I believe that mimicking authors is a great way not only to learn to write better, but also to learn to see the world in a different perspective. I felt myself looking through the eyes of the authors and I found that what I saw was different than what I had seen moments before when my own eyes remained my looking glass. Perspective is what makes the world what it is to each of us and taking on a new perspective allows us to better understand the world around us in multiple facets.

She sees nature anew by observing nature through a different textual lens, which then transforms her own writing (a psychological and textual rupture that inspires new life). George's ability to take on new perspectives is wonderfully portrayed in the following essay that won a national Walden Woods essay contest:

> First I feel the tiny feet of a small bird that rests his weight gently upon a thin branch. To him I must be a hulking monster, yet perhaps less terrifying than the bitter cold of winter which he likely feels lucky to have evaded today. From his tree branch I am as strange and intriguing to him as he is to me. He knows not, nor would he understand any of my thoughts. The "priorities" of human life would be lost on him. To him I am the object of observation.
>
> Next I morph into a gentle giant: an oak tree. I feel invigorated by the sun as my branches stretch out toward the warmth and energy it offers. Towering high I look down on my human-self in pity. What a short lifespan almighty man is cursed with. And such a fragile body. Yet my human-self trudges so destructively, so heavily over the smaller creatures of the woods; careless. To the tree I am just another human, an animal who thinks herself greater than the rest who pass through the trees' home; by species I am an enemy of the forest. Yet the tree doesn't fear me but instead pities me for my quick transition from life to death; my quick turnover to fertilizer on which his roots can feed.
>
> After taking over the tree's persona I imagine myself as the squirrel who relies on the tree so heavily, the lake whose permanence is of greatest contrast to my mortal being and finally the sun whose light and warmth give life to every being and enchantment to every child. It is renewing, and humbling to picture not only myself, but also the world, from their point of view. To see the world not speckled by nature, but instead as the embodiment of nature. It is empowering to see the fantasy world of wilderness as the real world and the only world and invigorating to be again captured and swept away by the power of the planet. If only this were the world we looked for maybe then this would be the world we see.

George's perspective-taking captures the essence of sustainability in the writing classroom. She is composing; she is composting. As Whitman would say, "Behold this compost! behold it well!"

Like Laura George, Morgan Beavers insistently observed the remarkable observation of Annie Dillard, relentlessly stalking her insight. In her paper on Dillard's theme of seeing, she offers a complex compost of perspectives, of seeing and not-seeing, of truth and falsehood, of truth found in rupture:

> Dillard introduces us first to an intentional and learned way of seeing as she searches for frogs along the pond's banks. Not naturally inclined to notice them, Dillard must train herself to distinguish the amphibians from their matching surroundings. She writes, "I got better and better at seeing frogs both in and out of the water. I learned to recognize." Sharing a sense of entertainment, Dillard writes, "Incredibly, this amused me, and, incredibly, it amuses me still." The frogs are little hidden treasures just like the pennies Dillard hid for strangers to find. Now "seeker" in the game of hide and seek, she finds equivalent entertainment in both roles. Dillard's amusement with her game now as an adult conveys a childlike naivety in her newfound sight. Finding frog after frog each time just as pleased as a child who found a penny, Dillard's game ends when the last frog she finds is, to her surprise, nothing but the dead remains of a waterbug attack. Dillard writes, "I noticed a small green frog" and, with a playful sense of pride, adds, "and he didn't jump." Inching closer to see more clearly, Dillard continues, "And just as I looked at him, he slowly crumpled and began to sag. The spirit vanished from his eyes. . . . He was shrinking before my eyes like a deflated football." Dillard's proud moment of seeing is disparaged by the grim realization that her frog is just an empty body. Moreover, the hollowness of the frog, which represents the ultimate prize of Dillard's searching, imparts the common notion that appearance may differ greatly from reality, and what we see is not always true.[32]

From this exposition of nature observation that leads to the illumination of false insight, Beavers leads the reader through an array of "seeing" in Dillard's pilgrimage. She concludes her essay, writing,

> Dillard ends "Seeing" by conveying the beauty of this ephemeral truth of vision. Though ideally we would see this way all the time, the awe that accompanies those rare moments makes them all the more desirable. Blind to her own lack of true sight until this moment, Dillard reveals—both to the reader and to herself— "I had been my whole life a bell, and never knew it until at that moment I was lifted and struck." Dillard defines her epiphanic moment as she takes the form of a bell and, subtly abandoning all previous attention to sight and shifting significance to sound, shows us the folly of idolizing one sense alone. Seeing is not a singular sensual ability but an experience indefinable by our limited experience. Writing, "The vision comes and goes, mostly goes, but I live for it," Dillard conveys her anticipation of the rare moments when she truly sees. Her portrayal of this truth as fleeting moments of bliss suggests a nearly prophetic sight into the truth of the supernatural world. She goes on, describing this

transcendent sight as "the moment when the mountains open and a new light roars in." Dillard's use of this image is suggestive of a story in Exodus; Moses asks to see God's face, and God replies that Moses cannot see his face but that God will cover Moses with His hand and, from Moses' place "in a cleft in the rock," he may catch a glimpse of God passing by. But for Moses, even this passing glimpse is more incredible than anything he has seen before. Similarly, Dillard finds herself overcome with awe by the mere slices of light that make their way through the mountain's cracks. As Dillard paints for us this image of light, she reveals the allure of truly seeing: even our most capturing moments of awareness expose only a fraction of the ultimate truth. And the glimpse of light in those moments when we do see, for even just a short time, invigorates our quiet but constant search for truth.[33]

In the introduction to the meditative biologist David Haskell's book *The Forest Unseen*, he tells of taking his introductory ecology class to the making of a Buddhist mandala, the infinitely detailed sand sculptures created by monks that represent a re-creation of the path of life, the cosmos, and the enlightenment of the Buddha. He suggests that "the monks and the students are engaged in the same work," that they all are exploring "community," in the richest, broadest sense. Moreover, playing on mandala as ecological metaphor, he writes, "The search for the universal within the infinitesimally small is a quiet theme playing through most cultures," noting Blake, St. John of the Cross, Julian of Norwich, and Saint Francis as the great mystical advocates of this theme.[34] Thus, in a perfectly Thoreauvian turn, he asks, "Can the whole forest be seen through a small contemplative window of leaves, rocks, and water?" His book is his answer, an elegant investigation of ecology based on sitting still, regularly, and observing a one-meter circle in a forest. Haskell sees the insights offered in observation of nature as a way of enlivening the awareness of and affection for the total biological community. As these three remarkable students show, composing is predicated on observation, particularly observation richly aware of context but also richly aware of natural limits; composing is based on conversations, on ecologies biotic and abiotic; composing is seeing the deep interconnections and permeable boundaries between selves (regardless of species); composing at its best seeks new truth and instantiates new hope. It's a lot like gardening.

NOTES

1. Alexander Pope, "Epistles to Several Persons: Epistle IV," *The Poetry Foundation*, accessed August 30, 2016, https://www.poetryfoundation.org/poems-and-poets/poems/detail/44894.

2. Wendell Berry, "The Want of Peace," *The Selected Poems of Wendell Berry* (Washington, D.C.: Counterpoint, 1998).

3. *Oxford English Dictionary* (OED) online, "radish, n.," Oxford University Press, accessed June 2016. (Note: One must have a subscription to access content in the OED, so no links are provided here.)

4. OED, "root, n.1," Oxford University Press, accessed June 2016.

5. Betty Jean Craige, *Eugene Odum: Ecosystem Ecologist and Environmentalist* (Athens, GA: University of Georgia Press, 2001), xii.

6. OED, "book, n.," Oxford University Press, accessed June 2016.

7. Ellen F. Davis, *Scripture, Culture, and Agriculture: An Agrarian Reading of the Bible* (Cambridge; New York: Cambridge University Press, 2009), 29.

8. OED, "compose, v.," Oxford University Press, accessed June 2016.

9. Jed Rasula, *This Compost: Ecological Imperatives in American Poetry* (Athens: University of Georgia Press, 2002), 1.

10. Henry David Thoreau, "Brute Neighbors," *Walden, The Thoreau Reader*, accessed August 29, 2016, http://thoreau.eserver.org/walden12.html.

11. Edward O Wilson, *The Future of Life* (New York: Alfred A. Knopf, 2002), Kindle edition, loc. 146.

12. Walt Whitman, "This Compost!" *The Walt Whitman Archive*, ed. Ed Folsom and Kenneth M. Price, accessed August 29, 2016, http://whitmanarchive.org/published/LG/1871/poems/170.

13. "Cholera in 1832," *Virtual New York*, accessed August 30, 2016, http://www.virtualny.cuny.edu/cholera/1832/cholera_1832_set.html.

14. Robert Frost, "Mowing," *The Poetry Foundation*, accessed August 30, 2016, https://www.poetryfoundation.org/poems-and-poets/poems/detail/53001.

15. Paul Kingsnorth, "Dark Ecology," *Orion Magazine*, accessed August 30, 2016, https://orionmagazine.org/article/dark-ecology/.

16. Peter Kareiva, Michelle Marvier, and Robert Lalasz, "Conservation in the Anthropocene: Beyond Solitude and Fragility," *The Breakthrough*, accessed August 30, 2016, http://thebreakthrough.org/index.php/journal/past-issues/issue-2/conservation-in-the-anthropocene.

17. Jedediah Purdy, "In the Shit with Thoreau: A Walden for the Anthropocene," *Huffington Post*, June 6, 2013, accessed August 30, 2016, http://www.huffingtonpost.com/jedediah-purdy/in-the-shit-with-thoreau_b_3526416.html.

18. OED, "sustain, v," Oxford University Press, accessed June 2016.

19. Henry David Thoreau, "Spring," *Walden, The Thoreau Reader*, accessed August 30, 2016, http://thoreau.eserver.org/walden17.html.

20. Joanna Macy, *World as Lover, World as Self: Courage for Global Justice and Ecological Renewal* (Berkeley, CA: Parallax Press, 2007), Kindle edition, loc. 2229.

21. William J. Wolf, *Thoreau: Mystic, Prophet, Ecologist* (Philadelphia: United Church Press, 1974), 100.

22. Quoted in Wolf, *Thoreau: Mystic, Prophet, Ecologist*, 118.

23. Henry David Thoreau and Bradley P. Dean, *Faith in a Seed: The Dispersion of Seeds and Other Late Natural History Writings* (Washington, D.C.: Island Press/Shearwater Books, 1993), 63.

24. Discussed in Edward O. Wilson, "Biophilia and the Conservation Ethic," *The Biophilia Hypothesis*, ed. Stephen R. Kellert and Edward O. Wilson (Washington, D.C.: Island Press, 1993).

25. Richard Schneider, "'An emblem of all progress': Ecological Succession in Thoreau's *A Week on the Concord and Merrimack River*," *The Concord Saunterer* 19, no. 20 (2011–2012): 98.

26. Thoreau and Dean, *Faith in a Seed*, 23–24.

27. Annie Dillard, *Pilgrim at Tinker Creek* (New York: Harper's Magazine Press, 1974; repr., Harper Collins e-books, 2009), Kindle edition, loc. 186.

28. UNESCO, *Educating for a Sustainable Future: A Transdisciplinary Vision for Concerted Action*, November 1997, accessed August 30, 2016, http://www.unesco.org/education/tlsf/mods/theme_a/popups/mod01t05s01.html.

29. "Sustainability Curriculum in Higher Education: A Call to Action," *Association for the Advancement of Sustainability in Higher Education*, 2010, accessed August 30, 2016, http://wwwp.oakland.edu/Assets/upload/docs/AIS/Conference/2010_Documents_A_Call_to_Action.pdf.

30. Neil B. Weissman, "Sustainability and Liberal Education: Partners by Nature," *Liberal Education* 98, no. 4 (2012), accessed August 30, 2016, https://www.aacu.org/publications-research/periodicals/sustainability-liberal-education-partners-nature.

31. Henry David Thoreau, "Walking," *The Thoreau Reader*, http://thoreau.eserver.org/walking1.html.

32. Annie Dillard, *Pilgrim at Tinker Creek*, loc. 7–8, quoted in Mary Morgan Beavers, "Ecological Wonder in Annie Dillard's Pilgrim at Tinker Creek," *Graduate Student Theses, Dissertations, & Professional Papers*, 11360, 2019, https://scholarworks.umt.edu/etd/11360.

33. Beavers quoting Dillard, *Pilgrim at Tinker Creek*, loc. 36.

34. David George Haskell, *The Forest Unseen: A Year's Watch in Nature* (New York: Penguin. 20130), xii.

Chapter Two

Ecotopia Revisited in Image

The Imagined (and Enacted) Peril and Promise of Portland

Hill Taylor

We need utopias to help us see, envision rather, the possibilities and perils that face us intragenerationally and intergenerationally. Envisioning and enacting sustainability in place-based ways is more essential than ever, as the stakes are more dire than ever. Our very existence is at stake, not to mention the existence of any future generations. That said, it is overwhelming to think about climate change, degradation of our various environments, and increased scarcity of resources like food and clean air and water. This chapter will show, through student practices of image-based invention strategies, how sustainability, stewardship, and environmental gratitude can come together as meaningful curricular components in the space of a writing classroom. Such ambition faces a daunting task.

   Close to twenty years have passed since Christian Weisser and Sidney Dobrin published their opening salvo into the field of ecocomposition with their edited collection, *Ecocomposition: Theoretical and Pedagogical Approaches*.[1] Since the publication of *Ecocomposition*, much has been written on the relationship "between nature, place, environment, habitat, location, and discourse," and I'd assert that both those inside and outside the field of composition understand the saliency of ecological inquiry from a humanistic, as well as scientific perspective.[2] This track record should not come off as a dismissal of the reality that many students (like the broader populous) often find themselves bleary-eyed from the barrage of platitudes about sustainability and basically anything "eco." The importance and opportunity for environmental consciousness and action are as imperative as ever, even if attitudes conducive to felt and effective change ebb and flow. Granted, we find ourselves amid environmental crisis, but we also find ourselves with tools and curricular foundations to make solidarity and success possible.

The development and multivarious trajectories of composition have enabled ecocomposition to sustain and be sustained. The advent of writing in the disciplines and writing across the curriculum, combined with concern over environment and issues of environmental health, plays well with the multidisciplinarity of ecocomposition. That said, there is an unfulfilled prophecy of ecocomposition, one that hinges on drawing attention "to the ideas of context and social construction of identity to include physical realities of place, and of natural and constructed space, both ideological constructs that often seem ignored in favor of more conceptual ideological structures such as gender and race."[3] This partition is a false one and need not exist.

Thinking geographically, spatially rather, necessitates ecocompositionists underscore new conceptualizations of how situated materialities and contestations of materiality enable engagement with the local aspects of place and environment, without neglecting the multitude of ecologies that make up our identities and dictate our envisioning of possibilities. Previously, I have asserted the need for a new conceptual frame, one required to reroute the scripts and texts of our everyday realities, so that we can achieve new possibilities predicated on dismantled systems of oppression (e.g., race and gender) as well as realizing heath and healing of our environments.[4] This visioning of utopias, this "calling in" of better realities, means interrupting and rearticulating systems of oppression while attending to the health of our land base and waterways. Dobrin argues in *Ecology, Writing Theory, and New Media: Writing Ecology* for a preference that we think expansively about ecology and writing; I read his call as a mandate to make our conceptual thinking anchor to a real situated environment if we are to have any sort of praxis or real-world impact.[5]

Ecocomposition has to make an argument, through rational inquiry but with extreme passion, nothing short of speaking for "the soil, and for nerve and muscle."[6] From my vantage, this plea for urgency is situated and focused argument, and rhetorical acumen is the unfulfilled promise of ecocomposition as a field. And, at least curricularly, this is what I aim to suggest is possible with this chapter's ecotopian engagement through a themed composition course focusing on Ecotopia. Pedagogically, students are stymied when asked to write essays from an unsituated rhetorical position. Teaching composition, intentionally or otherwise, from a modes method, one that "focuses on formal practice without an understanding of the purpose for the practice" leaves the student "divorced from any real reason to write."[7] Even though composition has evolved tremendously over the past decades, there are often classrooms and assignments where students develop writing skills, often as technical expertise or craft, but fail to make the connection to skilled rhetorical assessment. Such a charge is always already present, regardless of the theoretical progress any field or discipline has made. Effective engagement with the challenges of our day means that one must be able to deftly execute rhetorical assessment, and reach an audience with meaning and message, then hopefully see movement into action. Conceptualizations of ways to achieve this rhetorical situatedness are plentiful. For my themed composition curriculum I have chosen to go the route of combining students' everyday practice with the possibilities and thoughts of a better, more utopian, environment.

For a utopia to be meaningful enough that individuals feel compelled to enact it, to turn spatial practice and aspirations (e.g., behaviors, practices, expressions, and values) into a real place, the utopia must evoke some sort of emotion. Jacques Cousteau's famous observation that "people protect what they love" rings true here. If a curriculum can evoke emotion through investedness, situatedness, and collective envisioning of place, then we are well on our way to making strong appeals and observations that may foster utopias. For sure, we are well on our way to harnessing pathos in our rhetorical maneuvers.

Concepts of language, text, and emotion must soar beyond historical definitions that have been given play in the classroom; a new path to make connections between realities and possibilities must come to bear in ways that exhilarate and encourage our threatened generations to dream and behave passionately so as to call in new worlds and ways. This is an emotional path, one that does use the head space but ultimately sinks into the heart space. Emotion and environment, fortunately, work quite well together. Emotion somehow gets connected to a physical place, where things happen, memories get made, and hopes or goals get played out. One could argue that the terrain of really good curriculum does this same thing. Impactful curriculum evokes emotion—so much so that one embodies the curricular tenets—the curriculum inspires us on a variety of levels and registers. Psychologically, we are "rooted in place" by our dreams and emotional connections to the various environments of our place and what we want it to be.

This chapter sets course based on a "need to recognize fundamental interconnections between culture, survival, body, and place."[8] For teachers, the aim is to highlight the ongoing usefulness of literature and image as a means to enact and perform place-based inquiry and possibility. By using the historical and pedagogical precedent of place-based inquiry and action, one can articulate a curriculum that can avoid the default to a modes-based composition that Sumner so thoroughly warns us of in his insistence upon "argument pedagogy" fostered by a classroom that is really a "community of inquirers."[9] I use a place-centric piece of literature, *Ecotopia* by Ernest Callenbahk, that has been referred to as the novel that predicted Portland[10]; Ecotopia, as a manifesto and as a piece of fiction, has seen a renaissance in recent years just as population and "pride in place" have increased in the Cascadia region of North America. However, the utility of this text as a springboard to sustainability and environmental connectedness, as well as a text for envisioning better futures, can be much more expansive in geographic resonance. My hope is that *Ecotopia* can be used anywhere, in any classroom.

ROOTED IN PLACE, ROOTED IN TEXT

Here, I pause to note that my own engagement with place vis-à-vis *Ecotopia* is impacted by my positionality as a relocated southerner. Portland has been my home for close to a decade, but I'm still learning about "The Rose City" and digging in . . . still becoming rooted. One of my favorite Gary Snyder quotes is, "Find your place on the planet. Dig in, and take responsibility from there."[11] There is a mythos to any place, with Portland being no exception. I'm still unpacking, juxtaposing, and discerning the real, the fictional, and the imagined Portland as I try to calibrate my daily experiences with what I thought Portland was before I moved here, how it's represented in the news and media, and even how it's envisioned in others' texts. *Ecotopia* is a useful text for such consciousness-raising juxtaposition as it examines the prescience, and absurdity, of the ecological utopia portrayed in the novel.

My assumption is that most readers of this chapter possess at least a passing familiarity with the plot and storyline of *Ecotopia*, as well as a bit of awareness as to the reception and renaissance of Callenbach's novel. As I mention, *Ecotopia* could function as a core text in curriculum regardless of geographic location; however, I did choose the novel quite frankly because of its prescience in "predicting Portland" with the hope that as my students go through their daily lives they might note "much of Portland, Ore., with its public transport, slow-growth planning and eat-local restaurants, can seem like Ecotopia made reality."[12] When placing my order with the campus bookstore, my aspiration was that reading and writing about themes and everyday life in Portland in *Ecotopia* would be a "way in" for students to look closely and critically at the place in which they live, specifically through an environmental and aspirational/utopian lens. My essay sequences were designed to facilitate such an inquiry, and were set up so that composing would occur through a variety of registers (logocentric and otherwise). By sharing compositions that examine narratives of ecological utopia and possibility, my composition classroom would aspire for daily presentations that profile how student critique vis-à-vis ecotopian literature enables a situated environmental reflective practice and approach. Sometimes this noble goal was met, and other times things just dragged.

Our first step, as a class, was to read and simply synthesize *Ecotopia* as a novel. Prior to introducing our classroom takeaways of key themes and interactions, I will start with a brief summary of the novel. Ernest Callenbach's *Ecotopia* is set in 1999, which is twenty-five years after it was written in 1974. Callenbach's novel consists of diary entries and reports from the protagonist, journalist William Weston. Weston is the first American reporter to visit Ecotopia, a small country that seceded from the United States in 1980. Ecotopia is made up of what used to be Washington, Oregon, and Northern California. Ecotopia has been an independent nation for nineteen years, and most Americans, including the US government, still do not know very much about their northwestern neighbor. The Ecotopians are secretive and cut off from their American counterparts, and this has bred hostility from many on both sides of the border. The Times-Post of New York, with the approval of the president of the United States, sends Weston to Ecotopia.

HISTORICAL, ECOLOGICAL, AND LITERARY CONNECTIONS

When I first began to grapple with my concern over what sort of eco-place Portland actually is, or what Portland's potential might have been (or will be), I nearly immediately thought of Benedict Anderson's concept of "imagined communities."[13] There is one quote specifically that I find useful; it is when Anderson writes about the power of imagining as a process that unifies (as much as the actual product of the collective imagining). Imagining as process seems apropos to a classroom where there is much pedagogical attention given to writing as process. *Ecotopia*, and Portland, both serve as useful texts to examine how we compose our communities and their attendant possibilities. Anderson operationalizes a definition of nation in relation to community as follows:

> I propose the following definition of the nation: it is an imagined political community—and imagined as both inherently limited and sovereign. It is imagined because the members of even the smallest nation will never know most of their fellow-members, meet them, or even hear of them, yet in the minds of each lives the image of their communion. . . . Communities are to be distinguished, not by their falsity/genuineness, but by the style in which they are imagined.[14]

It is useful, for me, to see Anderson's emphasis on "style." One could take such a notion to reading Callenbach's *Ecotopia*, namely in an analysis of the collective identity that the citizens project and enact. The same analysis could be asserted when reading Portland as a text and examining the qualities that appear to be foregrounded in Portland's dominant identities (e.g., real-life Ecotopia, hipster haven, liberal mecca).

For instance, before moving to Portland, I (like many others I've met) had bought into the notion of Portland as shining city on a hill . . . an ultra-creative, progressive, and eco-friendly place. I imagined Portland as a place that I'd love and fit right in with kindred spirits and like minds. And, yes, I was generally correct in this self-indulgent assumption. I do love Portland, and the people here are wonderful. I'm grateful and lucky to live here. I have become a Portland booster; and, I'd argue that Portland is not a city that shies away from self-aggrandizing and boosterism. There is a certain style in which Portlanders imagine themselves and how we choose to see and re/present our community. A discernable aesthetic to Portland exists; it's palpable. When students read *Ecotopia*, they remark on a similar aesthetic that permeates the imagined nation in Callenbach's novel. Interestingly, students are often turned off by the style of imaging and representation that takes place in *Ecotopia*; there is a smugness and self-righteousness that does not quite sit well with some students when reading the novel. When these same students turn to "reading" Portland as a text they sometimes discover contradictions as well as a similar smugness and self-righteousness, qualities of Portland's collective imagined identity that they may not have picked up on previously, enabling a new perspective on the reality and possibility of the place known as home.

While the use of Anderson's "imagined communities" premise by itself is productive, a bit of theoretical scaffolding allows an even more incisive critique of Portland's various place-based articulations. Here, I suggest a turn to other conceptualizations of the imaginary to serve as foil to my premise that Portland really was a reasonably apt manifestation of Callenbach's vision in *Ecotopia*.

In his work *The Language of the Self: The Function of Language in Psychoanalysis*, coming from a Marxist tradition that emphasizes the imaginary as illusion and a Freudian one that treats illusion as fantasy, Lacan articulates an illusion as created in response to a psychological need.[15] Do we "need" Portland to be Ecotopia? To not be Seattle or San Francisco, or even Berkeley? Do we find ourselves beholden to an illusion that Portland is Ecotopia, even if the materiality of everyday life here shows us something different? Lacan's contention is that the unconscious functions linguistically (as opposed to symbolically or instinctually) and that the unconscious is fundamentally a discourse upon itself preoccupied with antagonism of the Other as a referent or foil. Such a foil can serve as an attraction or ideal, or oppositely as something to revile or toil against. As you will see from my students' narratives, there is a case for this assertion and application of both possibilities when figuring whether Ecotopia is an exacting illusion or sincere possibility.

THEMES AND ARTIFACTS:
A NOD TOWARD THE MULTIMODALITY OF *ECOTOPIA*

In my course, as we read and debriefed each class about what was "going on" in Callenbach's piece of fiction, my students and I collectively identified several key themes that drove the storyline in *Ecotopia*. Under each theme, the class became invested in noting specific exemplars of the stated theme. Later, when it came time to compose essay feeders, and ultimately formal polished essays, students returned to these identified themes as actionable touchstones. When returning to the themes and exemplars, I encouraged students to either write "against" the theme, in juxtaposition with what they might be seeing and experiencing on a daily basis in Portland, or to write "with" the theme as an affirmation of Callenbach's *Ecotopia* having become manifest in (or maybe even predicting) Portland.

In "Cultures, Contexts, Images, and Texts: Materials for a New Age of Meaning Making," Kathleen Blake Yancey asserts that effective recognition of the tension between print and digital composition and representation is appropriate, much needed, and ultimately unavoidable. Yancey, in using the metaphor of geology, delineates the tectonic shift that has occurred due to technology, the digital turn, and multimodal composition. Writers are working differently and in tension with historical paradigms, curricular and otherwise, to create a dynamic and changed landscape. In sum, the digital and multimodal is comprehensively "re-forming the academy; pointing us to new ways to write, new kinds of projects, new ways of circulating scholarship."[16] To many a reader, such observations are stating the obvious. I agree. These are things that we all have known for some time. Such statements are passe. That is, until educators are pressed to identify how our curriculum has kept up with this shift both technically and cognitively.

In my curricular engagement with *Ecotopia*, the classroom analysis is informed by multimodal student reflections on Ecotopia, as used as a supplemental text in an undergraduate writing course. In addition to collectively discussing the themes of *Ecotopia*, students were to respond to the reading in a journal. This was as much an opportunity for them to engage in low-stakes reflective writing as it was anything else like textual analysis or interpretation. That said, I did ask (or mandate, rather) that they experiment while journaling with various invention strategies explained in class to explore and gather materials for class discussions and essays. We would use our reflections from journaling to suss out *Ecotopia*'s theme and juxtapose our everyday observations of life in Portland.

The first theme was "transportation." Students noticed specific examples of Callenbach's concern over sustainable transportation. Namely, our classroom community kept returning to instances where citizens of *Ecotopia* utilized electric minivans and taxis, rode zero-emission trains or magnetic rail, and reveled in the omnipresence of free bikes for citizen use. We grouped architecture under the theme of "transportation." The reality of sustainable architecture, much like current LEED certification, struck a chord with students, as did Callenbach's preoccupation with connecting buildings by way of sky bridges. Portland is a city famous for its bridges, and the concept of sustainable, health-oriented activity inducing vis-à-vis walking, spatial connectedness resonated with each class I taught the novel in. As a new immigrant to Portland, this particular consciousness of bridge and salubrious lifestyle was striking to me. Students also remarked on the fact that air traffic over Ecotopia was forbidden.

As we read and discussed *Ecotopia*, students were also required to share photos of places and characteristics in their everyday life that, in some way, paralleled or contrasted what was being described and mapped out through the narrative. Students could share photos they took themselves or ones they discovered while information foraging on the internet. The photos that appear in this chapter are ones that were "discovered" on the photo sharing site Flickr. All the images in this chapter are available for sharing based on Creative Commons copyright agreement. Using such images in class also provided an opportunity to discuss issues of copyright and fair use in academic writing and publishing.

During the first quarter that I used *Ecotopia* as the cornerstone of curriculum, Portland's much anticipated new no-car bridge opened. Tilikum Crossing, aka Bridge of the People, is the first major bridge in the United States designed to allow access to transit vehicles, cyclists, and pedestrians but not cars; Tilikum Crossing has been lauded as the "bridge to the future" and to date has been embraced with the sentiment appropriate with such fanfare.[17] Portlanders like their bridges, especially when the bridge memorializes the city's commitment to cutting-edge architecture and sustainability. Many students made this connection immediately and submitted photos of Tilikum Crossing (see figure 2.1).

Other themes under the umbrella of transportation seemed to obviously fly in the proverbial face of everyday life in Portland. The two most striking were students' observations that there most certainly is air traffic in the skies over Portland and the fact that Portland's traffic is horrific. A couple of students noted that traffic in Portland was recently ranked tenth worst in the country as reported by the Oregonian.[18] (See figure 2.2.)

At the same instance, however, nearly every student in my courses remarks on the expansiveness . . . the comprehensiveness rather of public transportation in Portland, Oregon. It feels safe to say that there has been a bit of

Figure 2.1. Tilikum Crossing
Photo Credit: Eric Prado (no modifications made).

Figure 2.2. Traffic on I-5 Northbound
Photo Credit: John Russell (no modifications made).

self-generated hullabaloo detailing the alternative transportation options in Portland. Tri-Met, the metropolitan transit authority in Portland Metro offers robust mass transit services ranging from bus, light rail, streetcar, aerial tram, and bike programs. Students found ample images (as evidenced in figure 2.3) to generate comparisons between everyday Portland and Callenbach's *Ecotopia*.

And, Portlanders are known for their love of cycling. Many students circulated images of bikes. But, among the most striking was that of a "ghost bike" shared by one of my students (see figure 2.4). The ghost bike illuminates the night in this picture, warning passersby that roads are dangerous places. Ghost bikes are placed to memorialize a rider who has been killed or seriously injured in collision with a car, bus, or another motorized vehicle on the streets of Portland.

When discussing these memorials, students underscore the increasingly dangerous traffic conditions, worsening with Portland's population increase. The class sentiment (in just about every class) seemed to be, at least at the end of the quarter, that even though Portland still exudes an image of an alternative transportation Shangri-la, the reality is much different. With the city's popularity has come a critical mass of congestion, releasing the genie

Figure 2.3. Portland, Oregon, Tri-Met Streetcar
Photo Credit: Jasperdo (no modifications made).

Figure 2.4. Ghost Bike
Photo Credit: Sean Bonner (no modifications made).

of urbanization, placing Portland on par with other hip and popular West Coast metropolises like Seattle and forcing a reframing of how residents will see and experience their city. To be fair, (at least for now) the incidence of death, as well as serious injury, while riding a bike in Portland is well below the national and international average, according to the 2015 Portland Traffic Safety Report.[19]

Another iconic image that students would quite often share as their composition prompts, when discussing cutting-edge and *Ecotopian* transportation, is the Portland aerial tram (pictured in figure 2.5).

The aerial tram connects Portland's Southwest Waterfront neighborhood, and riverfront campus of Oregon Health & Science University with the main hospitals and education buildings of Oregon Health & Science University. I work at Oregon Health & Science University, so I ride the tram a few times a week, and I'm able to ride it free of charge. So for me, a bit of the novelty has receded. However, I seem to be in the minority here as each day Portland's aerial tram serves as a major tourist attraction for residents and visitors alike, willing to pay $4.50 for a round-trip ride. My students seem to like the tram as well, both for its exciting ride replete with vistas of Mount Hood and Mount St. Helens as well as what they described the tram to represent. Many students felt that the Portland aerial tram was quite similar to a type of transportation that one might encounter in the fictional world of *Ecotopia*. Such a form of transport intimates futurism, green transport, and a (quite literally) connection between nature, urbanization, technology, and health.

Figure 2.5. Portland Aerial Tram
Photo Credit: Paul Kimo McGregor (no modifications made).

The beauty of the rhetoric and mythos of *Ecotopia* is that it can be "read" and enacted anywhere. One of the curricular goals I have is to show how such reading can be put upon actual places as they exist as well as how we'd like for them to. Looking at the allure of the Portland aerial tram serves as a nice jumping off point for such an application. Place, even utopian mythical ones, can be enacted . . . making or producing preference and performance (aka space) and physical built place. An article in *The Oregonian* notes that Chicago may soon have an aerial tram network inspired by, but surpassing, Portland's. The idea is that there would be "a 17-story-high aerial gondola network that would ferry tourists and Chicagoans around the city's downtown, providing eye-popping views of its iconic skyline."[20] The description of Chicago's tram network sounds strikingly similar to the aerial bridges and connections of Callenbach's *Ecotopia*. Maybe there is mimicry at work here, but even if that is not the case there is a certain affective and inspirational sensibility present. During our class discussions, we would endeavor to apprehend the qualities and possibilities that go along with such a "structure of feeling."[21] Namely, we looked to such communal consciousness as "defined as social experiences in solution."[22] Students often remarked that a large part of their social identity, as a resident of Portland (and more broadly as an Oregonian), was bound up in a certain orientation or advocacy for progressive attitudes and approaches to solutions for problems.

Our next theme epitomizes such felt advocacy and attitude as much as any area that I can envision. This theme, identified in *Ecotopia*, was "energy and technology," and I hazard that progressive efforts at energy and technology reflect the sort of shared historical consciousness of certain communities that Williams describes. In our particular case it is the nation of *Ecotopia* or the "green" and "sustainable" city of Portland. There is a consensus, seemingly, in certain geographic areas as well as virtual communities over the viability and necessity of alternative energy technologies and renewable energy (i.e., two of five themes students agreed upon). These two topics, of energy technologies and renewable energy, are, or can be, quite polarizing, sparking strong debates among individuals and groups. Certain places may tend to produce an identity that suggests a strong affinity for alternative energy technologies and renewable energy; students agreed that *Ecotopia* underscored this premise and that Portland (maybe even the Pacific Northwest categorically) made such preferences into reality.

For their multimodal artifacts, submitted in support of this theme, students shared everything from the grandiose to the pedestrian. One of the more striking images of the Oregon landscape appears as one drives through the Columbia River Gorge on Interstate 84. Pretty much as soon as one passes the town of Hood River, beginning to leave the rain shadow of Mount Hood and the Willamette Valley and entering the edges of Oregon's high desert region, the sight of hundreds of windmills grips any observant traveler. At times, the windmills perched atop the walls of the gorge and not-so-distant hills, seem to go on forever. The windmills are numerous and striking; they are also huge, underscoring the totem-like quality and context of Oregon's windmills, as well as the undeniable reminder of a changed energy and natural landscape.

In class, we'd share comparisons of other similarly striking landscapes, such as oil derricks or fields of solar panels (neither of which populate a significant portion of Portland or the Pacific Northwest for that matter). But, all of these energy technologies possess a certain environmental rhetoric to them; just about all the students in the class got this concept pretty easily and were eager to map identity and attitude onto such places. Oftentimes, students perilously compressed the identity of entire states into caricature when discussing how a preference for particular forms of energy can be tied to collective consciousness and identity. Texas, for its oil, and West Virginia for its coal seemed to be favorites of the students.

In a sense, this is a glimpse into the art and practice of critical geography as advocated by Doreen Massey. I particularly like Massey's notion of stretched out social relations, where she suggests places can be "imagined as articulated moments in networks of social relations and understandings."[23] Such envisioning is invaluable when mapping the affinity and felt connectedness of individuals and groups over polarizing issues like energy and technology. Individuals may congregate in certain places, like Portland, if they are lucky enough to be able to relocate (similar to the citizens of *Ecotopia*), or individuals may find themselves relegated to a geographic environ that runs counter to their individual affinity for such things as alternative energy technologies and renewable energy. In such cases, physical distance mandates that such connections to community exist in Massey's "stretched out" way, but exist as an affinity nonetheless. Individuals with such affinities may even endeavor to enact their affinities counter to the dominant articulation of their physical surroundings. In sum, they would aim to produce space, making do in a tactical way against their (environmental) conditions of engagement. For such individuals the community and promise of real places like Portland, or imagined ones like Ecotopia, may serve as a strong and consistently present inspiration.

Such inspiration sets in motion the city as "in process" and "as possibilities machine" as Henri Lefebvre would describe it.[24] Edward Soja decodes what Lefebvre intimates better than most when he suggests the power of "Thirdspace" thinking. Soja argues that Thirdspace "must be additionally guided by some form of potentially emancipatory *praxis*, the translation of knowledge into action in a conscious—and consciously spatial—effort to improve the world in some significant way."[25] When decoding themes in *Ecotopia*, the class would often come up with examples and particularities from everyday life—simple practices that define community identity as well as social and environmental possibility. One such example clarified the approach to waste management in the Portland Metro area, which still amazes me even though I have resided here for some time. Trash is collected every two weeks; however, compost and comprehensive mixed-use recycling are collected weekly. This is a radical departure from some of the other places I've lived. In fact, the genesis for *Ecotopia* emerged with Ernest Callenbach deliberating over what could be done with all the waste that contemporary society was producing. From image and compositional reflection, students did concede Portland's preoccupation and outright zeal for low-waste production/recycling, sustainability, and renewable energy sources.

The fervor for low-impact waste is apparent in the options students have, including the drying of their hands at school with an air dryer versus paper towels; students submitted multiple images of this. Compostable products, including bags of all types, appear just about everywhere. In 2012, Portland also became one of several cities on the West Coast to limit, and ban in certain situations, the use of plastic bags in grocery stores.[26] Students, during class discussion, often appeared to see this as a quite normal and logical existence. When the topic came up that other geographic areas lacked similar mandates there were always a few students to which this was surprising.

Oftentimes, progressives will lament the participation of neoliberal government or private enterprise when involved in environmental or social justice efforts. The preference seems to be that "real" environmentalism is organic (pun intended) and forms from the masses of like-minded grassroots organizers. Yes, this is true. However, one thing that Callenbach shows us in *Ecotopia* is that such groups create governmental (capitalistic even) organizations and institutions. In fact, Callenbach does not subvert the capitalist paradigm per se; rather, he envisions a functioning democratic socialist nation with strong eco-sensibilities and ethics. In *Ecotopia*, institutions form consensus when it comes to environmental ethics. Here, I quote at length a passage from an earlier article where I assert that ethics form and articulate in a dialectic, and engaging in a "purity debate" about such ethics negates the possibility for meaningful reform:

> Even if our agency has been reduced to what we consume, by shopping at Whole Foods Market and supporting their practices of sound environmental stewardship and employee equality we are engaging and experiencing different possibilities driven by different ethics and logics. The responsibility of the progressive in organizations of any kind is to direct the discourse to areas of importance, especially ones not predicated on the benefit of the minority at the expense and exploitation of the few. If this sort of economic participation is not palatable, one should entertain the possibility of supporting multiple economies on a community or local level (i.e., coops or alternative currencies). Regardless, it would be a mistake not to consider all possibilities (even ones with the "enemy" or "oppressor") when one is precariously positioned in undesirable hegemonic relations.[27]

In simple form, this statement asks that we aim to change (and support change) structurally and strategically, just and as we organize and maneuver tactically in conditions not necessarily of our own making. Participation and proliferation of environmentally minded practices must be tied to both strategy and tactics, predisposed to include individuals, groups, and institutions both public and private.

The next theme, addressed by the class, focuses on the "way people live" in the words of my students. It was at this point that I offered up an explanation of Pierre Bourdieu's concept of habitus. In Bourdieu's *Distinction*, he suggests that habitus encompasses our "taste" for cultural objects—art, food, and clothing. He asserts that aesthetic sensibilities are shaped by the culturally ingrained habitus.[28] Upper classes, for instance, possess a taste for fine art due to the fact they have been socialized to appreciate art from an early age. Conversely, the working classes lack historical access to "high art," consequently lacking cultivated habitus suited to play and "feel" the fine art "game." Bourdieu often reminds readers that habitus is so ingrained that people nearly always mistake the "feel for the game" as natural instead as opposed to culturally developed. One could extend such notions of distinction, taste, preference, and bias to the citizenry of Ecotopia and Portland.

Ecotopia's, and Portland's, zeal for local and often organic food and products was an obvious touchstone for students. Images depicting co-ops and farmers markets always abound when discussing and defining preferences for food and the relationship people have with it, be these people Portlanders or Ecotopians. Per capita, Portland ranks second in the United States for farmer's markets, just behind Washington, DC, surprisingly.[29] Even though Portland is number two, its locavore culture and boosterism "feels" (a la Bourdieu) unrivaled.

When Callenbach penned *Ecotopia* in the early 1970s, legalization of marijuana was a pipe dream, literally and figuratively. Legal pot in Oregon and Washington today, seems as much as any correlation to mirror Callenbach's fictional utopia. Students shared quite a few photos of "pot shops" from around the Portland area. In fact, marijuana dispensaries in Oregon now outnumber McDonald's and Starbucks.[30] Having grown up in a time where even medical marijuana was circumspect, I continue to be amazed at how my students view legal marijuana as "no big deal" and how they take for granted its ubiquity.

Ecotopians live in a land where foodways resemble those of present-day Portland. Significantly, Ecotopians privilege foods without sugar and preservatives, which students easily map onto the contemporary preference for clean, whole, and gluten-free (as well as local) food. Characters in Callenbach's novel also fetishize local arts and indigenous spiritual practices, both core components of habitus in present-day Portland. While Callenbach paints a utopian portrait on most fronts, the one piece of the novel that students always stumble with is the inconsistency of his insertion of the mock warfare games played by Ecotopians The enthusiasm for outdoor and athletic activity is characteristically Portland and Pacific Northwest, however the fake (supposedly more peaceful) war games played by Ecotopians just about always gets labeled as the dark underbelly of Ecotopia when we parse out themes as a class.

Gender, relationships, and race serve as hallmarks of Ecotopia's progressivism. However, like contemporary Portland, all is not as well as it seems. Ecotopians often live in extended families, and tend to live by choice in ethnically separated localities. Their economic enterprises are generally employee owned and controlled. There seems to be much tolerance and sincere empathy for multiple perspectives; however, segregation occurs along lines of race and ethnicity.

By reading text, image, and place against (and with) *Ecotopia*, students can juxtapose the utopian and dystopian realities. Such critical juxtaposition can be set up to bear upon one of the United States' hallmark green cities (i.e., Portland) or any other place of one's choosing. Students would often submit photos that epitomize such juxtaposition when it comes to injustices centered on gentrification and discrimination along lines of race and gender. On the surface, all may seem well (and even progressive) in Portland, Ecotopia, and elsewhere; however, further (multimodal and multifaceted) scrutiny shows that systemic forms of oppression and exploitation thrive albeit with a different veneer.

The final set of themes we usually address, when dissecting *Ecotopia*, deals with political representation and economic relations. Again, Callenbach's prescience is uncanny yet flawed in parts. We saw the first nomination of a woman by a major political party in 2016; in Callenbach's *Ecotopia* the current governmental administration is woman-led (but not exclusively female) and government structures are highly decentralized. Strikingly and quite nonutopian, the national defense strategy has focused on developing a highly advanced arms industry, while also allegedly maintaining hidden weapons of mass destruction within major US population centers to discourage conquest and annexation.

Students usually seem readily available and capable of identifying these themes in everyday life, both locally and especially nationally. Ecotopia, as a nation, operationalizes a modus operandi that is contradictory but completely plausible (maybe palatable) with what many of my students see on a daily basis, either in person or through media.

In *Ecotopia*, science and technology aren't related to economic growth, however students would often offer up images that show a (supposed) correlation between technology and wealth. In sum, such a correlation plays out, though it creates pretty significant income disparity (e.g., San Francisco, Seattle, and Portland).

To this end, notice figure 2.6, which depicts the homeless crisis that many West Coast cities are now endeavoring to grapple with. The crisis has reached epic proportion and has resulted in many states making emergency declarations.[31] This is certainly not very Ecotopian, where there is basic income for everyone.

ENVOI: CLOSING THOUGHTS ON PRAXIS

Lawrence Buell, in his seminal work of ecocriticism, *The Environmental Imagination: Thoreau, Nature Writing, and the Formation of American*

Figure 2.6. Homeless Camp
Photo Credit: UrbexNW (no modifications made).

Culture, emphasizes that the environmental crisis is "a crisis of the imagination" and that solving the environmental crisis hinges on imagining nature and humanity's relation to it.[32] Buell underscores the role of the arts (especially literature) in collective cultural imagining of our spaces and places in the natural world. The use of *Ecotopia* in a college writing course, where we are asked to show students the world through the lens of various academic discourses, holds the possibility for operationalizing a variety of experiential registers. Here, aptly, we might usefully turn to James Gee's advocacy for thinking expansively about discourse.

Specifically, Gee explodes the concept of *Discourse* ("big D" Discourse). For Gee, *discourse* ("little d") refers to language-in-use. When discussing the combination of language with other social practices (behavior, values, ways of thinking, clothes, food, customs, perspectives) within a specific group, Gee refers to that as Discourse. Individuals may be part of many different Discourse communities, for example "when you 'pull-off' being a culturally specific sort of 'everyday' person, a 'regular' at the local bar . . . a teacher or a student of a certain sort, or any of a great many other 'ways of being in the world.'"[33]

Ecotopia, and similar narratives of ecological utopia and possibility, can be read (and realized) through a lens of being and observation. Specifically, such a lens would assert a privileging of emotional connection with, and action toward, imagined and enacted spaces. Through engagement with a variety of, both high and low stakes, writing assignments, students were able to build an experiential register with their own writing while developing voice and imagination as they relate to aspects and possibilities for sustainability. From my time with the text of *Ecotopia* and students' readings of it, I am left with a firm belief that *Ecotopia* can serve as a strong platform for the study of the relationships (and their implications) between human beings and the natural world.

E. O. Wilson, in his seminal work *Biophilia*, observes that the human mind is affected and shaped by an urbanized, modern, social world (saturated with image and information); the deep structure of the mind is inevitably adapted to, and informed by, the natural environment in which it evolved.[34] But, human beings have an innate instinct to connect emotionally with nature. In an extension of this analysis, my assignment is praxis driven and encourages (through text and image) that students articulate a connection with the pursuit of ecological utopias through a theory of ecopsychological "structure of feeling."[35] How does it "feel" to recognize, to look for, or to experience the opposite of what one seems to be conjuring in one's mind when reading *Ecotopia* and living our daily lives? Hopefully, my pedagogical sharing underscores ways that place-based readings of utopian texts enable, foster rather, student writing and reflection on situated ecological possibility and peril.

NOTES

1. Christian Weisser and Sidney I. Dobrin, *Ecocomposition: Theoretical and Pedagogical Approaches* (Albany: State University of New York Press, 2001), 101.
2. Weisser and Dobrin, *Ecocomposition*, 10.
3. Weisser and Dobrin, *Ecocomposition*, 12.
4. L. Hill Taylor Jr., and Robert J. Helfenbein, "Mapping Everyday: Gender, Blackness, and Discourse in Urban Contexts," *Educational Studies: Journal of the American Educational Studies Association* 45, no. 3 (2009): 319–29.
5. Sidney I. Dobrin, "Ecology, Writing Theory, and New Media: Writing Ecology," in *Routledge Studies in Rhetoric and Communication* (Florence: Taylor and Francis, 2011), 1–23.
6. David Thomas Sumner, "Don't Forget to Argue: Problems, Possibilities, and Ecocomposition," in Christian R. Weisser and Sidney I. Dobrin, eds., *Ecocomposition: Theoretical and Pedagogical Approaches* (Albany: State University Press of New York, 2001), 278.
7. Sumner, "Don't Forget to Argue," 271.
8. Derek Owens, *Composition and Sustainability: Teaching for a Threatened Generation* (Urbana, IL: NCTE, 2001).

9. Owens, *Composition and Sustainability*, 273.

10. Scott Timberg, "The Novel That Predicted Portland," *New York Times*, December 12, 2008, accessed August 22, 2016, http://www.nytimes.com/2008/12/14/fashion/14ecotopia.html?_r=0.

11. Gary Snyder, *Turtle Island* (New York: New Directions, 1974), 101.

12. Timberg, "The Novel That Predicted Portland," par. 14.

13. Benedict R. Anderson, *Imagined Communities: Reflections on the Origin and Spread of Nationalism*, rev. ed. (London/New York: Verso, 2006).

14. Anderson, *Imagined Communities*, 6.

15. Jacques Lacan and Anthony Wilden, *The Language of the Self: The Function of Language in Psychoanalysis*, ed. Johns Hopkins Paperbacks (Baltimore: Johns Hopkins University Press, 1981).

16. Kathleen B. Yancy, "Cultures, Contexts, Images, and Texts: Materials for a New Age of Meaning-Making," *South Atlantic Review* 33 (Winter 2013): 4.

17. Brian Libby, "Bridge to the Future (the Bridge That Bans Cars)," *The Atlantic* 316, no. 3 (2015): 42–43.

18. Joseph Rose, "Portland Traffic Jams Ranked Nation's 10th Worst (If You Can Believe It)," *The Oregonian*, March 31, 2015, http://www.oregonlive.com/commuting/index.ssf/2015/03/portland_traffic_ranked_nation.html.

19. Margi Bradway, *2015 Portland Traffic Safety Report*, Portland Bureau of Transportation, February 8, 2016, efiles.portlandoregon.gov/Record/8991354/File/Document.

20. Douglas Perry, "Love Portland's Aerial Tram? It'll Pale Compared to Chicago's Magical 17-Story-High Gondola Network," *The Oregonian*, May 9, 2016, accessed August 22, 2016, http://www.oregonlive.com/today/index.ssf/2016/05/love_portlands_aerial_tram_itl.html.

21. Raymond Williams, *Marxism and Literature. Marxist Introductions* (Oxford, England: Oxford University Press, 1977).

22. Williams, *Marxism and Literature*, 133–34.

23. Doreen B. Massey, *Space, Place, and Gender* (Minneapolis: University of Minnesota Press, 1994), 154.

24. Henri Lefebvre, *The Production of Space*, ed. D. Nicholson-Smith (Oxford: Blackwell, 1991); *Writings on Cities*, ed. E. Kofman and E. Lebas (Oxford: Blackwell, 1996).

25. Edward W. Soja, *Thirdspace: Journeys to Los Angeles and Other Real-and-Imagined Places* (Cambridge: Blackwell, 1996), 22.

26. City of Portland, "Frequently Asked Questions about Portland's Plastic Bag Ban," 2016, https://www.portlandoregon.gov/bps/article/402484.

27. Hill Taylor, "Articulating Reform and the Hegemony Game," *Workplace: A Journal for Academic Labor* 10 (2003): 7.

28. Pierre Bourdieu, "Distinction (English Translation 1984)," *English Studies in Canada* 41, no. 4 (1979): 12.

29. Kate Rabinowitz, "DC #1 in Farmer's Markets Per Capita," *Data Lens DC*, August 31, 2015, http://www.datalensdc.com/farmers-mkt-per-capita.html.

30. Emily G. Brosious, "Marijuana Shops Now Outnumber McDonald's and Starbucks in Oregon," *Chicago Sun-Times*, November 8, 2015, accessed August 22, 2016, http://extract.suntimes.com/news/10/153/7281/more-marijuana-shops-oregon-than-mcdonalds-starbucks/.

31. Rebecca Beitsch, "Cities, States Turn to Emergency Declarations to Tackle Homeless Crisis," Pew Charitable Trusts, November 11, 2015, http://www.pewtrusts.org/en/research-and-analysis/blogs/stateline/2015/11/11/cities-states-turn-to-emergency-declarations-to-tackle-homeless-crisis.

32. Lawrence Buell, *The Environmental Imagination: Thoreau, Nature Writing, and the Formation of American Culture* (Cambridge, MA: Belknap Press of Harvard University Press, 1996), 2.

33. James Paul Gee, *An Introduction to Discourse Analysis: Theory and Method*, 3rd ed (New York: Routledge, 2011), 7; *Social Linguistics and Literacies: Ideology in Discourses*, 4th ed. (Abingdon, Oxon; New York: Routledge, 2012).

34. Edward O. Wilson, *Biophilia* (1984; repr., Cambridge, MA: Harvard University Press, 2003).

35. Williams, *Marxism and Literature*, 132.

Chapter Three

"meanderings to the river"

A Sustainable Approach to Teaching Sustainability in First-Year Composition

Deborah Church Miller,
Lindsay Tigue, and Kim Waters

> The site of the University is on the south side, and half a mile from the river. On one side the land is cleared; the other is wood-land. . . . About two hundred yards from the site, and at least three hundred feet above the level of the river, in the midst of an extensive bed of rock, issues a copious spring of excellent water; and, in its meanderings to the river, several others are discovered.
>
> —"Report on the Siting of the University of Georgia," *Augusta Chronicle,* July 25, 1801

For most of the twentieth century, a spring at the corner of Fulton and Spring Streets, in Athens, Georgia, lay hidden between two parking lots, choking under deposits of trash and debris (see figure 3.1). Despite the aptly named location—"Spring Street"—the "copious spring" was only rediscovered and restored to its unique historical role in the university's siting late in 2008.[1] I first learned of the tiny wetland while attending a 2012 faculty development workshop sponsored by the University of Georgia's (UGA) Office of Sustainability, a workshop that led to the course and other program developments described in this chapter. In 2012, our visit to the town spring on Spring Street captured many imaginations, providing a living connection between history, language, and narrative in a hidden local landscape; today, the spring also furnishes a convenient metaphor, mirroring the impact of that workshop and the way it has "meander[ed]" through our First-Year Composition (FYC) program, "discover"ing other springs of energy and talent.

Bringing our diverse skills and disciplines to the task—as a writing program administrator, a creative writer, and a linguist—in this chapter we reflect on the ways we have variously incorporated sustainability into our FYC program. We each chose to adopt an emphasis on sustainability for different

Figure 3.1. Town Spring at Spring Street and Fulton
Photo Credit: Deborah Miller.

reasons, some pragmatic and some idealistic or idiosyncratic, but in one way or another, we found ourselves agreeing with Victor Nolet in his introduction to *Educating for Sustainability: Principles and Practices for Teachers*, that the "goal of achieving sustainability is the defining idea of our era."[2]

As the FYC writing program administrator, I open the chapter with a broad discussion of what it actually means to "teach sustainability" in FYC. I survey precedents, rationales, and debates on this topic and explore some of the challenges of introducing particular themes, like sustainability, in a writing course, especially in a general studies course such as FYC. In exploring broader definitions of sustainability, intersections between national and local FYC outcomes within the sustainability "paradigm" outlined by Nolet become clear.[3] I conclude my section by taking a close look at the challenges in designing a sample program-wide sustainability syllabus as a "deliverable" for the original 2012 faculty workshop and by sharing how some surprising, simple changes in training and orientation led to more productive and sustainable developments in our FYC program. The remainder of the chapter is given over to my two coauthors whose sustainability-focused course offerings were made possible, nurtured, or inspired by the program-level adjustments that have provided a constant energy source for sustainability's role in our FYC program.

TEACHING FIRST-YEAR COMPOSITION: WAYS INTO SUSTAINABILITY

Sustainability proves to be especially effective as a paradigm for teaching an introductory, general education writing course such as FYC because, in addition to embracing disciplinary knowledge from throughout the university, sustainability is now typically viewed as a values paradigm rather than a topic. As a paradigm, sustainability is capable of accommodating the proclivities, materials, and interests of a large and diverse FYC teaching staff and encompassing an even larger and more diverse student population pursuing majors in a range of disciplines. The idea of sustainability, far from its original roots in environmental and ecological studies, is now often defined as a "worldview," roughly described by a set of four shared characteristics. As summarized by Nolet, the characteristic sustainability "paradigm"

- considers environmental, economic, social, and political systems as interconnected systems rather than discrete entities;
- involves transformation of values and belief systems as well as technological, market, or policy approaches to problem solving;
- views social and economic justice and intergenerational equity as inextricable from environmental stewardship;
- emphasizes personal and collective practices consistent with responsible global citizenship.[4]

Perhaps even more comprehensively, the World Commission on Environment and Development defines sustainability as "meeting the needs of the present without compromising the ability of future generations to meet their own needs."[5] In order to "meet the needs of the present" and the future, students need practice in clear critical thinking, analysis, and, perhaps most of all, reflection—all skills practiced regularly in any FYC class. Teaching sustainability in a writing course can and should involve more than composing debates about recycling.

On the other hand, choosing any particular themed or "special topics" approach to FYC—including the embrace of a broad paradigmatic theme such as sustainability—demands a clear rationale and some justification for several reasons. First, in "special topics" composition courses when a course theme is allowed to dominate, teachers and students can easily lose track of the primary purpose of teaching composition, that is, to teach and learn the vocabulary, habits, and practices of college level writing.

For example, in summer 2002, I taught an oil crisis themed FYC class and the final evaluative comments revealed student's confusion (and resentment) about the course's purpose. In that course, students worked with a series of primary documents about the 1970s oil crisis (Jimmy Carter's speeches, news reports, images of gas station lines, letters and reports from OPEC negotiations), watched related films (*Syriana; Who Killed the Electric Car*), and discussed some secondary commentary (Thomas Friedman's essays on oil "addiction"). Alongside the topic contents, I worked hard to keep students' attention focused on writing in response to these materials and toward their writing processes. Students wrote summaries, syntheses, analyses, and carried out researched writing in addition to producing peer reviews, revision, reflection, and final portfolios. While I judged students' work in the course to be surprisingly sophisticated and thoughtful, students' evaluations were a mixed bag of grumbling and defensiveness: "I signed up for a regular English 1101 class." "In this English 1101 class I did not know that we would be buying history books about the oil crisis." "It did not make sense to me why we had been talking about the oil crisis all semester when really we should have been focusing on our writting [sic] skills." "I was not at all very fond of the idea of my 1101 class being based on the oil crisis. Although it is a subject that is very important to American society, I believe it made the class more difficult to complete." "I found it hard to write about the oil crisis over and over again and constantly found myself very bored of the subject." As these comments reveal, first-year students can be a psychologically conservative bunch, as William Perry pointed out years ago. According to Perry, our students typically enter college with a "Dualistic" world view; this means, that when they sign up for English 1101, they want it to meet their expectations and assumptions about a college writing course and can easily feel cheated and overwhelmed if they do not care for a particular "special" topic.[6]

A second concern with themed composition courses is that the discipline (dating back to Aristotle) is fraught with concerns over the proper "subject" of composition. Those familiar with composition's history will remember the discipline's rise in the 1980s with its concomitant struggle to distinguish itself from literature studies within English departments. They will also recall the culture wars fought in the 1990s and be aware of recent arguments advising that "writing about writing" is the best and most fitting subject matter for composition classes. Then, too, they will understand fears about the loss of control of our "franchise" and will acknowledge the increasing fragmentation of our discipline in the twenty-first century.[7] These are debates that continue, but from a purely disciplinary, professional perspective, composition instructors and administrators need to be sure that composition instruction is primarily concerned with teaching writing processes and that it can be clearly identified as composition instruction whatever topic or "subject" students may be writing about.

Finally, getting the approach to FYC "right" is particularly important because the two-course, six-hour FYC sequence, such as that required in the University of Georgia System core and typical in programs across the country, is the only extended, general, analytical writing instruction and practice in academic discourse many college students will receive. In addition to the limits of FYC's tenuous six-credit hour foothold within student's college writing experience, even this slim six-hour purchase on college writing practice and instruction is fragile: exam-based placement exempts the majority of entering students—currently 60 percent of students entering UGA—from at least half of their six hour composition requirement.[8]

In the 2016 instructional landscape then, a landscape of limited opportunities for writing instruction and practice among college students, it seems essential not only to keep the focus on writing practice in our limited time with incoming college students, but also to find ways to both ethically incorporate the essential themes of sustainability into our FYC courses and to keep FYC courses themselves, sustainable.

THE 2012 SUSTAINABILITY WORKSHOP: LOCATING DEFINITIONS, GOALS, AND MATERIALS

Most of the issues described above were still below the radar when I applied in May 2012 to join a syllabus workshop offered by the UGA's Office of Sustainability. This workshop was designed in response to the Sustainability Office Curriculum Committee's goal to

> provide inspiration, strategies, and examples for engaging students to prepare them to address the challenges of sustainability in their professional, civic, and personal lives regardless of discipline. . . . Provide resources and programs that assist faculty in integrating sustainability into their courses.[9]

I applied for the workshop for two reasons: one personal and one administrative. The personal reason was influenced by my then-limited definition of sustainability, which coincided conveniently with a desire to indulge my historical interest in science, ecology, and environmental issues. As my application stated: "Years ago I completed a BS in Wildlife Biology at Purdue University and have always had an interest in environmental activities." On the other hand, my administrative rationale was aimed toward curricular development. As the associate director for FYC, training and orienting new teachers is a key responsibility, as well as designing and delivering curricular materials.

In developing curricula, our office's administrative philosophy provides for both a reasonable degree of program standardization while, at the same time, allows our teachers the broadest possible range of choices and approaches. We believe that offering an open syllabus template and many examples and models of successful syllabi, rather than a "standard" syllabus, boosts our teachers' professional investment and creative reward; they adapt their distinctive interests and specializations to program standards by creating their own syllabi. In participating in the workshop, I hoped to develop a new sample FYC syllabus, one that would invite some of our ninety-plus teachers to incorporate sustainability themes into their composition courses in unique ways while still fulfilling the specific goals and objectives of our program.

Going into the sustainability workshop, I had few specific ideas about the syllabus I hoped to develop and a very limited notion of sustainability, mostly related to composting and recycling and, uneasily, to the moderately unsuccessful oil crisis topic I described above. I had not even decided whether I would try to work toward an English 1101 syllabus—which in our case is a nonfiction genre and analysis-based composition course—or an English 1102 syllabus—which has many of the same goals as English 1101 but works with *literary* texts: poems, stories, and plays. I hoped the workshop would clarify the key elements of sustainability and would offer, as promised, some ideas and examples of ways to incorporate those elements into a composition course.

The workshop leaders encouraged participants to begin syllabus development by identifying their course's key goals and objectives. By outlining our objectives, we could then identify potential venues and assignments where sustainability themes and topics could be introduced. For example, a math professor exchanged standard practice problems for "sustainability" calculations such as determining decomposition rates for compostable organics; a consumer sciences professor used environmental limit case studies to replace the generic qualitative research cases found in her textbook, and a romance languages instructor replaced many of her standard translation exercises with Italian and French news articles about climate change, oil prices, and carbon footprints. My definition of sustainability began to shift and expand when a materials engineering professor declared his intention to study sustainable manufacturing practices and a landscape architect shared her approaches to sustainable design in "hardscapes." In every case the workshop leaders encouraged us to first identify our own course goals and standards and then to use them as guides for responsibly adapting and adopting sustainability themes and concepts into our normal course material.

In FYC, our goals and standards are defined at the national level by the Council of Writing Program Administrators (CWPA) and the National Council of Teachers of English (NCTE), at the state level by our university system and board of regents, and at the university and program level by our own local FYC program's interpretation of these various national and state standards, which we publish explicitly as course goals and include implicitly in our grading rubrics.

At the national level, the CWPA's "Framework for Success in Postsecondary Writing" and the related "WPA Outcomes Statement for First-Year Composition" were developed collaboratively with representatives from the CWPA, NCTE, and the National Writing Project.[10] These two documents together represent national touchstones for first-year writing instruction. The framework outlines the "rhetorical and twenty-first-century skills as well as habits of mind and experiences that are critical for college success" while the "Outcomes Statement" "describes the writing knowledge, practices, and attitudes that undergraduate students develop in first-year composition." Neither document sets standards for local programs; in fact, the collaborators specifically reject any attempt to set local standards. On the other hand, both sets of standards attempt to "represent and regularize writing program priorities for first-year composition."[11] In brief then, the framework lays out the attitudes and behaviors that lead to success in college writing while the outcomes point the way toward assessing the achievement of those attitudes and behaviors.

The framework identifies eight habits of mind essential for success in college writing:

- Curiosity—the desire to know more about the world.
- Openness—the willingness to consider new ways of being and thinking in the world.
- Engagement—a sense of investment and involvement in learning.
- Creativity—the ability to use novel approaches for generating, investigating, and representing ideas.
- Persistence—the ability to sustain interest in and attention to short- and long-term projects.
- Responsibility—the ability to take ownership of one's actions and understand the consequences of those actions for oneself and others.
- Flexibility—the ability to adapt to situations, expectations, or demands.
- Metacognition—the ability to reflect on one's own thinking as well as on the individual and cultural processes used to structure knowledge.[12]

The framework leads to the practices described by the CWPA outcomes, which includes these five skill groups:

1. Rhetorical knowledge—the ability to analyze and act on understandings of audiences, purposes, and contexts in creating and comprehending texts;
2. Critical thinking—the ability to analyze a situation or text and make thoughtful decisions based on that analysis, through writing, reading, and research;
3. Writing processes—multiple strategies to approach and undertake writing and research;
4. Knowledge of conventions—the formal and informal guidelines that define what is considered to be correct and appropriate, or incorrect and inappropriate, in a piece of writing;
5. Abilities to compose in multiple environments—from using traditional pen and paper to electronic technologies.[13]

Both the WPA framework and the WPA outcomes directly mirror Nolet's sustainability paradigm outlined above. The framework's eight "habits of mind"—curiosity, openness, engagement, creativity, persistence, responsibility, flexibility, and metacognition—intersect repeatedly with the behaviors accounted for in the four-part sustainability paradigm Nolet describes. For example, the framework's "curiosity," "flexibility," and "openness" map closely onto the sustainability paradigm's "transformational problem solving"; the framework's "persistence" and "responsibility," clearly align with the sustainability paradigm's "personally and collectively responsible practices"; and the framework's "creativity" and "metacognition" are essential to developing the sustainability paradigm's "desire for integrity" and "social and economic justice" while also stirring "recognition of the interconnectedness of systems."

The ease with which this sustainability paradigm intersects with the goals and standards of the composition community make sense when we think of the "rules" of engagement for academic discourse, which are, in most ways, simply a heightened, more logical and more extended form of civil communication. Like academic discourse, sustainability is a conscious and consistent form of civility toward the resources of planet earth to "meet the needs of the present without compromising the ability of future generations to meet their own needs."[14] It is safe to conclude that FYC, as a discipline, provides an excellent venue for conveying the sustainability paradigm and, in fact, adopts a priori a sustainability perspective.

Finally, in preparing to integrate sustainability into a standardized syllabus, the leaders of the workshop encouraged participants to explore and share sustainability materials: textbooks, websites, and other useful teaching resources. We worked through parts of a UNESCO website, Teaching and Learning for a Sustainable Future: A Multimedia Teacher Education Programme, a series of general education materials on Bloom's taxonomy and course objectives, and brought in and shared texts related to sustainability in our own disciplines. My goal in syllabus development at the time was to use our program's standard texts and materials as a basis for a simple integration of sustainability themes or topics that anyone could adopt without ordering special materials (or for that matter that students might mistake for "history" texts!). I also made a decision relatively early in the workshop to design my syllabus for our literature based FYC course, English 1102, both because it seemed like more of a challenge, but also and more importantly because, as noted above, a major percentage of our incoming students take just this one course. I found it especially helpful to make an individual review of the available resources aimed at writing classes and explored textbooks that might be useful in a supporting or guiding role for a sustainability-focused FYC course. These could be fairly represented by three basic genres of sustainability or sustainability-related textbooks.

The first group includes *general* readers. These topical nonfiction readers comprise a mix of nonfiction articles, excerpts, and literary essays related specifically to sustainability or more generally to environmental issues and topics. Writing apparatus is usually limited, if there is any, but may include prompts for discussion, thinking, and writing. General readers also often introduce individual texts or entire sections with short contextualizing headnotes and explanations. *Green*, edited by Brooke Rollins and Lee Bauknight, is a good example of a brief reader, along with *Sustainability: A Bedford Spotlight Reader,* edited by Christian Weisser, and *Sustainability: A Reader for Writers,* edited by Carl Herndl.

Each of these collections emphasize slightly different perspectives. For example, *Green* highlights short contemporary writings in a variety of accessible genres, such as excerpts from contemporary books like Colin Beavan's article "Life After a Year Without Toilet Paper," an excerpt from *As the World Burns: 50 Things You Can Do to Stay in Denial*, a graphic text by Derrick Jensen and Stephanie McMillan; and lists and links to films and music. Weisser's collection starts with foundational environmental and political texts from Muir, Thoreau, and Leopold and then branches out through time into essays on political commentary, environmental crisis response, and urban and global sustainability. Herndl's collection also covers ground thematically, but sticks to contemporary texts and journalistic commentary essays by authors such as Michael Pollan and Thomas Friedman. Herndl's collection, like Weisser's, groups articles by theme, but focuses on specific content areas: trash, food, soil, and climate change. Teachers might also look to the *Best American Science and Nature Writing* series in this category.

Specific collections such as *At Home on This Earth: Two Centuries of US Women & Nature Writing*, edited by Lorraine Anderson and Thomas S. Edwards, takes a diachronic view of women's nature writing, represents a specialized reader subset. There are also available a fairly large group of environmentally focused, specifically literary readers. Poetry, especially poetry concentrated on particular themes, seems to be very popular. For example, *The Ecopoetry Anthology*, edited by Ann Fisher-Wirth and Laura-Gray Street; *Can Poetry Save the Earth: A Field Guide to Nature Poems*, by John Felstiner; *Black Nature: Four Centuries of African American Nature Poetry*, by Camille T. Dungy and Sibley Alexander; and *Bright Wings: An Illustrated Anthology of Poems About Birds*, by Billy Collins and David Allen.

After general and specialized readers, the second text group embraces collections that practice or teach *rhetorical criticism* around and through environmental literature. Many of these texts might provide source ideas or readings for a first-year class, but would likely be too advanced and specific to use as a stand-alone textbook. Among these, we could include specific explorations of environmental rhetoric such as Killingsworth and Palmer's 1992 examination of political rhetoric *Ecospeak: Rhetoric and Environmental Politics in America*, or Daniel Philippon's 2004 study of historical rhetoric *Conserving Words: How American Nature Writers Shaped the Environmental Movement.* Sydney Dobrin and Christian Weisser's *Natural Discourse: Toward Ecocomposition* is one of a series of books they have authored or coauthored developing the concept "ecocomposition." Lawrence Buell's 2005 reflection on the impact of continued environmental calamities on literary works, *The Future of Environmental Criticism: Environmental Crisis and Literary Imagination* would also belong in this group, as would Timothy Clark's, *The Cambridge Introduction to Literature and the Environment.* Herndl and Brown's 1996 collection, *Green Culture: Environmental Rhetoric in Contemporary America* or Waddell's 1998 *Landmark Essays on Rhetoric and the Environment*, both collections of rhetorical analysis, criticism, and commentary, would also belong here.

A third major group of texts is specifically meant *to guide writing instruction*, and the three representatives described here all encourage students to produce texts. This group includes Cox and Pezzullo's *Environmental Communication and the Public Sphere*. This text specifically teaches writing/communicating as environmental advocacy. It introduces major movements, historical trends, and key definitions and prepares students for the "markets, campaigns, media forums, and messaging strategies that will allow them to inform and influence public opinion on matters related to the environment."[15] While this text might be more suitable for a journalism or professional writing course, it provides useful background for teachers in other fields.

Saving Place: An Ecocomposition Reader, Sidney Dobrin's 2005 text, lays out the principles of eco-composition discussed also in *Natural Discourse*, which Dobrin co-wrote with Christian Weisser. *Saving Place*, however, was written specifically for introductory composition courses. In *Saving Place*, Dobrin encourages teachers and their students to see that "writing and environment are deeply enmeshed."[16] Dobrin uses the tools of traditional composition courses (including incorporation of the WPA outcomes described above) to help students engage with the rhetorical environment *within* the written text at the same time that they encounter texts *about* the natural environment. As Dobrin describes it, "ecocomposition combines the study of writing—composition—with the study of relationships between organisms and their environment—ecology."[17] The readings are primarily literary essays (broadly, "nature writing"): Emerson, Thoreau, Muir, and Leopold, Edward Abbey, Annie Dillard, Gary Snyder, Janisse Ray, Terry Tempest Williams, and Wendell Berry.

The third major text in this writing instruction group, while geared to composition teachers, is meant also for a broader audience of "researchers and practitioners outside the realms of composition and English studies—namely, any postsecondary educator willing to consider the potential impact of sustainability on his or her research and teaching."[18] Published in 2001, Derek Owens' *Composition and Sustainability: Teaching for a Threatened Generation* aims to encourage a "pedagogy of sustainability" through writing and composition that will reach across the curriculum. Owens calls it "sustainability across the curriculum"—an SAC to complement WAC (Writing Across the Curriculum).

Many of the texts above informed and influenced my eventual course design and syllabus, as did the workshop's emphasis on sharing ideas, defining goals, and expanding our concepts of sustainability. In the final analysis though, it was one of our final workshop activities, a simple stroll through campus learning about the history of our campus landscape and the effect of sustainable design on our academic setting, that was to, eventually, have the greatest impact and the most sustained influence on our FYC program. My first task after the workshop, however, was to design an open-ended and flexible FYC syllabus incorporating sustainability themes and ideas.

DEVELOPING AN ENGLISH 1102 COURSE WITH A SUSTAINABILITY THEME: THREE ASSIGNMENTS

Incorporating sustainability themes in English 1101, which draws on nonfiction reading, can be straightforward. In fact, as Derek Owens points out, the "contextual freedom and disciplinary flexibility" of the typical English 1101 course gives a "writing teacher more leverage" for providing "an introductory arena where students begin to view their personal and academic needs and desires through the lens of sustainability."[19] He points out, too, that the interdisciplinary nature of English 1101 fits the sustainability paradigm and "in this sense, we can envision composition studies as environmental studies—not an offshoot of ecology but as the study of one's immediate and future environs."[20] Finally, Owens simply declares that introductory composition courses provide a perfect subject-neutral arena for introducing students to sustainability concepts; Owens asks, "If you can make them read and write about anything, why not a subject that is crucial to their intellectual, spiritual, economic, and physical survival?"[21] In other words, and despite the caveats described above, English 1101 with its focus on nonfiction texts can be readily redesigned to accommodate various themes. So, recalling the numbers of students who move directly to English 1102 as described above, I set to work on integrating sustainability themes into a more challenging area—our literature-based English 1102 curriculum.

At our institution, English 1102 takes a traditional (some might say old-fashioned) approach to teaching composition through the close reading and analysis of literary texts: stories, poems, and plays. In a recent defense of literature as primary content in FYC, Christine Farris nevertheless worries that teaching argument through literature may force FYC teachers to "return to literary interpretation at the expense of attention to students' writing processes and production of texts, which are central to what composition does."[22] Yet, Farris primarily argues that finding a way to preserve the relationship between literary study and composition is "central to pedagogical and political issues in English studies."[23] Adding a third component—sustainability—to literary interpretation and writing processes, seems to hold the potential to both overload and further confuse course goals.

The English 1102 "sustainability" course I developed was sparked to some degree by the questions raised on the UNESCO website about storytelling and sustainability. The authors point out that an increased interest by educators in storytelling

> has led [them] to think about ways in which storytelling can be used to explore important shared themes and visions. . . . Not only do such stories offer a source of inspiration, they also contain a potential for understanding the many ways in

which we value and devalue our beautiful green and blue planet. Stories provide us with practical insight into approaches to our most persistent environmental difficulties.[24]

Exploring that connection between stories and sustainability was reflected in the course's eventual title question: "Is There a Sustainable Narrative?"

In designing the course, I challenged myself to produce a "standard" section of English 1102—using only our standard texts (at that time, John Schilb's *Making Literature Matter* and Andrea Lunsford's *St. Martin's Handbook*), and meeting all our standard FYC program requirements such as requiring three longer staged and scaffolded papers with opportunities for revision, frequent peer review, a final portfolio, the use of a standard grading rubric, and over all, a methodology of encouraging appreciation for "literary texts through reading fiction, drama, and poetry" and of writing "analytically about them."[25] At the same time, I hoped to use those requirements to explore the way students answered core questions about sustainability: How can a narrative support or undermine sustainability? How do literary works define and demonstrate sustainability? Is there such a thing as a sustainability narrative or a sustainable narrative? My major task lay in developing three core writing assignments; these three assignments would integrate the standard goals of English 1102 and the FYC program with some of the goals of the sustainability workshop and begin to answer these essential questions.

The first major project remixed several assignments and involved a series of four sequenced and related low-stakes writing tasks culminating with composing an original narrative. For the first task in the series, I adapted Derek Owens' "Campus Profile" assignment.[26] Students researched, compiled, and summarized information about a "special place" of their choosing. Often they chose their home neighborhood, but this varied. One student chose a special vacation retreat, another chose a grandparent's farm, and another chose the rear-loading dock of a local pizza place. To complete the assignment, they found and archived information about their "places":

- municipality
- water shed
- power source and/or fuel source
- names of their government officials from local to national
- soil types in the area
- climate, topography, yearly rainfall
- products and industries
- when the area was settled or discovered or incorporated
- pictures, maps, or images of the surrounding area

After they completed this researched "place report," they next answered a series of questions leading to an exploratory, descriptive essay about this special location.

Working with the profile archive and exploratory descriptive essay, students would next design and chart a plot scheme that could incorporate their "place" as the setting. The fourth and final task was to compose a brief imaginative narrative using their archives of detail to found a story in this particular setting. This assignment met many standard English 1102 goals, including practice completing extensive research and documentation, practice in first person observation, practice in writing specific, detailed description, and finally practice in plot analysis and definition. While I had to adapt our standard rubric to evaluate their completed project, I was still able to work within our basic evaluative categories: unity, evidence, presentation and design, coherence, and audience.

The story archives were often illustrated with the students' own photos and included neighborhood scenes as varied as a brilliantly graffitied tenement in Brooklyn, an exclusive gated high rise in Hong Kong, and a Montana prairie farmscape.

We called the final element in these collections—their stories—their "place narratives." The main requirement for the narrative was that the students would use their archive to provide backstory and to flesh out elements of their story's setting. This brief story was actually the least important element in the project overall, but writing it gave them a chance to have some creative play, incorporating their descriptions and research archives. They also exercised their understanding of plot, character, and most importantly, of their familiar setting. They loved the creative space and put a good deal of energy into their stories.

One student's story, Kate's, recounted her imagined version of a well-known family tale: how her great-grandmother and great-grandfather met, fell in love, and founded a small but successful family farm, where they lived together for sixty-nine years and where Kate spent her summers and holidays growing up. Most of Kate's classmates, however, developed dramatic stories of confrontation and conflict in their home neighborhoods: getting chased by wild dogs, getting knocked out, nearly drowning, fighting monsters and evil gnomes, being in dangerous fires, and having nightmares. I will have more to say about this later, but I will also say that most of their stories—at least—had happy endings.

The second major project I developed for the new syllabus was a digital poetry anthology: a collection of five poems the students self-selected to represent, define, and/or illustrate the general topic "sustainability" from the several hundred poems in their standard text, John Schilb and John Clifford's *Making*

Literature Matter. For their digital anthology, students researched and wrote headnotes, made audio recordings of their readings, chose illustrative images, researched and wrote annotations, wrote line-by-line paraphrases, and, in some cases, prepared creative or personal responses to the selections. The major written product of the project was an introductory reflective essay explaining and defining the relationship of the chosen poems to the sustainability theme. In completing this project, the students engaged deeply with poetry as a genre, while also practicing the "collecting, selecting, reflecting" activities that would later be required in their capstone course portfolio. Meanwhile, they were broadening their understanding of sustainability by developing and illustrating their own unique definitions of sustainability in their collection essays. As a key step in the process of drafting their anthology, students wrote out brief definitions of sustainability. Here's a sample of the definitions the students composed and then used to select their anthology poems:

- Poets can write about century old ideas and still have a heavy impact on modern day people. Even if things disappear and are tarnished, ideas will still remain. That is true sustainability.—*Melissa*
- The idea of sustainability is most consistent with the balance of the yin and yang involving the whole universe.—*Sylvia*
- Sustainability is the opposite of apocalyptic.—*Ujash*
- When I think of sustainability I think of the term "surviving": surviving to live until old age, your soul surviving past your body's decay, your love surviving the test of time, and the Earth surviving to encompass it all.—*Katy*
- Sustainability through literature gives hope through words in a subtle way we may not realize. There will be a tomorrow, and that sense of *more*—more time, more chances, more love—will drive us forward.—*Amanda*
- The main driving factors in this ability to sustain are hope and love.—*Sheryle*

The third and final major project attempted to make connections with sustainability through a traditional literary analysis of a play, in this case Chekov's *The Cherry Orchard*. The selection of Chekov's *The Cherry Orchard* was primarily based on its open source digital availability, which made it possible to perform searches in the text, but, in addition, the play's central focus on property, changing political times, and the titular cherry orchard on the Ranevsky estate offered a potentially productive connection to our sustainability theme. The students read the play's first and third acts aloud in class, watched selections from the hyperrealistic 1999 filmed production (directed by Michael Caccoyannis), read and summarized a series of performance reviews, and analyzed the functions of each of the characters. For the final analysis essay, they selected a single image or word from the play and used the search function to trace every instance of that word/motif. While I hoped the setting, and specifically the orchard, would produce some interesting related analyses, only a few of the students chose to focus on the landscape of the play, and some of the better papers worked on the ideas of guilt, money, and mobility. As it turned out, while Chekov's cherry trees certainly carry the burden of an extended metaphor throughout all the business of the play, they seem to function, for my students at least, entirely as the "tokens" Wendell Berry describes in his 2014 South Atlantic Modern Language Association plenary address.[27] That is, the trees are never seen as real trees; they are a token, or substitute, for the thing actually valued—in this case, money.

The final project in our class—as in all our program's FYC courses—is an ePortfolio. Our ePortfolio is a digital collection including two of three major projects/papers polished and revised, an exhibit demonstrating the student's revising process, an exhibit demonstrating his or her ability to peer review, a brief biographical headnote as a homepage, and a wild card exhibit to act as a concluding frame. These exhibits are all introduced and woven together thoughtfully (we hope) in an introductory reflective essay. I encouraged this class to incorporate sustainability as a theme for their final collections.

The introduction from one of my favorite portfolios opens with an image of the author, a young man aspiring to a degree in elementary education, with a couple of school kids on his shoulders. The portfolio's author, Chris, writes, "This portfolio catches the essence of my new found definition of sustainability: the ability of humans to use love to endure through tough situations in hope of achieving a better future."[28] Compare Chris's definition to the one from the World Commission on Environment and Development (WCED) wherein sustainability means "meeting the needs of the present without compromising the ability of future generations to meet their own needs."[29] In other words, through the work of the course, Chris was able to formulate a personal sustainability definition that aligns closely to that of the WCED.

Overall, the course I designed was moderately successful. On the positive side, students worked in both scholarly and creative written genres to reflect on what sustainability might mean in relation to their own lives and environments. Sustainability did not feel like a tacked-on recycling concept and no one complained about buying the standard texts or felt as if they had missed taking English 1102. Also, students engaged with most of the goals of our FYC program, if not always consciously. On the negative side, the course felt rushed and overburdened for a summer eight-week class; my major projects were all lengthy, involving many steps and intermediate writing assignments. Students could have used additional weeks to read, absorb, discuss, reflect, and revise the material they were turning in. In other words, the primary product of the original sustainability workshop, a new course syllabus, still needed a good bit of modification and revision to be useful as a curricular model.

On the other hand, the byproducts of the workshop proved to be the real and primary source for making sustainability a continual theme in our FYC program. As it turned out, the key element in making "sustainability" viable in our program was not by providing a sample syllabus or new scaffolded assignments, but instead by introducing those sustainability workshop ideas and resources to our new teachers each year. This approach gives our teachers the freedom to develop an entire sustainability-related syllabus, to foster a single sustainability-themed assignment, or simply to share those sustainability workshop resources and connections with interested students in their classes. A particularly effective strategy was taking new teachers on a "sustainability walk" through campus. Starting that first August in 2012 and each year since, our new teaching assistants and teachers enjoy a break from classroom orientation hours to enjoy a sweaty walk around their new academic home. At stops along the way, our guide from the Sustainability Office answers questions, describes the underground cisterns next to a rain garden, points out solar installations on the roof of a design studio, tells stories about hidden streams in our campus watershed (one that runs, weirdly, under the middle of our football field in Sanford Stadium), explains how sustainability projects are funded and how students can win small grants by proposing sustainable projects, and more. He sometimes demonstrates the latest installation of the mobile goat herd, funded by one of those grants, and always takes us to the tiny rehabilitated wetland, the town spring, and tells the story of the university's founding. After the walks, these campus places, impressions, and resources just naturally begin to "meander" through our program, uncovering new springs of energy willing to place sustainability at course center.

My coauthors, two of the doctoral students inspired by the introduction of sustainability in their teaching orientations and by the programmatic freedom to develop their own syllabi, describe below the very different ways they incorporated sustainability themes in their FYC courses. Here are their stories.

MEANDERING TOWARD SUSTAINABILITY: LINDSAY TIGUE'S ENGLISH 1101

Before coming to the University of Georgia to complete a PhD in English and creative writing, I completed a master of fine arts (MFA) in creative writing and environment at Iowa State University. This master's program had a unique interdisciplinary focus on sustainability and the environment. The idea behind the program at Iowa State is that good communicators—good writers—must take the crucial, dire, and powerful information about the state of the environment and share it in meaningful ways with the public. Taking this further is the idea that, if you give a place (or the earth) its proper story—its due—then people will care. People will act. This core idea of communicating what sustainability *is*, what it means, has been central to my own teaching. At Iowa State, I taught several sustainability themed composition courses. I was interested in getting students to discuss what the term means and how people talk about this buzzword. I was careful to distinguish between my composition courses and an environmental studies course. I explained that we would be focusing on writing and, when reading, we would discuss the inherent issues, but that we would access them by thinking about various rhetorical strategies the authors employed.

When I first taught the course, I broke the class into several thematic units—connecting to place, environmental justice, sustainable agriculture, and environmental activism. During each section I chose readings that went along with the outlined umbrella topic. While we covered this content, we also moved through various written, oral, visual, and electronic rhetorical units. During the first week, I began with an environmental biography. This was an in-class writing assignment that had students read a brief Annie Dillard excerpt from *An American Childhood* and then write about their own connections to the natural world. This early in-class writing project served as a diagnostic that I could use when moving forward. It also served to tell me where students were in terms of their engagement with the natural world, providing a backbone for introducing other sustainability topics.

One thing I found when first teaching an environmentally themed course was that the students really enjoyed thinking about the connections between sustainability and a sense of place. They engaged with the idea that, in order to get people to care about sustainability, they first need to care about places. People are more apt to fight to save their home, their community, and this connection can serve as a window to talk about larger, global environmental issues. We would begin by talking about the students' homes and, since we were in Iowa, we would discuss the original landscape of the plains and the tiny amount of remnant prairie still around them. It was fascinating to talk with students about the definition of "nature" as many of them came from agricultural areas that they considered full of "natural" beauty, but which were actually completely transformed from their original state. That being said, many others also connected with wooded areas, rivers, and parks that they wanted to see protected. Later in the semester we moved toward more global issues, and we talked about the "not in my backyard" issues that environmental justice advocacy organizations are trying to bring to light. We read an essay by Nydia Valasquez called "In Search of Justice" that revealed to them the amount of Superfund sites in or near underserved neighborhoods. Many of them were appalled and had never really thought about the crossovers between sustainability and social justice. After that, we read Tegan Nia Swanson's "Everything Rises on an Atoll," an essay about an American woman's experience living on the Marshall Islands, and they learned about the environmental issues plaguing these islands and atolls. They learned how the Marshallese will eventually become climate change refugees due to rising waters. The author of this essay came to visit my class and they were able to consider the atrocity of having to leave one's home and what it really means to be connected to a place.

When I came to the University of Georgia, I began teaching introductory composition (English 1101) within their well established FYC curricular framework. I thought about my experiences teaching an environmentally themed composition course, and I brainstormed ways I could adapt the course to fit into this new program. I recalled the ways my former students had connected to place as an entry point into larger sustainability topics, and I decided to theme my course around "a sense of place." This was an exceptionally relevant topic for most of my students as a large portion of them were freshmen who had relocated from elsewhere in Georgia, the United States, or internationally to attend the university. I wanted them to think about a place that they connected with (it could be their home, but it might not be) and to think about how they might connect with the environment around them. On my course overview and syllabus, I included a Gary Snyder quote that encapsulated my reasoning behind the course theme, "Find your place on the planet. Dig in, and take responsibility from there."[30] This quote demonstrates the way a sense of place can be a jumping-off point for a larger environmental accountability. Early on in the semester, I also had a representative from the sustainability office give my students a sustainability tour around campus so that they could see the recycling, green space, and energy and projects happening around them. I had originally gone on this tour during my teaching assistantship orientation, and I was impressed by many of the initiatives the office was sponsoring. This also allowed students to see what the money in their "green fee" (a part of the matriculation fees for the semester) goes toward firsthand.

Iowa State's composition program's main projects are a five hundred-word summary, a textual rhetorical analysis, a visual rhetorical analysis (which I incorporated as a group presentation wherein they analyzed a documentary about an environmental issue), a researched argumentative paper (about an environmental issue of their choosing) and an accompanying individual presentation, and a final portfolio. At the University of Georgia, the FYC program for English 1101 includes three main projects and a final portfolio. Prior to any of the official projects, I assigned a similar diagnostic that served as kind of an environmental place-based narrative. The students completed an in-class writing project where they described a place they've connected to, whether it be their home, someplace they have lived or stayed temporarily, or some place they have visited and been impacted by. For the first project, I did a genre analysis paper and the students rhetorically analyzed the official tourism website for a state of their choosing within the United States. For the second project, the students researched an environmental topic and wrote an argumentative research paper. I provided a list of potential topics such as, environmental justice, sustainable agriculture, bike lanes and public transit, alternative energies, supermarket waste and dumpster diving, overfishing, deforestation, and species extinction. I required that students zero in their topic in a particular place. So, for example they might choose how overfishing is affecting food culture in Japan, or how deforestation is impacting particular communities in Brazil. This went along nicely with the overall course theme of a sense of place, and it really encouraged the students to be specific. It narrowed their topics and helped them focus their research. In this way, sustainability topics can be a great choice in a composition classroom because they make that local to global connection clear. In composition instruction, I am always trying to encourage my students to be more specific, to use more concrete evidence, and to explicitly make connections between the specific evidence and larger issues and ideas. One student, in a reflection, wrote about her process of choosing a topic and making sure her evidence actually supported a specific argument. She said:

> To me, creating bike lanes is one of the most important processes in the nation. I had the chance to read more about the topic and learn the unbelievable benefits that could be generated from such projects. . . . It took me a while to write my thesis for this paper. I was not sure exactly what the message I want to deliver here is. I wanted to state to people that riding a bike could save their lives but then I realized that I have to be aware that my topic is bike lanes not riding bikes. This was a little challenging for me. This was tricky because I could easily relate bike lanes to so many different issues but I had to stay on topic. I tried not to get off topic as much as possible and I ended up writing my thesis to be addressing the issue of riding bikes versus riding cars.

Having students focus on these specific place-based topics helped them to better avoid the generalities, abstractions, and vague language that can often plague beginning composition projects. It also helps students to think about bias and how to avoid it in their papers, how they need to avoid logical fallacies in their arguments and rely on evidence. One student reflected:

> For the second paper in the class, we choose a sustainability topic to write about. Being the outdoorsman I am, I chose to write about the growing deer population in suburban areas. Writing about something I relate to and experience everyday would make it easier to develop my voice. However, my subject matter was more controversial than other sustainability topics like oil pipelines or reducing industrial waste, so I had to make sure my voice was professional. I found a few very interesting articles from reliable sources that presented very useful information for my augment. However, I started to run into a problem. Being professional, calling for action and developing my voice do not fit together very well. Despite my best efforts, my own bias and opinions crept into my paper more than I would have liked. In my defense, I was trying to persuade readers to take action, so I needed to appeal to their reason and emotions. I appealed to their reason respectively, but I was a little overwhelming with my emotional appeal. I also was not as organized in this paper. I earned an 83 on this paper which was lower than I was expecting. However, this was still a learning experience for me, and I have the rest of my portfolio to continue to work on my writing.

For this student, the researched argument project was a chance to discover his own bias and to see how to avoid it in a researched paper. He also understood the course's focus on process as he mentioned his plans for revision.

In addition to the primary projects I assigned in my "Sense of Place" composition class, I also assigned weekly journal assignments responding to our readings. One assignment asked the students to volunteer somewhere or attend a cultural activity in town—an art museum or exhibit, the farmer's market, the student organic farm, or youth shelter, etc. The idea with this assignment was to increase students' sense of place by having them explore and connect with this (possibly) new place around them. I also offered extra credit to students who went on one of the historical self-guided walking or driving tours put together by the Athens Welcome Center, which included tours about African American history, Civil War history, and local music history. Students who went on these tours found it a worthwhile way to learn more about where they were living.

Throughout the semester I assigned a variety of readings from both our rhetoric textbook (*The Bedford Book of Genres*) and also a course pack of readings about sustainability and a sense of place. I assigned Michael Martone's essay about living in the Midwest "The Flatness," which teaches students about closely seeing the places around them. This essay came early in the semester and served as a good introduction for close reading and analyzing an author's strategies. In a later reflection, one student wrote:

> At the beginning of the semester, I read some of the assignments and thought that the author's point was one thing but in reality it was another. One such reading assignment was by author Michael Martone. In his essay "The Flatness"

he writes about the terrain of the Midwest. When I first read this essay, I thought he was only describing the land as flat with slight changes in elevation that no one noticed. When we discussed this paper in class I realized that the paper was saying even though to most people the land was flat, because he was so accustomed to the land, he became so in tune that he could feel every change in the terrain and knew of every bump. This changed the meaning of the essay from the land is flat and uneventful to the author describing that even though the land is flat, he knows everything about it because it is a part of his sense of place. Doing exercises like these helped me think critically on the papers I read in order to get the correct meaning of a paper.

I also assigned the article "What is Sense of Place" by Jennifer E. Cross, professor in the Department of Sociology at Colorado State University. Cross outlines how various academic disciplines define this term and then also the various kinds of relationships people have to place. Other authors the class read include Joan Didion, Barbara Kingsolver, Pico Iyer, Wendell Berry, Rebecca Solnit, and Richard Louv. We also read some more technical articles and data that broke down the idea of "livable" cities, and we discussed what livability really means.

Overall, I found that the concept of "a sense of place" as a window into sustainability provided a great framework for teaching rhetorical concepts. We talked about visual strategies and how places are used in persuasive and informational genres as well as how to "read" visuals and determine what appeals and strategies are at play. The students got practice in applying specific and interesting research toward developing a focused thesis that connects to a larger theme of cultural importance. And finally, the students, in their third project, practiced remixing that research into a presentation that included a multimodal component that they created (a video, a website or blog, an electronic advertisement, or animation). In a course evaluation, a student said, "The course was well organized and every assignment was toward a sense of place. . . . I thought it was a well-structured system of assignments." And another student said, "She did a good job explaining and helping us understand how each assignment was connected to a sense of place. Each assignment was geared toward this theme. I thought this was a good way to teach us on our own what a sense of place is to us."

At the end of the course, as a part of the FYC curriculum, the students put together a portfolio that included revised versions of their original papers. In their portfolios, they included a reflective essay and many students used this assignment to comment upon the theme of the course and the various assignments. One student wrote:

> Our class was focused around the idea that each person creates their own "sense of place," which was applicable to my life, as this is my first semester of col-

lege, and my first time having to make a new home for myself. I was able to learn, through the writing of others, that no matter what the circumstance is, or where the person is located, a sense of place is created, and that everything affects sense of place. This idea was always in the back of my mind during my first semester, as I tried to make Athens my new home.

This idea of how people affect places came up in other reflections as well and demonstrated to me that students understood this connection between sense of place and sustainability. Another student commented, "In the second paper, I show a sense of place that is falling apart due to people's actions. The paper shows that someone's sense of place can be lost, and that people should thoroughly think how their acts will affect others."

It was my goal to design a class that students could apply to their lives beyond the classroom. It was my hope that when students saw environmental arguments and sustainability initiatives and responses to those initiatives in the media and around them, that they could feel they had a knowledge base to understand and analyze them. One student wrote, about choosing a project and the class generally:

> I remembered a video I saw online earlier this year about solar roadways. This topic was immensely interesting to me and, as I began to plan and write my paper, I became passionate about it. I developed that connection and ended up enjoying this paper a lot more than my first. This plus what we read and talked about in class caused me to think about the cups I was using, notice the plastic bags that crossed my path, see all the faults with our current roadway system, and so much more. I appreciate this. I appreciate the fact that this class has come home with me. I haven't just been going to class and leaving behind everything we talked about once I was out of the classroom. This is a class that will stay with me forever.

The students in my English 1101 class at the University of Georgia ultimately understood that environmental responsibility is intimately connected to place and how one relates to the surrounding world. In addition, my students successfully practiced rhetorical analysis and were able to develop successful argumentative and analytic papers while engaging with a critical and timely topic.

ANOTHER MEANDER: DEVELOPING INDIVIDUAL ASSIGNMENTS—KIM WATERS'S NARRATIVE "A GOOD PLANET IS HARD TO FIND: THERE IS NO PLANET B"

I grew up in the woods—playing in the tree house with my sister and brother—and camping with my family, especially in the cold months when the bug population had gone down for the season. My dad and brother hunted. I didn't, but I ate the game: venison (*Odocoileus virginianus*), bobwhite quail (*Colinus virginianus*), dove (*Zenaida macroura*), rattlesnake (*Crotalus adamanteus*), rabbit (*Sylvilagus floridanus*), and wild turkey (*Meleagris gallopavo silvestris*), to name a few of my favorites (venison tenderloin in a pinot-sour cherry reduction on angel biscuits . . . nothing finer). But my dad was clear, we only kill what we will eat. It's not sport; it's providing sustenance. Well, what he actually said was, "Hit's puttin' food on tha table." All this by way of saying, I have a long, rich, and continuing connection to the natural world. I understand now, more than ever, that there is no Planet B. We must endeavor to protect and sustain this one.

An example from my daily life: Few natural predators exist for deer in our region. Not anymore. Deer populations are growing and many deer have trouble finding food and water in the woods so they move into the suburbs. Day lilies (*Hemerocallis fulva*) and roses (*Floribunda*) are favorites, as is my Harry Lauder's Walking Stick (*Corylus avellana*). And the birdbath (*Concretus genericus*) is popular in times of drought. My experience is not unique. Clearly, nature and civilization are out of balance.

Fast Forward >>

Having abandoned the private sector for the academy, I found myself one hot August afternoon hiking around North Campus at the University of Georgia. I marveled at how the spring, around which this great land grant university, the oldest publicly chartered university in the United States, now trickled out of a drainage pipe. Trickled. The usual suspects are to blame: soil run off, invasive nonindigenous plant species, and litter. I remember standing with my mouth open, my gaze fixated on that trickle. I stood among a cohort of new English teaching assistants (TAs), as Kevin Kirsche, director of UGA's Office of Sustainability (OOS) and leader of our tour, explained how Spring Street has all but lost its eponymous link. I had no way of knowing how *the trickle* was affecting the other neophyte TAs. Most were not *from* here. Alabama, North Carolina, Missouri, New York, Maryland, California, Ohio, Louisiana, Columbia (the one in South America)—all had delegates among us. But I grew up here, *right* here, about fifteen miles from where I was standing. My grandparents were farmers, for goodness sake. My history, my family's history, is tied to this *place*. I was depressed.

As the sustainability tour continued, we turned from a project in progress (revitalizing the Spring Street spring) to success stories in progress: underground cisterns filled with captured rainwater, a fountain spouting captured air-conditioner condensate from the law school, roof top solar panels, water-

Figure 3.2. A Pair of Chew Crew Program Goats Outside
Photo Credit: University of Georgia Marketing & Communications. All Rights Reserved.

permeable ground surfaces . . . on and on. But by far, the success story that captured my imagination was . . . the Chew Crew (see figure 3.2).

The Chew Crew, brainchild of environmental design student Zach Richardson and funded by a campus sustainability grant from the OOS, began chewing in 2012. These hoofed crusaders are deployed each fall and spring along campus stream banks to eradicate kudzu, English ivy, privet, and other invasive plants. The Chew Crew are popular participants in annual Earth Day celebrations and serve as beloved ambassadors for the university's sustainability program (see figure 3.3).

Depression left the building. I was impressed.

Fast Forward >>

A daunting prospect for any new TA: develop a course syllabus. Also, decide on obligatory research paper angle . . .

<< Rewind

I'm not an English Department grad student. I'm a doctoral student in the Linguistics Department teaching in the English Department. As a linguist,

Figure 3.3. Chew Crew button
Photo Credit: Kim Waters.

I study endangered languages, indigenous languages, as well as pidgins and creoles, especially those native to my home state of Georgia and Cherokee and Gullah-Geechee. Both the Cherokee and Gullah-Geechee are displaced peoples. The Cherokee were forcibly removed from the Southeast and stripped of their ancestral homelands in 1838–1839 by the Jackson administration. Gullah-Geechee speakers are descendants of formerly enslaved people who were forcibly removed from West Africa beginning in the 1600s and brought to colonial plantations (forced labor camps) in Georgia and South Carolina. Property rights continue to be central issues in both cultures.

As an acoustic phonologist, I don't have Jane Austin, Shakespeare, or Henry James in my hip pocket. I'm not a poet. Or a novelist. Or a medievalist. So what can I teach? I decided to become the maven of pop culture, well, old school pop culture. We'll read Hunter S. Thompson, I think to myself, and David Foster Wallace. We'll watch *I AM*, a 2010 documentary by Tom Shadyac, best known for blockbusters *Ace Ventura, Liar Liar, The Nutty Professor,* and *Bruce Almighty.* Through these voices, we'll investigate personal choice. We'll find our own voices. We'll be better informed about the planet that sustains us all. And if we (here, the royal *We*) are lucky and the seed takes root in fertile soil, some of us will become activists. But all of us—*all* of us— in this threatened generation will become more informed, more thoughtful, and more deliberate about how we live our lives. *That's* my plan.

Fast Forward >>

Round One: Fall 2014 ENGL1101, My First Time Teaching First-year Composition

On day one I conducted an ice-breaker exercise with students in pairs. The instructions were, "Ask your partner to answer the questions (projected on the screen) and then introduce your partner to the class." The last question, question five, is the lynchpin for the semester's work: How *green* are you?

I see a raised hand, "Ms. Waters, what do you mean by *green*?"

Fast Forward >>

Writing makes better writers, right? That's the idea. So it's time to write . . . but first . . . we must read for inspiration, for insight. I have a few tricks up my sleeve, that is, a few readings as ways into reflection and personal responsibility. The first reading I assign as prelude for the introductory essay comes from a twenty-one-year-old Hunter S. Thompson. We read a letter he wrote to a friend where Thompson debates the utility of giving life advice wherein he employs the float or swim metaphor (and evokes Prince Hamlet): Is it better to float on the tide (take what comes) or swim (against the easy option, toward your own goals)? I ask students to write a reflective essay adopting the "float or swim" metaphor. I ask them to reflect on a decision made either to float or swim and how that decision feels in retrospect. They must answer the question, "Would you make the same choice now?"

Our second reading for class discussion was David Foster Wallace's 2004 essay for *Gourmet* magazine, "Consider the Lobster." I ask students, "What were your expectations about a piece on lobsters in a food magazine before reading the article?" (This is not an essay featuring recipes.) I ask students to comment on Wallace's use of ethos, pathos, and logos and to say which was most compelling. As a class, we discuss the quality of Wallace's thought process and the nature of his "voice." I ask students to observe how this piece becomes a narrative adventure and to note how Wallace weaves concern for our oceans and the creatures who live there into his narrative.

Next up: sustainability prep. Step one for our second writing assignment, the compulsory research paper, was to introduce the class to Kevin Kirsche, director of the OOS, who takes the class on the sustainability walk, similar to the walk we took as fledgling TAs. The walk and Kevin's narration of sustainability projects on campus was a huge success. The students seemed engaged and in awe of the programs already in place on campus.

For step two, I scheduled a lab appointment for the class to meet with a research librarian. I sent our research librarian a draft of the prompt and let her know my objective: each student will propose a new sustainability project for UGA to adopt. Their research papers will be written as proposals addressed to the director of the OOS. The result: our research librarian did a wonderful job preparing a research guide for the class on topics ranging from air quality initiatives and bio-swales to rooftop beehives and urban butterfly gardens.

Step three was a screening and class discussion of Tom Shadyac's film, *I AM*. The feature-length documentary chronicles Shadyac's rebirth, from a highly conspicuous, automaton-ic consumer to a human being who understands life as something deeper and more precious (and precarious) than consumerism and acquisitiveness. The film challenges us to figure out how we can make the leap from being part of the problem to becoming part of the solution.

Result: students were rattled. I could see it in their faces. They were challenged to reconsider their goals and aspirations and to decide why they have made the choices they've made about majors and future plans. They were also asked to consider where the tracks they're on will lead them . . . and whether they really want to go there. In other words, are their goals their own or are their goals proxies for accomplishing what their parents want them to accomplish.

Now we're ready to write a sustainability research paper. Here's a summary of the first semester's research paper prompt:

> Your research will help you gain insight into a sustainability topic. Based on your research, you will propose a new program for UGA to adopt in its ever-growing sustainability efforts. Review links provided for information on many RRR (reduce reuse recycle) programs and other efforts already in place around the country. It's important to note that the program you propose should resonate with you. It should be something that you really care about in a deeply personal way. There are many areas for you to consider: Air quality, water quality & use, energy conservation and new sources of energy, green space, wildlife habitats, responsible land use, etc.

Results were discouraging: Out of two classes of twenty-two students each (forty-four papers), thirty were on the benefits of using more efficient light bulbs. Another seven were about installing more efficient showerheads in dorms. Takeaway learning for TA: be more specific and yes, more prescriptive!

Round Two—Fall 2015

Toward being more prescriptive regarding research paper topics, I trolled the internet for lists of greenest colleges and universities across the nation. What are they doing that UGA *could* be doing? I created a spreadsheet with twenty-two topics (see figure 3.4). This time, each student would select a topic from the list, each choosing a different one. I held an email lottery wherein students had to email me after midnight the following day to claim a topic. Earliest time stamp wins the topic. This "competition" clicked. I had many emails posted between midnight and 1:00 a.m. To flesh out the spreadsheet and provide additional resources for students, I interviewed a few sustainability gurus on campus to identify local experts for each of the topics I'd selected. I populated the spreadsheet with contact names, email addresses, and websites for one or two local experts on each topic as jumping-off points for students. I required that each student schedule a face-to-face interview with the local expert.

A few words on the benefits of face-to-face interviews. To my way of thinking, face-to-face interviews are multipurpose in a jar:

1. Students get out of their comfort zones.
2. Students become familiar with departments and resources on campus.
3. Students hear dedication and passion about environmental issues first-hand.
4. Students learn perseverance and tenacity: "Ms. Waters, my contact hasn't emailed me back. What do I do?"
5. Students learn how to approach people in positions of authority and ask for a few minutes of their time.

The Bottom Line: Face-to-face Interviews Teach Life Skills

Below are excerpts from three fine student papers: two from fall 2015 and one from spring 2016. In the first, Kenneth Brock recommends options for off-grid housing; in the second, Jarod Sjogren highlights the health benefits (in addition to reducing energy consumption) of outdoor classrooms; and in the third, Anthony Zenere advocates for a major watershed clean-up operation and explains how dredging can help restore a degraded manmade lake, previously used for recreational purposes.

ENGL1101 Sustainability Research Paper - List of Topics

Project No.	Project Topic	UGA office / source of info
1	Bioswales & rain gardens	Horticulture
2	Butterfly gardens	UGArdens
3	Wildlife habitats	Odum School of Ecology
4	Energy-saving software for building monitoring	College of Environmental Design; College of Engineering
5	US Green Building Council certification for all new buildings	College of Environmental Design; College of Engineering
6	Reduce cars on campus	Parking Services
7	Alternative (off-grid) residential housing	Housing Office
8	Only recyclable/biodegradable bags, cups and containers at campus sporting events	UGA Athletic Association, UGA Facilities Management Divison
9	Agricultural Methane Harvesting	UGA in Costa Rica
10	Purchase of carbon-offsets	UGA in Costa Rica
11	Harvesting wind energy	Office of Sustainability
12	Air quality improvement	Office of Sustainability
13	Water quality (point-source pollution vs non-point source pollution)	UGA Watershed
14	Roof-top beehives	College of Agriculture and Environmental Science
15	Out-door classrooms	Ground Department (FMD)
16	"Living machines" for waste treatment	Real Estate and Space Management
17	Gently used "free" store	Department of Student Services
18	Dawgs Ditch the Dumpster **upgrade** (to a sale-based approach and alternative revenue stream)	Housing Office
19	Students for Enviromental Action (SEA) **upgrade** - Student Organization	Center for Student Organizations
20	The Energy Concept **upgrade** - Student Organization	Center for Student Organizations
21	Bag the Bag **upgrade** - Student Organization	Center for Student Organizations
22	Student Environmental Planning Organization **upgrade** - Student Organization	Center for Student Organizations

Figure 3.4. Sustainability Topic List
Image Credit: Kim Waters.

Yurty Field by Kenneth Brock

For the University of Georgia, I propose a solution to be named, "Yurty Field." ["Yurty" is play on the name of the "Herty" field, where UGA played its first football game.] My proposal will place yurts on campus where students can live;

although this would not completely solve the residential housing problem, Yurty Field will become a place that offers environmental, economic, and educational benefits. . . . These homes take advantage of the sun in the winter by facing south and absorbing the sun's heat. During the summer, air flows through the windows and out through the hole, otherwise known as a toon, at the top of the domed ceiling. This creates a vacuum effect to keep the inside cool. During the cold parts of the year, the toon is covered with a felt piece to keep the heat inside (Mauvieux 152).[31] Because of this, yurts have no need for air conditioning or heating.

Outdoor Classrooms: Nature's Influence on Education by Jarod Sjogren

These [outdoor] classrooms would also produce countless health benefits for the students. In an attempt to get these classrooms implemented, innumerable studies, experiments and surveys have been conducted; each focused on finding the hidden benefits of learning outdoors. Some of these studies discovered benefits including: increased productivity, increased team-mentality, and lessened ADHD symptoms. Despite the economic inhibitors, this project holds great potential for the University of Georgia to increase its ability to provide a superb education for its students during their four years on campus.

Our Water Quality is Running Away by Anthony Zenere

Lake Herrick at the Intramural Fields is one of the most recognizable features of the UGA campus. The park is a fantastic recreational resource for faculty, staff and students, and in the past the lake itself has been part of that. Since the lake was closed for swimming and boating in 2002, the park has lost some of its allure. The fields are still popular, and the trails are still a fantastic resource, but the lake remains a dismal reminder of how quickly something beautiful can be lost to pollution and inattention. This is not a lifetime sentence. The UGA Office of Sustainability has been working to restore the park for over ten years, and is thinking about ways to restore the water quality and remove the bacteria that have made the lake a waste instead of a recreational area (Cavallaro).

. . . sediment increases the turbidity of the water, preventing light from reaching flora and fauna in the depths of the lake. It also aids in the growth of bacteria, including fecal coliform, which has been cited consistently as a major problem, and a primary reason to close the lake to swimming.

The solution requires drastic steps. The first is a full scale dredging operation. Dredging is a long, involved process, but Lake Herrick is much smaller and shallower than some bodies of water that have been dredged in the past (Henshaw 241.) The purpose of a dredging operation is to remove unwanted sediment from a body of water. Using a large excavator with a clamshell bucket attachment, a trained operator will carefully scoop sediment from the lake bed onto a barge, or some other vehicle that will transport the sediment away from the lake. The sediment is filtered to remove boulders and tree stumps, then rocks, and finally gravel, until all that remains is a slurry. The slurry will be pressed to remove any excess water, and then dumped in a landfill (Rankine). If the slurry is too contaminated to be dumped in a landfill, it will be transported to a government approved storage area.[32]

Excerpts from Brock and Sjogren demonstrate how diverse project proposals not only improve sustainability by taking some routine energy-intensive functions such as housing and classroom space off-grid to reduce energy consumption, but they can also provide value-added health benefits and educational opportunities. Zenere's research shows how lessons from water cleanup operations on rivers and lakes across the globe can inform watershed projects at UGA.

Each semester, I encourage students to capitalize on the opportunity to showcase their sustainability research during the OOS-sponsored Semester-in-Review luncheon. The luncheon features a Georgia-grown, seasonal menu and offers OOS interns an opportunity to present their work. Students who have done sustainability-related work during the semester are invited to prepare posters with highlights from their research for display during the event. Such events keep diverse university community groups that are engaged in sustainability efforts informed, connected, and inspired.

Finally, I close with comments on personal growth from students, precipitated by their sustainability research.

> Fall 2014 mid-term evaluation (9AM class): I like viewing activities like the *I AM* film we watched because *it gets us thinking more deeply*.

> Fall 2014 final course evaluation (8AM class): Ms. Water's [sic] is fantastic. I love her energy, enthusiasm, and the way she presents herself every day. I also love how she tried to connect with each individual student as the course went on. I feel as though she actually cared about *who we are and what we do with our lives*. As a result, I was more inclined to put forth the work she required.

Overall, I felt my excursions into sustainability topics helped me make the kind of individual connections with my students that teachers can only make in a writing-intensive, experientially focused course. Using sustainability topics helped my students—University of Georgia first-year students—connect with their new environment and to begin to think critically, specifically, and creatively about the space they now occupied. We live in troubled times. But how many generations have made the same observation. One aspect of our times that gives me hope is the rise of social activism. Sometimes what is required is a situation so desperate that people cannot bear to be silent. We can all be activists, whether in small ways or grand ways. But we must all act to ensure a better life on Planet A.

SUSTAINABLE SUSTAINABILITY IN THE UNIVERSITY OF GEORGIA FIRST-YEAR COMPOSITION PROGRAM

In the years since that first faculty workshop, we have arrived at two main conclusions about incorporating a sustainability focus in FYC, one quite certain and the other more of a curious observation. First, we have firmly concluded that working with specifics, especially specific locations, is crucial. In the South Altantic Modern Language Association plenary mentioned above, Wendell Berry emphasizes the necessity of keeping an eye on the local landscape—not just preserving wilderness or managing ecological crises, those distant and difficult issues, but, more importantly, keeping an "attentive and loving" watch on our "economic landscapes," our neighborhood land, our farms and managed forests.[33] Likewise, in James Lang's *Chronicle of Higher Education* essay, "The Grounded Curriculum," he explores the ironic problem—much in evidence at UGA—of carrying out huge construction projects on our physical campuses while offering more and more virtual substitutes such as hybrid, online, and distance courses. Lang writes: "Sometimes I feel like jumping into the fray and founding or joining a new technology-driven initiative in course design or delivery. At other times, I feel like locking myself in a room with twenty Web-deprived undergraduates and a copy of *The Brothers Karamazov*, and forcing everyone to look one another in the eye and discuss the meaning of life for a few hours."[34] In Lang's essay, he urges us to "place" ourselves and to "ground" our curriculum in our place. In our experience, grounding ourselves in the local texture of this specific campus environment right here in Athens, Georgia, through the simple act of taking a walk and taking a close look around—preferably with a knowledgeable guide!—can provide new motives and energy for both teachers and students as we focus our collective gaze on the local landscape. Grounding our curriculum sustains us. And, as we have all discovered, narrowing our lens by seeing, describing, and studying specific places inspires students to do the same in their writing. Student's writing becomes more focused, specific, and interesting.

Our second observation is simply offered up for your consideration. While at least one of us has incorporated a sustainability thread in our English 1102 lit-related curriculum with moderate success, we have all noticed the increase in students' engagement when classwork is founded on or in narrative. However, in the creative work done for the first assignment in the original, summer 2012, English 1102 sample syllabus, the class activities uncovered a concern about the general trend of narrative plots. As one student pointed out—sustainability is "like, the opposite of apocalyptic!" We might argue further that, as an image, the idea of sustainability evokes, perhaps, a

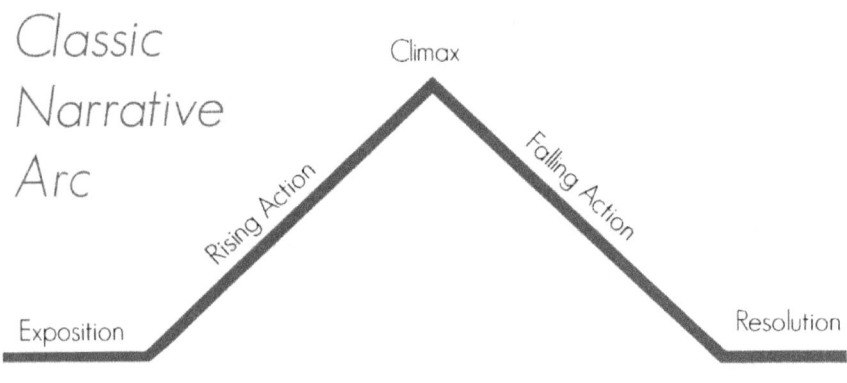

Figure 3.5. Classic Narrative Arc
Image Credit: Cheryl Brumley. Creative Commons License. Available at https://blogs.lse.ac.uk/impactof socialsciences/2014/08/27/academic-storytelling-risk-reduction/.

gentle series of waves, mirroring the idea of consistency or persistence. The familiar narrative "arc," as represented by figure 3.5, on the other hand is typically evoked with a sharp, dramatic angle, representing conflict, crisis, and resolution.

This typical narrative structure, originating in conflict, is also represented by the many lists of common narrative plots. A common list—the "seven" basic plots—reveals the essential role of conflict in our most basic narratives:

[wo]man vs. nature
[wo]man vs. [wo]man
[wo]man vs. the environment
[wo]man vs. machines/technology
[wo]man vs. the supernatural
[wo]man vs. self
[wo]man vs. god/religion[35]

Reading this list brings to mind the fact that when the 2012 students wrote narratives based in their special places, using the information derived from their archives, only two composed "comedies," both love stories. As Jerome Bruner posits, "place is crucial and its shapes and constrains the stories."[36] Why then did the majority of the class write *apocalyptic,* conflict-thick narratives in these special settings, their own "special" places? There were monsters in quiet suburban home neighborhoods, fights in the cul-de-sac at the end of the drive, carnivorous gnomes in the bedroom, wild dogs running through clipped backyards, and zombies among the neighborhood park swings and picnic tables. What might be the connection, or is there any connection, between these "apocalyptic" narratives and the potential for sustainability? Do humans crave crises? Does the narrative of crisis and apocalypse undermine, or does it support our desire for peaceful sustainability?[37]

In David Orr's 2003 lecture on sustainability, "The Four Challenges of Sustainability," he describes the fourth challenge as purely metaphysical—a spiritual challenge. We must have some hope, he argues, "that we [humans] may grow into something more than a planetary plague."[38] He concludes that we must find a way to challenge the narrative of apocalypse, leaving us with a call to find a sustainable narrative of "celebration":

> No culture has gone farther than our own to deny individual mortality and this denying is killing the planet. A spirituality that allows us to face our own mortality honestly without denial or terror contains the seeds of the daily heroism necessary to preserve life on Earth. Instead of terror, a deeper spirituality would lead us to a place of gratitude and celebration. It would also energize us to act.[39]

To make sustainability a sustainable and viable topic in our FYC program, we have found that success results from providing teachers with resources, inspiration, and, most importantly, freedom from rigid course requirements and required, prepackaged syllabi. As our varying narratives in this chapter have, we hope, shown, letting individual teachers find their own unique ways to deliver the topic of sustainability is perhaps the surest way to find that place of "gratitude and celebration" as well as the energy to act and to continue to act.

NOTES

1. Larry B. Dendy writes, "The 1784 General Assembly of Georgia allocated 40,000 acres to endow a college or seminary of learning; the following year, Abraham Baldwin, a Yale graduate, wrote the University of Georgia's charter. However, it was not until 1801 that lawyer and legislator John Milledge bought 633 acres along the Oconee River and donated the land as a site for the school. Josiah Meigs, another Yale graduate, was appointed president and sole faculty member and in September 1801 taught the first university classes. The first permanent university building, a three-story brick structure, was completed in 1806 and named Franklin College in honor of Benjamin Franklin. It was the only university building until 1821, and for many years the university was commonly known as Franklin College, though its official name was the University of Georgia" ("University of Georgia," *New Georgia Encyclopedia*, December 2, 2003, last edited by NGE staff on September 15, 2015, http://www.georgiaencyclopedia.org/articles/education/university-georgia).

2. Victor Nolet, "Introduction," to *Educating for Sustainability: Principles and Practices for Teachers* (New York: Routledge, 2015), 3.

3. Nolet, "Introduction," 1.
4. Nolet, "Introduction," 1.
5. World Commission on Environment and Development (WCED), *Our Common Future* (Oxford: Oxford University Press, 1985), 42.
6. Patricia Bizzell, "William Perry and Liberal Education," *College English* 46, no. 55 (1984): 447–54.
7. For a review of the culture wars see Maxine Hairston, "Diversity, Ideology, and Teaching Writing," *College Composition and Communication* 43 (1992): 179–93; and John Trimbur et al., "Responses to Maxine Hairston: 'Diversity, Ideology, and Teaching Writing,'" *College Composition and Communication,* 44, no. 2 (1993), 248–56. For an introduction to the argument for "writing about writing," see Douglas Downs and Elizabeth Wardle, "Teaching about Writing, Righting Misconceptions: (Re)Envisioning 'First-Year Composition' as 'Introduction to Writing Studies,'" *College Composition and Communication* 58, no. 4 (2007): 552–84. See a recent discussion about controlling the franchise, or boundaries, of composition as a discipline in Gregory Columb, "Franchising the Future," *College Composition and Communication* 62, no. 1 (2010): 11–30. For a discussion of the fragmentation of composition as a discipline in the twenty-first century, see Richard Fulkerson, "Composition at the Turn of the Twenty-First Century," *College Composition and Communication* 56, no. 4 (2005): 654–87.
8. Audrey W Shinner, email message to Deborah Miller, November 24, 2015.
9. "Curriculum Committee," *Sustainability UGA,* 2012, UGA Office of Sustainability, accessed 2 December 2015, http://sustainability.uga.edu/what-were-doing/academics-research/curriculum_committee/.
10. Council of Writing Program Administrators, "Framework for Success in Postsecondary Writing," accessed November 21, 2015, http://wpacouncil.org/framework; "WPA Outcomes Statement for First-Year Composition (3.0), Approved July 17, 2014," accessed November 21, 2015, http://wpacouncil.org/positions/outcomes.html.
11. "WPA Outcomes Statement."
12. Introduction to "WPA Outcomes Statement."
13. "Framework for Success in Postsecondary Writing."
14. World Commission, *Our Common Future.*
15. Robert Cox and P. C. Pezzullo , *Environmental Communication and the Public Sphere,* 3rd ed. (London: Sage Publications, 2013), 6.
16. Sidney I. Dobrin, *Saving Place: An Ecocomposition Reader* (New York: McGraw Hill, 2005), vi.
17. Dobrin, *Saving Place,* xiii.
18. Derek Owens, *Composition and Sustainability: Teaching for a Threatened Generation* (Urbana, IL: NCTE, 2001), xiv.
19. Owens, *Composition and Sustainability,* 5–6.
20. Owens, *Composition and Sustainability,* 6.
21. Owens, *Composition and Sustainability,* 7.
22. Christine Farris, "Literature and Composition," in Tate et al., eds., *Guide to Composition Pedagogies* (New York: Oxford UP, 2014), 165.
23. Farris, "Literature and Composition," 163.

24. UNESCO, introduction to "Storytelling," *Teaching and Learning for a Sustainable Future,* 2010, http://www.unesco.org/education/tlsf/mods/theme_d/mod21.html.

25. Christy Desmet et al., *A Guide to First-Year Composition at University of Georgia* (Sweetwater, TX: Fountainhead, 2015), 11.

26. Owens, *Composition and Sustainability*, 27–35.

27. Wendell Berry, Plenary Address, South Atlantic Modern Language Association, Atlanta, 2014 (personal notes by author).

28. Chris A. Emma Portfolio, Summer 2012, ENGL1102.

29. World Commission, *Our Common Future*, 42.

30. Gary Snyder, *Turtle Island* (New York: New Directions, 1975), 101.

31. The in-text MLA citation refers to Benoit Mauvieux, Alain Reinberg, and Yvan Touitou, "The Yurt: A Mobile Home Of Nomadic Populations Dwelling in the Mongolian Steppe Is Still Used Both as a Sun Clock and a Calendar," *Chronobiology International: The Journal of Biological & Medical Rhythm Research* 31 (2014): 151–56.

32. The MLA in-text citations in this excerpt from "Our Water Quality Is Running Away" by Anthony Zenere are as follows: Gabe Cavallaro, "Office of Sustainability Plans to Revitalize Lake Herrick for Recreational Use," *The Red and Black*, November 21, 2014, http://www.redandblack.com/uganews/office-of-sustainability-plans-to-revitalize-lake-herrick-for-recreational/article_e585bb62-70f7-11e4-ab5b-7b54c87a11c1.html; Paul Henshaw, Stephen Cervi, Alex J. McCorquodale, "Simple Cost Estimator for Environmental Dredging in the Great Lakes," *Journal of Waterway, Port, Coastal and Ocean Engineering* 124 (1999): 241–46; Craig Rankine, Diana Smith, Joyce Mercuri, "Cleaning Up: How Dredging Is Cleaning Up Ridgefield's Lake River," Department of Ecology, State of Washington, December 30, 2014, http://ecologywa.blogspot.com/2014/12/cleaning-up-how-dredging-is-cleaning-up.html; and Rhetoric @reno, "Western States Rhetoric and Literacy Conference: Literacies and Rhetorics of Crisis," University of Nevada at Reno, October 3, 2013.

33. Wendell Berry, Plenary Address (personal notes by author).

34. James Lang, "The Grounded Curriculum," *Chronicle of Higher Education*, July 3, 2012, http://www.ipl.org/div/farq/plotFARQ.html.

35. "Basic Plots of Literature: Special Collections Created by IPL2," the I-School at Drexel College of Information Science and Technology, 2012, accessed November 6, 2014, http://www.ipl.org/div/farq/plotFARQ.html. See a collection of other standard lists of these conflict-driven "basic plots"—20 by Tobias, 36 by Polti, and more (Drexel i-school librarians: IPL2) http://www.ipl.org/div/farq/plotFARQ.html.

36. Jerome Bruner, "Research Currents: Life as Narrative," *Language Arts* 65 (1988): 578.

37. See Killingsworth and Palmer, "The Discourse of Environmentalist Hysteria," as well as Peterson and Horton, "Rooted in the Soil," about using story to make a point and the importance of myth. Also, see Killingsworth and Palmer, "Millennial Ecology: The Apocalyptic Narrative from Silent Spring to Global Warming," in *Green Culture*.

38. David W. Orr, "Four Challenges of Sustainability," *Ecological Economics*, Spring Seminar Series 2003, School of Natural Resources, University of Vermont, https://ratical.org/co-globalize/4CofS.html.

39. Orr, "Four Challenges of Sustainability," paragraph 15.

Chapter Four

Reflecting on Action and Acting on Reflection

High-Impact Practices for Transformative Learning in Sustainability

Justin Rademaekers and Cheryl Wanko

In the spring semester of 2015, twenty-nine English studies students across two separate seminar courses committed themselves to a challenge: Could they live a "no impact" lifestyle? For just one week, students were asked to eliminate purchasing, make no trash, use eco-friendly transportation, eat locally, eliminate or reduce electricity use, cut back on water consumption, and give back to the community. During the course of the experiment, students reported through required reflective writing on their struggles living in this way, such as conflicts with family shopping traditions; the cheap, fast, and wrapper-cloaked food of campus life; the need to be constantly plugged in; and fitting community volunteerism into already busy lives. Student reflections during this week revealed not just their tribulations but the deeply embedded nature of identity in the economic, environmental, and social pillars of sustainability. From a sustainability educator's standpoint, the purpose of such an experiment, developed by *No Impact Man* author and sustainability educator Colin Beavan, is not just to learn about sustainability, but to experience sustainable living.

Experiential learning is just one of the eleven high-impact practices outlined by The Association of American Colleges and Universities (AACU) and the work of George Kuh, designed to "give students direct experience with issues they are studying in the curriculum and with ongoing efforts to analyze and solve problems in the community."[1] The promise of high-impact educational practices is that student engagement outside the classroom will lead to a deeper understanding of their subject, in this case the subject of sustainability. In turn, the complex nature of sustainability itself, we and others believe, urges sustainability educators toward the high-impact practices that foster deep learning. This complex relationship between subject and pedagogical methodology has caused many scholars to question the structures of the academy itself and the fractured surface learning those structures encourage. As Arjen Wals and Bob Jickling describe in their 2002 article "Sustainability in Higher Education," the concept of sustainability necessitates a pedagogical shift from "consumptive learning" to "discovery learning and creative problem solving"; from "teacher-centered" to "learner-centered arrangements"; from "individual learning" to "collaborative learning"; and from "theory dominated learning" to "praxis-oriented learning."[2] Action-based high-impact learning dissolves disciplinary boundaries to encourage "deep learning," which engages students' hands and hearts, as well as their heads.[3]

Writing-intensive courses are themselves high-impact practices, according to the AACU, and including them across the curriculum is a method by which institutions have tried to spur interdisciplinary learning. Writing-intensive courses offer the benefit of directly and deliberately engaging students' language systems in deep learning. Thus, a writing-intensive high-impact experience in sustainability, such as the one we will discuss in this chapter, offers an important avenue for invoking pedagogical shifts toward a praxis-oriented deep learning in sustainability education: students participating in high-impact No Impact Week (hereafter NIW) were not just learning about sustainability by way of experience, but were engaged as writers reflecting on their successes, challenges, and curiosities, and considering the possibilities and impossibilities for change. Experiential learning, scaffolded by reflective writing, can thus be *transformative*.

With this in mind, our chapter examines a writing-intensive high-impact practice which, as sustainability educators, we hoped would promote transformative learning.

PEDAGOGICAL CONTEXT

Both of us teach in the English Department at West Chester University, a four-year comprehensive public institution that is part of the Pennsylvania State System of Higher Education. We used NIW in two upper-level research-based English capstone classes, each taking slightly different approaches: one was more rhetoric oriented (Justin), and one was more literature oriented (Cheryl). Both classes, however, participated in NIW during the same week of the spring semester. NIW is a popular pedagogical activity based on Colin Beavan's memoir, *No Impact Man*, which relates Beavan and his family's attempt to reduce their impact on the environment to net zero over the course of a year. During the first month, they worked to eliminate their waste output; during subsequent months, they curtailed transportation emissions, electricity and water usage, as well as challenging themselves to eat only food from within 250 miles. Whole communities, campuses, and individual classes across the United States and around the world have testified to the experiment's difficulty and power via video.[4]

Our students replicated this activity over the course of a week that ran from Sunday to Sunday, and they had the choice of working only on that day's assigned topic (e.g., avoiding buying anything on Sunday), or attempting to do the activity cumulatively: ceasing to buy anything starting Sunday, then adding to this by eliminating trash starting on Monday, then eliminating fossil-fuel based transportation starting on Tuesday, then adding consumption of only local foods on Wednesday, etc. until unplugging for an "eco-sabbath" on Sunday. Because a class taught in our honors program also does NIW (not connected to our two classes), four out of the total of twenty-nine students had participated in NIW in the prior year.

To explore the effects of writing in relation to NIW, we asked our students to engage in reflective writing of various sorts: Justin's rhetoric-based class produced public reflective writing (blogs, Twitter), while Cheryl's literature-based class produced traditional personal reflective writing. Both types, of course, were shared with the instructor and thus even the "personal" reflective writing was to some degree mediated by the performative element necessitated by evaluation.

METHODOLOGY

Once we had collected the reflective writing, we studied it for evidence of a deeper understanding of sustainability and students' personal relationships to it. We did this by examining their writing in two ways. First, because we each discussed the "three pillars" of sustainability with our classes—environmental/ecological, economic, and social/cultural—we coded their writing according to this division. What we quickly realized was, like our own understanding of sustainability, students' comments did not divide neatly into these three categories; however, the categorization provided a useful way to look at how they may have understood their own experience.

The second examination we performed asked what kind of evidence constituted the deeper understanding that we were hoping to achieve. Would our students be able to consciously connect their experiences with the systems that structure their privileged, Western, and unsustainable lifestyle and lives, and, if so, how would we be able to notice this in their writing? Elizabeth Allan and Dana Driscoll assert that this is possible:

> When students reflect upon their learning, they engage in a potentially transformative act of responding to, connecting with, and analyzing an experience, event, process, or product. Reflection is one way to bridge the divide between thought and action—an opportunity for students to describe their internal processes, evaluate their challenges, and recognize their triumphs in ways that would otherwise remain unarticulated.[5]

To bring to the surface the various ways in which students may have understood their experiences and to see the components of their learning in their reflective writing, we turned to Jack Mezirow's theories of transformative learning, especially the often-cited (and critiqued) ten phases of transformative learning that are required in order for true transformation to take place. Janet Moore explains the overall impact of the process:

> Transformative learning is concerned with altering frames of reference through critical reflection of both habits of mind and points of view. For example, critically reflecting on patterns of consumption and production may have an impact on our own consumptive behaviours. . . . A learning experience that involves the questioning of structures, systems, and relationships is bound to enter personal and interpersonal areas that need to be carefully considered for all involved.[6]

We hoped that, through examining the "personal and interpersonal" in their reflective writing, students would move through questioning the structures to taking sustained critical action. Below are Mezirow's phases and some interpretative questions in reference to our NIW project:

1. *Experiencing a disorienting dilemma*: Did our students find and describe NIW as disorienting, or as presenting a dilemma?
2. *Performing self-examination*: Did NIW cause students to question and examine themselves and their habits? In doing so, did they feel fear, anger, guilt, or shame?
3. *Critically assessing assumptions*: Did our students move beyond the local, personal activities of NIW to think about the assumptions implicit in their actions and responses to those actions?
4. *Recognizing that others share similar discontent and a similar process of transformation*: Students found support in the fact that their peers were also doing NIW; Did they identify similar struggles in the lives of family and friends who were not doing NIW?
5. *Exploring options for new roles, relationships, and action*: During NIW, did students recognize their tasks as options for building new identities

and relationships and for taking action to address sustainability? Did they look for other models?
6. *Planning a course of action*: Did students make statements that would allow us to see what they planned to do after NIW was complete?
7. *Acquiring skills and information for implementing plans*: Did students show evidence of researching how to implement the lessons of NIW in their lives after the week was over?
8. *Provisional trying of new roles*: Did students state they would move beyond reflection to action because of NIW?
9. *Building competence and self-confidence in new roles and relationships*: Did NIW allow students to interact more confidently with family and peers in relation to changed habits learned via NIW?
10. *Reintegrating into one's life on the basis of conditions dictated by one's new perspective*: Six months later, did students continue to incorporate into their lives some of the actions they took during NIW?[7] Did they live more sustainably?

We didn't expect that a one-week writing-intensive high-impact practice like NIW would create a completely transformative learning experience for our students. Indeed, the aims of Mezirow's phases 5–10 were ambitious, given that NIW occurred at about midpoint in a fifteen-week semester, and that this class was, for the great majority, the only class to expose them to sustainability topics during their college careers. We did, however, see phase 5: *exploring options for new roles, relationships, and actions* as a pivotal phase in sustainability education; one that if some students could reach, might lead to a long-term transformative experience. As we will discuss in detail below, student writing primarily indicates that they mostly used their writing to process phases 1–3.

Because we introduced sustainability to our students via the "three pillars" model—though the two classes modified and complicated this model in different ways—this chapter proceeds through the pillars to note evidence of the stages of transformative learning. In our conclusion, we combine what we learned about student learning from their reflections with our later data set, the survey of continued sustainability-related activities. Finally, we address the larger questions this study evokes: How can writing-intensive high-impact practices effectively promote sustainability education in English studies? What are the implications for using high-impact practices coupled with reflective writing for sustainability education? How can we help such learning experiences become transformative? We begin with the assertion that practices like NIW can help students develop a deeper understanding of sustainability and its principles, and our conclusions can help others frame and carry out this type of activity to best harness English studies to serve the larger effort of sustainability education so that institutional change and social change may emerge through the efforts of individual faculty in their classes.

"BROKE" STUDENTS, BLATANT CONSUMERS: ECONOMIC TRANSFORMATIONS TOWARD SUSTAINABILITY

According to Mitchell Thomashow, "ecological identity" refers to "all the different ways people construe themselves in relationship to the earth as manifested in personality, values, actions and a sense of self."[8] His professional work with students who are considering changes to become more environmentally engaged suggests that experiential learning provides a path for their development and transformation. However, the NIW reflections our two classes collected showed that students were much more comfortable expressing their other "*eco*"-identities: their *economic* identities. While we will return to the idea of an ecological identity in later sections, it became clear to us that students understood themselves less as ecological—tied to the natural world—and much more as economic creatures as they processed their NIW experience. The labels students chose for themselves in these pieces are often economic: the "broke college student," for example, living the "penniless life of a college undergrad." Their language identifies personae or roles that they seem to believe are widely accepted, and their self-identification as undergrads with no money is a stereotype they seem proud to embody and reinforce, as though they are living through a time of struggle and challenge (which for many is, of course, true). Some of their comments imply that they see this as a natural stage of growth that students must pass through on their way to the "real world."

In doing NIW, many students saw their economic lives and identities as conflicting with the ability to embrace a low-impact lifestyle, *experiencing the week as disorienting*, according to Mezirow's first phase of transformation. We can understand students framing their NIW experience as an economic activity, as opposed to an environmental or social one, in order to defuse the perceived conflict between the pillars of sustainability. Rather than leading them in a transformational direction, often the economic identity simply allowed them to retreat into helplessness or deferment of action, in part because modern US discourse has traditionally pitted the economic and environmental against each other, and the effort of harmonizing them individually seemed insurmountable.

The reflections indicate that questions of economics and sustainability most often arose in relation to obtaining and eating locally produced food.

Since, for our junior- and senior-level students, food is one thing that they must purchase, this was the main active purchasing choice during their NIW. Most of students' other choices were framed negatively, in which they had to give something up or not do something.

One student in the rhetoric-focused course that required public reflections used tweets to share multiple reflections on spending:

> "Also, was planning on cleaning my room today anyway. I'll try not to cringe while I look at my blatant consumerism."

> "On the bright side, because I have limited funds, I typically don't buy a lot of superfluous things."

> "Realized that I constantly think about buying new things."

> "Eating local isn't really in my price budget at this point in my life. I understand why it's pricier but that doesn't mean I can swing it."

This series of tweets raises important economic themes that appear throughout our students' responses. First, we see two sides of this student's economic identity: "eating local isn't really in my price budget at this point in my life" and "limited funds" vs. "constantly thinking about buying" and "my blatant consumerism." These statements echo those in numerous other posts and reflections, exposing the contrast between self-knowledge about overconsumption (and the money involved) and an inability or unwillingness to consider items like more expensive local foods as something they could "constantly" or occasionally think about buying.

This student's tweets imply that there are simply some items that are *natural* for college students to buy and to overspend on—clothes, electronics, coffee, take-out—but then others require unusual effort and thus are optional or need conscious negotiation in order to purchase. Thus, his room is full of all kinds of stuff he doesn't need, but he does not acknowledge that not buying this other stuff would allow him to buy more meaningful items, such as local food.

Similarly, another identified herself and her roommates as "broke college students," but then later tweeted that she "Temporarily forgot about #noimpactweek as I bought a coffee this morning and an unnecessary pint of Ben&Jerry's tonight." She begins by referring to economic constraint of not enough money, but then when she transgresses against her "broke" status, she invokes the constraint of participating in NIW. Thus, "broke" seems not to conflict with the *cost* of coffee and ice cream; the definition of "broke" only applies to certain types of purchases, such as local foods. Mezirow's phase

2, *examination of self*, seems to occur in these public reflections, but not far enough that students' *assumptions of their economic identities* (phase 3), and the broader economy that helps mold them, are questioned.

Although he feels powerless in the face of larger food systems, the first student's series of tweets indicates that he understands some of the social/economic mechanisms that can increase the price of local foods. This is an important realization, one which indicates that learning about sustainability has indeed occurred and that social/economic assumptions are being reassessed: NIW changed this buying decision from automatic to one that required intentionality. One student's private reflective writing also showed evidence of understanding some of the complexities of our food system by hinting at the dual meanings of "free"—both in the sense of liberty as well as in the sense of cost: "Our 'free' country doesn't seem so free when you have to go so far just to find local foods." This student recognizes that *local* is in fact *far* and requires expending fuel, time, and effort to procure, as opposed to the fast food easily obtained at the convenience stores, Burger King, or other fast food near campus. She continues, "Perhaps, when I'm out of college and financially stable, I might give it a try." She connects her inability to access local foods with her economic identity: that once she passes out of the "broke student" stage and has achieved a certain socioeconomic status, she can "try" to eat local food. In this, she shows that she has accepted her society's preconceived stages of development and transformation, and does not see that other approaches are open to her.

To return to the original tweets, another tension is the internal struggle over spending money. This student realized that he "constantly" thought "about buying new things," but he also indicated that "because I have limited funds, I typically don't buy a lot of superfluous things." Living as a young person in a culture that tells you that acquiring new stuff is natural and desirable generates a constant internal monologue telling one that buying feels good, that buying will allow one to fit in more easily, and that thinking about buying is a productive use of one's mental energy. Yet this student's experience with NIW seems to indicate that he is uncomfortable in exposing this internal dialog, as Juliet Schor notes of others she studied in *The Overspent American*.[9] An inner imperative to buy is then stymied by a limited ability to buy, setting up a tension of want and frustration that generates the idea that the goal of maturing is to be able to buy *what* and *all* one wants.

We see the imperative to buy built into other comments as well. For example, "I didn't buy anything new which sometimes is hard—especially if I go on Amazon and look at my wish list." Students live in webs of habit, often structured by corporations, which naturalize consumption. Students are confronted not only by their current purchasing wants, but also with those from days or weeks past, even though letting them sit on a "wish list" indicates that those items are not that necessary or even desirable. This student points out the difficulty of not buying things, of not following that internal consumer imperative, and other students, too, pointed either to these "hardships" or to the triumph of not buying anything. Refraining from buying even those items acknowledged as unnecessary is difficult: "Forced myself to not go into Lush," tweeted one, "Hardest decision in a while." Allowing for exaggeration for humorous public effect, we can see here the force of the consumer imperative, if not going into a store is perceived as "hardest." In fact, the student's use of humor in this public post reiterates the perceived harmlessness of the consumer imperative. Humor would be lost if a student posted instead "Forced myself to not go into the bar. . . . Hardest decision in a while"; or "Forced myself to not go into church. . . . Hardest decision in a while," both statements to which peers might react with concern. The perceived frivolity of consumerism and buying as a choice is required context for the student's humor. Americans expect that they will have a wide choice in *what* they buy, but they are not used to thinking about buying *itself* as a choice.

Part of the role of the "broke college student" is imagining oneself as an autonomous economic being, albeit a cash-strapped one. At least one student, however, indicated that her father would be happy that she was not buying online during NIW, revealing the transitional economic status of most our students. Of the other students who acknowledged their parents, most noted that their parents would not understand or support NIW. While these reactions and those of friends will be analyzed more in our discussion of the social pillar of sustainability, it is important to note here that our students seemed to have most difficulty moving in and past phase 4, *recognizing that others share similar experiences*, and thus negotiating their experiences in relation to those of their family and peer groups. These groups most reinforce students' economic habits and thus their economic identities. Students' limited ability to critique their purchasing habits, especially in relation to local foods, may also relate to the problems college students encounter when having to budget for themselves for the first time: "changing budgeting tendencies may require changing an individual's feelings, cognitions, normative beliefs, habits and perceptions of control toward budgeting, and not merely increasing knowledge."[10] Thus changing even the smallest redistribution of funds from the typical college student purchases to something as politically laden as local food may require students to do wholesale reconceptualization of their economic lives, which rest on much more complex social formations, such as upbringing.

If cost and budgeting are not concerns, and if family background does not challenge the dominant model of consumerism, one must rely on other factors to change or reduce spending, and American society does not offer students many. Frugality for its own sake seems not only hard—it is hard not to buy—but unnecessary when there's no perceived consequence to not saving. The ethical imperative to do no harm is difficult to sustain when the harm is not immediate and does not directly affect the purchaser. The disgust of looking around one's domicile and "cringing" at one's consumerism, as the first student did, is difficult to sustain because it requires constant self-criticism instead of the pleasurable self-indulgence purchasing promotes. As another student explained, "I used to believe that I had a spending problem but I got down to understanding that I really just enjoy getting out of the house and being in the store looking at new things." Reveling in possibility is part of the enjoyment of purchasing—or the build-up to the purchase—which is then ritualized into a social activity.

Only one student, who had done NIW the year before, was fairly comfortable with the week and what it required of her in terms of economy. She said that "I almost never go shopping for fun." But even she, who seemed one of the least likely to view NIW negatively, stated that she consciously framed NIW for herself as an economic experiment. By not buying things, by turning off lights, and by reducing water usage, she was saving money: "Living on my own, money is important, so I also framed it as a way to live cheaper. . . . By changing how I use these resources, I can directly change how much I have to pay (since my roommates are also concerned with low-impact lifestyle as well as inexpensive living)." While this student seemed to be living in a supportive atmosphere, students who framed the week in terms of economic savings managed to fit better into their self-identified "broke college student" role, which may indicate a way in which some students were able to make NIW more socially acceptable among their friends and family. It is perhaps the case that a transformation of economic identity for the sake of sustainability is an easier shift for students to make than a shift in social or environmental identities. This could be because students are already accustomed to the virtue of frugality within their "broke college student" role. Of course, economic activity is intimately connected to social activity, since an economic system is a sociocultural construct, and it is related to the environment because of the necessary problems economic activity causes the natural world: as one student noted, moving into *critically assessing her assumptions*, her thinking "slowly transformed into a realization: the environmentally harmful habits I formed were an unsustainable symptom of the lifestyle I no longer wanted." Student reflections related to the economic pillar of sustainability are entangled with both the social and environmental threads of sustainability, and students ran up against similar roadblocks to transformation in each. It becomes increasingly clear that transformative learning in *one* of these areas necessarily relies on similar learning within the others.

ENVIRONMENTAL CHARITY AND GO-GREEN HIPPIES: ECOLOGICAL TRANSFORMATIONS TOWARD SUSTAINABILITY

The environmental pillar of sustainability underscores the importance of reducing environmental degradation and the ecological costs associated with the development of humanity. For the purpose of this study, we understood evidence of the environmental pillar to include student references to the ecological environment (i.e., "environment"; "nature"); as well as references to issues associated with the ecological environment, or environmental issues (i.e., "landfills"; "water quality"). Student references to the ecological environment exemplify a core component of their ecological identity. As Thomashow notes, "personality, values, actions and a sense of self" are manifest in ecological identities,[11] and as we see in the case of student reference to the ecological environment, one's sense of self is particularly wedded to one's sense of the human's position in the natural world. A range of themes emerged in student reflections on the relation between self, sustainability, and the ecological environment including an ecological identity supported by a victim/charity narrative of engagement in which the environment is described as a helpless other and the sustainability crusader participating in NIW becomes the charitable hero. We also see in these student reflections an ecological identity characterized by the creation of personal relationships to both tangible products and environmental issues, which is occasionally accompanied by a feeling of connectedness to the ecological environment, spiritual or otherwise.

Casting the environment as a *victim* to which students give *charity* and are positioned to either *help* or *harm* emerged as a common frame of reference for the ecological environment through which students portrayed an ecological identity. This creation of the environment as victim might be understood as an expression of Mezirow's first phase of transformation in sustainability education: *experiencing a disorienting dilemma*. The charity frame of understanding was evidenced by student use of the *help* verb, for example: "We *helped* the trees from the invasive vine"; or, we are "trying to *help* the environment" (emphasis added). Whereas the victim frame was evidenced by student acknowledgment of guilt or belief that human interactions with the ecological environment are generally negative. The dilemma in this case is not so much about the tribulations of living sustainably, but the guilt associated with a human's invisible, unpredictable, and seemingly unstoppable destruction of the environment. Clearly, student references to "guilt" and "trying to help" indicate both a dilemma/need to help and an uncertainty about whether that help will be sufficient.

In some students we did see reflections on the ecological environment move toward Mezirow's second phase of transformation in sustainability education: *performing and examination of self*. One student wrote, for example: "If I did leave the faucet on while brushing my teeth . . . I would feel a definite sense of guilt"; and another wrote: "When an individual is conscious of trying to conserve the amount of waste and engery [*sic*] that is created you truly realize what you do to the environment." Here we see an important shift take place from the environment as a victim due to the actions of others to the environment as a victim due to the actions of ourselves. These feelings of "guilt" and this acknowledgement of *consciousness* in student reflections are realizations that individual actions are detrimental to the environment, which is an essential transformative step if a student is to move toward the next phase of transformation: *critically assessing assumptions*.

We might also understand this ecological identity steeped in guilt that some students express as a component of one of the major barriers to sustainability education: feelings of futility. In Colin Beavan's digital extension of *No Impact Man*, Colinbeavan.com, the author blogs about sustainability issues and the reception of his No Impact projects. According to Beavan, feelings of futility were among the most commonly cited obstacles to "feeling useful" about the project among those who have responded to his No Impact surveys.[12] Feelings that one could never impact something so large and complex as sustainability within a cultural and economic system that seems to thrive in unabashed opposition to sustainable living, are clear deterrents to a transformational experience. When students reflect an ecological identity steeped in guilt and propelled toward helping the ecological environment, we see an othering of the environment that for some may increase their sense of futility but may encourage others to further transform.

We clearly see students *performing an examination of self* when they make reflections about their increasing feelings of connectedness to nature through the NIW project. One student reflected that this project "opened my mind to exploring my local environment"; and another that experiences like cooking were "bringing me closer to nature." Such passages represent a different kind of relation to the ecological environment that presumably comes from sustainability experiences that push students to think critically about the ways in which they are connecting to the environment. Students reflecting on this connectedness use words that indicate some form of embodiment of nature such as the mind *opening,* the individual moving *closer,* and the *embracing* of the ecological environment. Indeed, this increased embodiment of the ecological environment represents an ideal of a high-impact pedagogical practice. In these reflections on connectedness, we might understand students' critical engagement with materiality in NIW as a means by which some push to reconsider material as a form of interaction with the ecological environment rather than the environment as something *other than* humans and *other than* consumer products. As discussed elsewhere in this chapter, this embodiment of the ecological environment is where the interconnectedness of humans to environmental, economic, and social relations to sustainability emerge and the boundaries among these pillars begin to vanish. It may also be that sustainability requires multiple forms of transformation: a transformation of the student as consumer; of the human as harmer of the environment; and of the human as the disconnected, symbol-using animal. At its best, sustainability education seeks to imbue students with a realization of their interconnectedness to the environment, which requires a transformation. What's less clear is whether there is a singular, particular transformation for students to experience in learning about sustainability, or whether multiple transformations are required across the multiple identities and relations of individuals.

One indication that some students did not reach Mezirow's third phase of transformation—*critically assessing assumptions*—that rather than extending both their economic and ecological critiques to assess problems of consumer culture, consumerism remained a foregone conclusion, and instead products were placed in relation (good relations and bad relations) to environmental quality. One student wrote, for example: "I already do a lot of environmentally friendly things like using plant based cleaning supplies free of chemicals and eating organically whenever possible." In passages like these the human action of *friendliness* toward the ecological environment is mediated by their choices as consumers—which cleaning supplies to buy and where the apple came from. The most commonly discussed product-environment relations were water bottles, which students related to the ecological environment with reflections such as: "Plastic water bottles seem to be the biggest problem"; "Reusable water bottles are better for the environment"; and, "Sustaining the environment doesn't have to mean being a go green hippie, it could simply start with a reusable water bottle."

Vehicles are products also frequently related to the ecological environment, with reflections such as, "I drive to my friends' apartment, which is just past town, when it is better for the environment and my health to walk." Product-environment relations in student reflections shouldn't be too surprising. These are, after all, the everyday items that students encounter (in addition to media and food). Student environmental reflections tended to highlight tangible products in place of the ubiquitous, less tangible consumer resources directly relating that product to the ecological environment, such as *lights* in place of *electricity*; *vehicle use* in place of *fossil fuel use*; *water bottles* in place of the ecological costs of *water purification* and *wastewater treatment*. As discussed elsewhere in this chapter, references to resource uses such as these were much more common in relation to economic cost than to the ecological environment.

This tendency to emphasize tangible products over intangible resources may indicate that student learning in this high-impact project was more focused on the *who* or *what* of sustainable living than the *how* or *why* of sustainable living. At times, student reflections on sustainability were surprisingly void of references to the environmental or ecological factors underlying the need for sustainable living in the first place. For example, in a time characterized by climate crisis, not a single student referenced "climate change," "global warming," or "greenhouse gases" in their reflections on living sustainably. In place of these ecological issues, students discussed cars/vehicles (128 times) and lights/light bulbs (80 times). Likewise, only one student referenced the importance of "clean water" while "water bottle" was mentioned twenty-nine times among student reflections.

As we examine student references to the ecological environment it becomes clear that NIW engages students with the ecological environment but mostly *through* not *beyond* consumer culture. That is, students reflect on the materiality of consumer culture in this project and its distancing of them from the ecological environment, but rarely relate to the ecological environment outside of reflections on materiality. As discussed earlier, on some occasions students did reference feeling a closeness to nature aside from their relations to tangible products, such as feelings of guilt or a need to help, but more commonly reflections on the ecological environment came through reflections on products. Student reflection on the ecological environment through NIW clearly revealed their critical engagement with products and those products' relations to the ecological environment. Much less clear was evidence of students' critical engagement with the ecological issues that emerge from consumer culture—in this regard, melting ice caps, rising seas, and polluted streams were disconnected from turned off lights, walks to campus, and three-minute showers.

The transformation of ecological identities in the case of the ecological environment clearly showed student awareness of disorienting ecological dilemmas (Mezirow's first phase). As we consider the inward turn of transformative learning, toward an *examination of self*, we see many students limit that examination to the framework of consumer culture by critiquing their ecological identity on the basis of product use, rather than as autonomous beings in the ecological environment. Some students did, however, reconsider their ecological identities outside the consumerist framework, and these students seemed to be rewarded with feelings of *closeness* and *embrace*. Sustainability educators in the English curriculum should consider how critique of consumer culture may both promote and limit transformation of students' ecological identities. One the one hand, reflections on consumer products and their connection to environmental degradation helps students critically assess their assumed lives as consumers, but on the other hand too much focus on the student's consumer identity may risk opportunities for students to critique their moral or philosophical assumptions about the human's relationship with the ecological environment.

"UNPLUGGING" IS NOT AN OPTION: SOCIOCULTURAL TRANSFORMATIONS TOWARD SUSTAINABILITY

The prior two discussions of students' ecological identities in relation to economic and environmental identities help expose the identity struggles of our students, and possibly all students. Because possible identities are symbolic acts constructed by culture, discussion of the final pillar—the sociocultural—is the most important and comprehensive, both in student writing and in this chapter. Our university students are at once children and adults, residents and transients, producers and consumers, all testing their social identities and determining where and how they fit into the social, cultural, economic, and environmental framework of American life. Student reflections during NIW are representative of this negotiation of social identity as students struggle to find harmony between sustainable living, social expectations, and personal responsibilities. In this study, we understand the sociocultural pillar of sustainability to include challenges to sustainable living ranging from larger issues of social organization (society) and what we see as issues of *infrastructure*; to social expectations and what we see as issues of *cultural norms*, especially as enforced by more intimate social groups. While some may not perceive infrastructural challenges like access to public transportation as part of the sociocultural dimension, we see issues of infrastructure as the product of sociocultural norms, such as the affordances of personal vehicle ownership. For many students participating in NIW, the assumptions and expectations of families, friends, and partners, as well as the cultural impact on infrastructure, present significant barriers to the transformation process.

Students in our study continually referenced social interactions constructed through physical infrastructure. Our university is located in an affluent suburb that is a geographic point between rural communities to the west and south, with a major US city to the east. The student body represents this amalgamation of rural, suburban, and urban, which makes transportation infrastructure a central issue for students seeking sustainable lives, echoed continually in our students' reflective pieces. For some students in the dorms, university living was seen as a benefit to living sustainably: for example, "Since I live most of the year at school, I can cut out transportation during that time by walking to class, carpooling with a friend to work when we have the same schedule, and making the decision to walk into town instead of driving." For those who commute or choose to live off-campus, transportation was a profound dilemma because of the lack of a reliable, efficient public transport system. One explained that she doesn't use public transportation because she has to

> make sure I get to campus on time for class, which potentially could have increased the overall time even more. This is an area that was much less of a concern for [my boyfriend] because he goes to [an urban university], and he was able to easily hop on the train to get to class with only a 40 minute ride. This reinforced what I already knew: 1) I drive too much and 2) public transportation would require a much longer commute than I'd be willing to commit to.

Such comments clearly delineate the transportation challenges associated with attending a suburban university, as they also enact Mezirow's phase 2, *self-examination*. Even in instances where access to the university didn't require use of a vehicle, students faced other problems, as one student reflects: "My friends and family do not live within walking distance. My home is not within walking distance from my work. The grocery store is definitely not within walking distance." While many students' reflections do seem to be complaints of inconvenience, to think of them solely as that would be a misjudgment since for some, personal vehicle use also is seen as a matter of safety. One student reflected on fear of crime during dark hours to explain her reluctance to walk across town to campus, and others discussed the dangers of roads without sidewalks. Yet in the same vein, as in the quotation above, students reflect that if they attended an urban university (where crime rates are higher), they would abandon personal vehicle use unless it is for the purpose of traveling home. None of these students balanced such safety concerns with death and injury rates due to automobile use.

Off-campus student housing in the college's town, within walking distance to campus, is an option. However, these arrangements could be fraught because of social habits. One student initially complains about renting in town: "When my friends and I first signed the lease . . . I was bitter that they had cars and could drive, but if my schedule didn't match theirs I would be left stranded and have to walk." As in this quotation, discussion of material conditions often brought up social norms, such as comparison with others and ensuing emotional reactions. Schor notes that although people often deny comparing themselves, their goods, and their habits with those of others, evidence shows that they clearly do.[13] Mezirow's stages of transformation would ask this student to consider the tension between her and her roommates' experiences, as this student does: "On the flip side, I'm never left stranded (I have great friends who got my back. . . . Especially at night). And I'm also not bitter anymore and been choosing to walk more." Others acknowledge how transportation issues were embedded in the cultural practices of their rural hometowns that they brought with them to college: "Driving around on the weekends with my dad has become tradition, not to mention I live in an area with no access to public transportation and really no use for alternative forms of transport." The idea of commuting home on weekends (clearly a product of ubiquitous use of personal vehicles) was discussed by other students: "I did drive 100 miles tonight, though I assure you it was necessary." Norms of "necessity" here are clearly culturally constructed.

Second to issues of transportation infrastructure were reflections on food infrastructure both on campus and off, as discussed in our economic section. One student reflects, "Food is hard to get locally on a college campus and I don't have a kitchen to cook in here," and another remarks, "The community kitchen in my dorm . . . would be a great service to myself and other students if it actually contained utensils needed to cook." While life in a dorm may ease transportation dilemmas, campus-bound students are given an infrastructure that disconnects them from other opportunities for agency. Students who eat on campus don't have choices about the food's origins or the wasteful distribution process, and those who choose to resist this process and cook on campus run into community kitchens that lack functionality. They perhaps can be seen as sites where culture and infrastructure outpace one another with the community kitchen becoming a dysfunctional relic of university life; however, as the student acknowledges, it could offer transformative opportunities.

When we look at student reflections on sustainable living, infrastructure and access are clear barriers to achieving sustainability. What's less clear is to what extent these issues of access and infrastructure prevail because students prefer the convenience of the status quo, or whether these barriers would dissipate if students countered the social norms subtending these problems. As we see in some of these reflections, because living sustainably means resisting—or, in their word, "sacrificing"—the conveniences and traditions/norms of family life, student life, and work life, limitations of infrastructure become an excuse for feelings of futility.

The student reflections expose the challenges that emerge from the responsibilities of social systems, including family, work, and school as they are currently structured. One student summarized this challenge, reflecting: "We live in a world where we are constantly on the go; on our way to work, school, second jobs, visiting friends and family, and taking part in the other various activities not only leaves us unable to slow down our lives, but unable to even think about giving back." This reflection is tinged with futility, displaying a sentiment shared widely among students: that sustainable living is an interesting and important challenge, but it always comes behind family, work, and school responsibilities. This fourth-place status of sustainable living emerged throughout student reflections in situations where social engagements were deemed nonnegotiable. For example, in relation to transportation: "I had to drive to my parent's to take part in a Fantasy Baseball Draft"; "I did, however, drive home . . . which uses a lot of gas in my 1987 Ford Ranger. My brother is in a play tomorrow night . . . and I simply refuse to miss it, even for No-Impact Week." Their identities as students and workers were also repeatedly referenced, especially in relation to the electrical grid: "'Unplugging' is not really an option when you are a student knee deep in school work"; "I needed my phone in case something happened on my way to work." And some social connections were simply too strong to break, even for one week: "Thursday is my free night in my weekly schedule and I could not give up the urge to join my friends on the internet. I understand the choice I had made in not following protocol but this was too hard of an event for me to give up. . . . Thursday and the Weekend are terrible times to give up internet (most likely the point though)."

Some, perhaps out of care or their concepts of other social roles, revealed that students sometimes viewed the conditions of others' lives as nonnegotiable. One of our most surprising social/infrastructure reflections came from a student who worked as a nanny. She commented, "For the baby, however, certain things were needed to make sure he was comfortable, such as a certain light in his room that needed to stay on as well as a humidifier and a noise machine. This made me really aware of the energy it takes when you have children because kids love electronics and when you have babies they may need certain things on at all times." Sustainable living was persistently presented as an antagonist to other, less negotiable, social contracts where things "had to" happen; were "not really an option" to avoid; or that students outright "refused" to miss, even when they recognized that the point of the lesson was to get them to examine the structures upon which they were dependent. Students *do* need lights, electronics, and phones to do social things, such as working, being with family, and doing homework because of the habits their society reinforces for them and the lack of a set of sustainable alternative methods for achieving the same goals. This then projects onto the conditions of others, such as infants, and relationships with others, such as between a parent and an infant.

Through these reflections we see an idea emerge that the social expectations of everyday life dictate whether students try to live in ways that are sustainable. In this sense, sustainability becomes an add-on lifestyle that works only if it complements existing needs, and where it doesn't, they apologize but pursue these *have to, must, and refuse not to* social contracts that they—and we all—treasure.

This is especially the case when we examine reflections that indicate a fear of sustainable living becoming a form of social exile. Numerous student reflections on NIW indicated that students worried how peers would perceive their attempts to live sustainably. On the topic of reducing water waste, students wrote: "Because I had an interview I also knew that my hygiene needed to be up to par so I watched my water use when taking a shower." Another wrote: "I also don't shower on the weekends unless I have somewhere that I need to go and be presentable for," and another mused, "This might be a little gross, but instead of flushing every time I went number 1, I would wait until I had gone a couple times so that I was [*sic*] flushing too often and using all that water." Here we see water clearly bound to expectations of social contracts. There is a sense that one must waste water in order to be "presentable" and "up to par," as not doing so would be "gross." In these word choices we see a differentiation between home and public, as though students could achieve sustainability if they never left the house, but the moment they enter the gaze of the public they feel compelled toward water waste to meet social standards of presentability. This is important because what we may observe here is a breakdown of student movement from Mezirow's third-phase, *critically assessing assumptions* (here, about water waste), to the fourth phase of transformation, *recognizing that others share similar experiences*. If students knew that others were also sharing the experience of not wanting to waste water, logically we would see less fear of social judgment with regard to showering and toilet use. To say: *I must waste because I am leaving the context of this course experiment*, is to say that *I feel others would not understand this dilemma or share in this experience of sustainable living.*

Other student reflections confessed as much, with one student writing: "It takes confidence to be different and not care what others think. I wish I was the type of person that didn't care what people thought but I'm not." Here again we see an apologetic pursuit of these *have to, must, and refuse not to* social contracts. Students reflect that sustainable living, while admirable, requires the confidence to forsake the social gaze, to not care if others judge one's hygiene, material possessions, relationship with food, etc. There is a real reason why *building self-confidence* is phase 9 of Mezirow's ten transformative phases: nonconformity takes real strength, especially for college students.

As in the case of references to the ecological environment and students' ecological identities, the tendency to interpret social norms as greater necessities than sustainable practices may indicate that student learning in this high-impact project was more focused on the who or what of sustainable living than its how or why. Few reflections discussed breaking treasured social contracts in pursuit of sustainable living. Students didn't reflect on not being able to go home for the weekend because they were committed to living sustainably; didn't reflect on why we have electronics "just in case"; and didn't reflect on the plugged-in nature of their education. These social contracts remained largely unexamined and nonnegotiable, even for a week.

Yet several students reflected on ways that the NIW experiment improved their engagement with others. All the students who took part in the optional service event at the end of the week—removing invasive vines in the campus's nature preserve—commented not only on how they were "helping" nature, but also on the supportive experience of working outside with others; student responses to activities during the week such as a nature walk (Justin) or a local foods potluck (Cheryl) were overwhelmingly positive. More important, however, are those comments that show students moving beyond their peers in the class to involve family and friends, which opened new opportunities for meaningful interpersonal contact. One student writes: "I thought it'd [no electricity] be especially difficult today because my favorite TV show has its finale tonight, but it's not been too bad. I've played Monopoly with my family, so anyone who has played it knows how long it takes." Another student's boyfriend got on board: "Bringing that [not wasting] to his attention was just as fun for me as it was eye opening for him. It was exciting to try some new things together, such as 'military showers' and exploring a local nature preserve for the first time." A third student got more out of a common economic transaction: "The feeling of buying something straight from the farmers was empowering. I actually felt good buying food, something that never actually happens every time I buy a tin can full of soup." In these reflections, we see an important shift in which those who export their sustainable living experience from the personal and classroom domains to their everyday interactions with family, friends, and fellow citizens, find that, contrary to fears of alienation, there is new fun and engagement with others.

In these reflections on engagement with others, we see evidence that some students approach Mezirow's fifth phase of transformation: *exploration of options for new roles, relationships, and actions*. This phase of transformation derives not from an individual's disposition, but also from phase 4, *recognizing that others share similar discontent and a similar process of transformation* which allows them to engage others in pursuit of sustainable living. One student found that the process of disconnecting from consumerism and reconnecting through sustainability allowed her to engage others with plans to change:

> It is important to understand what this constant presence of the media and constant attachment to others can do to myself as an individual. I think it's good that

our no impact week included a day devoted to introspection, and it seems like all outward change begins here. I hereby resolve to care less what others are doing and to devote more time to figuring out my place in it all.

This idea of "my place in it all" seems to be central to student transformation within the sociocultural pillar of sustainability, as if to ask: *Am I a child or adult, a resident or transient, a cyclist, carpooler, driver? Am I socially "presentable" and "up to par," or am I a "go green hippie?" Am I caught up on the latest shows, and movies, and internet hype, or am I okay playing board games instead?* Students who seemed to have had limited transformation in this sustainability education experiment were hindered by their refusal to extend the experience beyond themselves as individuals or the classroom assignment. For many this may have been a fear of being socially unacceptable if transformed by the sustainable living experience. Students who seem to have undergone the greatest transformation did so because they began developing competence or interest in modifying social relationships in response to the sustainable living effort, and were rewarded to find more engagement with others, not less.

Sustainability educators in using writing-intensive high-impact practices might look for ways to build more opportunities for student engagement with others outside the classroom as a way to best encourage the reinforcement of confidence that leads to greater transformation. For example, Beavan's experiment is often run campus-wide, which could help alleviate some of these social pressures and model for students a possible transformation to another, more sustainable set of social norms. As students work to find their place in it all, they find an alluring comfort in the sociocultural norms that define their identities and ways to engage with others. Considering that these sociocultural norms (extraordinary hygiene, fast and cheap food, personal vehicle use, ubiquitous electronic use) are often at odds with sustainable living, students must be encouraged to engage with others outside these norms where they might discover, as some students did, that sustainable living offers opportunities for different, sometimes more meaningful social connections.

CAN REFLECTIVE WRITING AND HIGH-IMPACT PRACTICES INDUCE TRANSFORMATIVE LEARNING IN SUSTAINABILITY EDUCATION?

It's clear that sustainability education requires the deep and transformative learning that writing-intensive high-impact practice can start to approximate. Whether this learning ever occurs or how to improve the likeliness of its occurrence is more difficult to assess. Our analysis of student reflections across this exercise shows that while we succeeded in using the high-impact experience of NIW to generate expressions that reflect early transformative learning (Mezirow's phases 1–4), evidence of later phases of transformation are rare.

To expose any lasting change in students' lives—any actual transformation, no matter how small—we developed a short survey that asked them whether and how they continued NIW habits of living six months later. Because we assumed from the initial information derived from the reflective writing that few respondents would have made radical changes to their lives or would have engaged in outright environmental activism, we deliberately limited our survey primarily to the types of lifestyle changes that Beavan discusses in his memoir. We presented participating students with a list of practices they would have been exposed to during NIW: personal habits such as recycling, eating more local foods, using transportation alternatives, unplugging more often, using a handkerchief, etc. as well as more probing options such as whether or not they "continued to remind family and friends about sustainable practices" or whether they "continued to question the systems that forced them into an unsustainable lifestyle." While the first set of options would be a good start for new action, combining the first with the second set would indicate more of the transformative, deep learning that we had hoped would be galvanized by reflecting on the week-long experience.

Out of our twenty-nine total students, eighteen completed the survey.[14] The survey indicated that, even among the fairly accessible range of options, students' continuing practices were minimal: 89 percent of students used a reusable water bottle, and as expected, most (83 percent) continued recycling. (Both instructors considered it a significant failure that 17 percent of the students chose not to recycle after NIW, since recycling is usually the main action that students believe is relevant to sustainability.) 50 percent reported eating more local foods, 28 percent reported using transportation other than cars more frequently, but no student admitted to using a cloth handkerchief.

The survey options that would indicate persistent critique beyond the NIW experience, on the whole, received lower scores. None of our students reported that they had continued any kind of sustainability-related community service, which Beavan suggests as the way to make up for the harm that one inevitably causes in other aspects of one's life. While 39 percent said that they continued to question the systems that forced them into an unsustainable lifestyle, a stronger 56 percent admitted that they "stop[ped] buying stuff [they] don't need," both of which may indicate that sustained questioning will continue, and which may even now manifest in some of the smaller actions students took. A more promising 61 percent said that they continued to remind family and friends about sustainable practices, indicating that they continued to explore Mezirow's fourth phase, comparing their experiences with those of others. This also reinforces what the reflective writing indicated: that it is the social that controls the other pillars, especially for college students. No participant developed his or her thinking further to implement any actions that were not introduced or stressed during NIW, and one student admitted, "I have not continued any No Impact Week practices."

Both the reflective writing and the survey indicate that a much more conscious reframing of NIW would be needed in order to get students to more advanced stages of transformational learning—if a one-week writing-intensive high-impact experience is capable of beginning such change at all. This is one of the larger implications for teaching sustainability: that such experiences need to address transformative learning head-on and students need the opportunities to process, discuss, and complain, both in class discussions and in public and private reflective writing. Writing-intensive courses create this opportunity in a way that high-impact practices alone could not.

What we have tried to explore here is student navigation of ecological identity during a writing-intensive high-impact practice, with particular attention to the transformative learning process needed for learning about sustainability, as communicated by their reflective writing. Sustainability is an inherently complex topic that, when taken seriously, challenges every aspect of an individual's sense of self. Thomashow admits there are "tensions, contradictions, uncertainties, and ambiguities of constructing an ecological identity in the shifting terrain of post-modern life. It is not easy to navigate this terrain, balancing conflicting feelings about technology, politics, faith, nature, and humans. . . . There are no easy answers, comprehensive programs, or miraculous blueprints" for the kind of transformative learning that must occur.[15]

Fortunately, the English studies curriculum has a proud history of pedagogical practices, including writing-intensive courses, designed to help students identify the "tensions, contradictions, uncertainties, and ambiguities" of their everyday lives, ecological and otherwise. The writing-intensive high-impact practice of NIW created an experience through which some students moved closer to a transformation of their ecological identities, while others did not.

Writing-intensive learning in any course provides students with an opportunity to think critically about the intersection of language and course content, and ideally to see language and content as inseparable in the construction of knowledge. Experiential learning provides students with an opportunity for action in a facilitated educational setting that connects action with course content. It's important to note that writing-intensive learning is not simply ancillary to experiential learning—each is a high-impact practice in its own right. By combining the two, as we did during our NIW exercise, students are positioned to learn about sustainable living by experiencing it, but also learning to critically examine their own language systems and how those systems impact their experiential learning about sustainability. The writing-intensive component of experiential learning in this case becomes a recursive learning process that can encourage transformative learning.

But while English studies may hold the key for helping students explore the intersections between their personal experiences and social structures, both in high-impact and other types of class-based activities, the complexity of sustainability requires that this cannot happen solely in English studies classrooms. Each sustainability pillar has its own embedded and interconnected set of transformations—to achieve economic agency and to transform one's idea of oneself from the consumerist economic identity that drives our unsustainable culture, for example, students need to go through stages of transformative learning in relation to economics. To uncouple themselves from the social norms that encourage stasis, they need to transform their ideas of community. Even further, to understand the geographical infrastructure and political systems that underpin environmental racism, students must experience transformational learning in relation to history and privilege. Transformation related to sustainability can only happen if these and other kinds of transformation also occur.

To facilitate this broad application of transformational learning, future writing-intensive high-impact practices in sustainability education can build on prior research on high-impact practices via the following suggestions:

- *Scaffold experiential learning* about sustainability to begin with identities most easy to negotiate (economic) and build gradually toward the more embedded and seemingly less negotiable issues of sociocultural identity. We found that the "broke college student" identity many students already utilize has the potential to fit comfortably with the sustainability experience. Easing into the sustainability experience in this way can help students more readily engage in the early phases of transformative learning.
- *Encourage critical engagement* with sustainability outside the domain of consumerism (relationships with products) alone, being sure to also encourage a renegotiation of moral and philosophical relations to the ecological environment. We found that ecological awareness was seldom connected to student reflections about sustainability. Writing prompts should encourage reflection on the *how* and *why* of sustainability, not just the *who* and *what*. Writing prompts should also provide opportunity for students to reflect on human relations with the ecological environment, broadly conceived, rather than solely human relations with environmental problems.
- Whenever possible, *emphasize social engagement* with others to encourage transformation. NIW can be narrowly practiced as a series of small, individual actions, when Beavan clearly articulates in his later chapters that

collective action is what is required. We found that students who kept their sustainability experiment private, rather than externalizing the experience and involving others, were less likely to advance in the transformative learning process. Several students who engaged with others, braving the fear of appearing socially unacceptable, often found reward in deeper engagement with others. These students were also more likely to overcome the debilitating feelings of futility. Writing prompts might require students explicitly to engage friends, families, and strangers in the sustainability experience; NIW could also build in rewards for doing so.

- *Acknowledge that sustainability requires a multitude of transformations* among economic, environmental, and sociocultural systems that cannot happen in a single writing-intensive high-impact experience. Instead, writing-intensive high-impact experiences in sustainability must happen across the curriculum throughout students' education. These experiences should be coordinated, scaffolded, and directed toward particular transformations through particular high-impact practices.

This list of recommendations shows why the institutional situation of educating for sustainability is so important and why sustainability studies mesh so well with, and even *require*, high-impact practices and institutional structures such as writing across the curriculum. To track transformation in all the areas that contribute to sustainability transformation, students should be reflecting on—and instructors should be monitoring—their questioning of received systems in their economics classes, in their biology classes, in their geography classes, in their kinesiology classes. One of our students reflected that "this experience has changed my view of society and sustainability because it has showed that our society is not really built or progressing to improve sustainability." Helping students advance to this type of critique requires creating multiple spaces and activities that ask them to reflect on what's possible or yet to be imagined in all disciplines and to know what a sustainable lifestyle will require of their attitudes, habits, bodies, and minds.

NOTES

1. "High-Impact Educational Practices," *Association of American Colleges & Universities,* accessed December 15, 2015, https://www.aacu.org/leap/hips.

2. Arjen E. J. Wals and Bob Jickling, "'Sustainability' in Higher Education: From Doublethink and Newspeak to Critical Thinking and Meaningful Learning," *International Journal of Sustainability in Higher Education* 3, no. 3 (2002): 229.

3. Sipos Yona, Bryce Battisti, and Kurt Grimm, "Achieving Transformative Sustainability Learning: Engaging Head, Hands and Heart," *International Journal of*

Sustainability in Higher Education 9, no. 1 (2008): 68–86; Kevin Warburton, "Deep Learning and Education for Sustainability," *International Journal of Sustainability in Higher Education* 4, no. 1 (2003): 45.

4. See the "No Impact Story!" feed, *YouTube,* accessed December 15, 2015, https://www.youtube.com/user/MyNoImpactStory/feed.

5. Elizabeth G. Allan and Dana Lynn Driscoll, "The Three-fold Benefit of Reflective Writing: Improving Program Assessment, Student Learning, and Faculty Professional Development," *Assessing Writing* 21 (2014): 37.

6. Janet Moore, "Is Higher Education Ready for Transformative Learning? A Question Explored in the Study of Sustainability," *Journal of Transformative Education* 3, no. 1 (2005): 82.

7. Jack Mezirow, "Learning to Think Like an Adult: Core Concepts of Transformation Theory," in *The Handbook of Transformational Learning*, ed. Edward W. Taylor, Patricia Cranton et al. (San Francisco: Jossey-Bass, 2012), 86.

8. Mitchell Thomashow, *Ecological Identity: Becoming a Reflective Environmentalist* (Cambridge, MA: MIT, 1995), 3.

9. Juliet B. Schor, *The Overspent American* (New York; Basic, 1998), especially chapter 4, "When Spending Becomes You."

10. Blair Kidwell and Robert Turrisi, "An Examination of College Student Money Management Tendencies," *Journal of Economic Psychology* 25, no. 5 (2004), 603.

11. Thomashow, *Ecological Identity*, 3.

12. Colin Beavan, "Ten Ways to Overcome Futility (About Life, Climate Change, or Anything Else)," *Colin Beavan: aka No Impact Man*, accessed December 16, 2015, http://colinbeavan.com/ten-ways-overcome-futility-life-climate-anything-else/.

13. Schor, *Overspent*, 92.

14. Out of the twenty-nine students enrolled, two students disappeared from the classes by the end of spring semester, one was taking the fall semester off, five had graduated, and one more seems to have left school, and so they may not have been able or may not have felt like they should take the survey; we assume that the two other nonrespondents would have taken the survey had they made substantial sustainability-related changes to their lives.

15. Thomashow, *Ecological Identity*, xv.

Chapter Five

Design Thinking and Sustainability Problem Solving

Reconceptualizing a First-Year Writing-Intensive Seminar

Joseph R. Lease, Matthew R. Martin, and Joanne Chu

Wesleyan College, located in Macon, Georgia, is perhaps best known for being "the first college in the world chartered to grant degrees to women."[1] As part of its mission to be a "pioneer in women's education" and to promote "[r]esponsible citizenship and ethical leadership in service to others,"[2] Wesleyan incorporated sustainability education into its last strategic plan (2012–2017) in several ways, but the most notable goals from a curricular standpoint were the need to "increase faculty eco-literacy for teaching sustainability principles" and to "increase student exposure to global perspectives within sustainability."[3] For the college's writing program, these goals created significant change through the decision to revise the second half of the two-semester long first-year seminar (named WISe for Wesleyan Integrated Seminar) to include a sustainability component in addition to the course's already established expectation of teaching research writing to all first-year students. The three authors of this chapter were all part of the team that planned and built the new WISe 102, and also worked to revise it in subsequent semesters after it was first taught.

The decision to implement these changes within WISe 102 was not a difficult one. WISe 101 and 102 were then the only courses the college offered that a majority of students enrolled in, so any attempt to implement sustainability education on a campus-wide scale would be most likely to succeed there. Moreover, as a writing-intensive course, WISe 102 benefits from the same flexibility of content as most other first-year composition courses, what Derek Owens refers to as "composition's little secret."[4] And the connective potential between composition and sustainability has been well established by Sidney Dobrin, who claims: "Writing is an ecological pursuit. In order to be successful, it must situate itself in context; it must grow from location (contextual, historical, and ideological).[5] Finally, sustainability is a broad enough topic that it can be explored by any faculty member on campus, allowing the teaching team to use their expertise and stay in their comfort zones, something Jeanie Allen notes as critical to the success of any first-year experience program.[6] A challenge for us was finding a way to connect the seemingly (from the students' perspectives) disparate goals of a sustainability-themed and writing-intensive course. To accomplish that goal, we turned to design thinking (DT).

In the fall of 2013, Wesleyan embarked upon its overhaul of WISe 102 led by Dr. Joanne Chu of EcoEthos Solutions, the college's sustainability consultant, and Dr. Matt Martin, director of WISe 102. Drs. Chu and Martin believe that design thinking could be an ideal bridge to connect WISe 102's sustainability and writing goals in part because of its focus on a single user. In addition, this focus on individual users could allow students to overcome feelings of compassion fade, which can be common in classes that focus on "big picture" issues. In studying this phenomenon of compassion fade within the realm of charitable giving, Daniel Västfjäll et al. "propose that decisions about saving lives depend heavily on affect," meaning that people must care about the information they are presented with when making a decision in order to use that information in decision making.[7] This factor helps explain why people often feel sympathy for and move to help one person in need when global-scale humanitarian crises do not receive the attention they deserve. The larger the group in need, the more statistical and impersonal it seems, and, therefore, the less empathy people tend to have toward that group, and the less likely they are to help. Deborah Small and George Loewenstein make a similar argument when studying whether people care more about victims they can identify versus ones they encounter through statistics, noting that people "react differently" toward the former: "Specific victims of misfortune often draw extraordinary attention and resources. But, it is often difficult to draw attention to, or raise money for, interventions that would prevent people from becoming victims in the first place."[8] Studying sustainability in the classroom can certainly be statistically overwhelming, and it can also be challenging for students to feel like they can do anything to help improve massive global problems. One of the central tenets of design thinking, however, is that by focusing on and helping meet the needs of one individual, a DT group can actually meet the needs of many people.

Beginning with a faculty-wide training workshop on DT held before the start of the semester, planning continued throughout the term with weekly meetings attended by Dr. Chu and the seven professors from the six disciplines who would pilot the course the following spring. As the workshop implied, the introduction of DT into the WISe curriculum was the most obvious change to the course that needed to be worked out. Two other areas of emphasis also emerged during the fall planning sessions: 1) making sure the class maintained its focus on research writing and on developing students' writing skills in general and 2) gaining faculty buy-in to generate enthusiasm for a cross-disciplinary writing-intensive course where some team members would be slotted into the role by their divisions rather than volunteering to teach the class. Dr. Lease was part of the initial WISe 102 teaching team, and he was given the task of designing shared writing assignments that would both meet the course's strategic outcomes for writing and help the rest of the teaching team feel confident enough to provide excellent writing instruction to the Wesleyan first-year students.

PLANNING THE COURSE: DESIGN THINKING

DT was introduced to Wesleyan by Dr. Chu in her role as a sustainability consultant to the college, but the methodology itself was in large part developed at Stanford's Hasco Plattner Institute of Design (d.school). The goal of design thinking, broadly speaking, is to provide a means of problem solving that can be both innovative and practical in today's increasingly complex global society. The steps of the process bring together "creative and analytical approaches" in an interdisciplinary way that "draws on methods from engineering and design and combines them with ideas from the arts, tools from the social sciences, and insights from the business world."[9] Participation in d.school courses is limited to Stanford graduate students, but the d.school generously shares its methods and best practices openly via its website, which has led to design thinking being used effectively by kindergartners, CEOs, and all levels of learners in between.[10]

DT works through a five-step, repeatable process focused on solving a problem for a single user (repetition is expected as discovering the best solution is unlikely on a first attempt). The stages of this process, and all materials necessary to conduct a workshop in DT, can be found on the "Resources" page of the d.school website.[11] The process begins with a step called "Empathize," in which the DT team identifies a design challenge, then seeks out and interviews people who are impacted by what will be redesigned. To move to the "Define" step, the team reviews its empathy work and chooses the person they think they can help the most as their "user." During "Define," they identify the problem that, if they can solve it, they think would have the biggest positive impact on their user's life. "Ideate," the third step, is a brainstorming process that aims to get ideas for potential solutions out quickly and in high volume, after which the group decides which one it likes best. Then, in "Prototype," the group builds a low-resolution model of the solution out of items such as cardboard, paperclips, pipe cleaners, and construction paper. The "low rez" aspect of this model is intentional as it is more likely to get honest feedback from the user than something that looks like the group put a lot of time and/or money into building. Finally, the group moves to the "Test" phase, showing the model to their user and recording their reactions and feedback. The purpose of testing is to gain more feedback from the user, and so in testing the iterative DT process starts all over again with an emphasis on empathy. Feedback from users can lead to minor tweaks or to the realization that the group has not even identified the problem with which the user most needs assistance, which may mean starting over from scratch. In either case, a reaction from a user that sends a team back to work is actually positive because it helps students get over a fear of failure and better understand that real-world problem solving often takes multiple attempts before the best solution is found.

As the teaching team worked together to revise WISe 102 into a course built around a shared pedagogical framework of DT for sustainability, we focused on the idea that the course would build on WISe 101(the first-semester first-year seminar) as a foundation for traditional students' Wesleyan education. The goals of WISe 101 are to help students make a successful transition to college, to work on academic skills (speaking, writing, critical thinking) crucial to college success, to help students understand the nature and value of a Wesleyan education, and to help students understand what they want from their education and how they are going to get it. The goals of WISe 102, as each instructor shared in a statement that started all course syllabi, are:

> To reinforce and expand the writing and critical thinking skills taught in WISe 101; to provide students with research writing skills and strategies needed to be successful in college; to have students identify, examine and work together toward solving problems in the world around them; to promote and model free and respectful academic inquiry.

Instructors went on in all syllabi to explain how this course would be different:

> WISe 102 takes a different tack from 101 and, using the lens of sustainability, explores larger, global issues and seeks innovative solutions to real-world problems. Sustainability teaches us to understand problems by considering the future as well as the present and taking into account the complex interaction of such things as economic development, environmental resource use, and human well-being. This year, WISe 102 sections will focus on food, approaching the topic from a variety of different academic disciplines and pedagogical approaches. At the same time, the course will instruct you in an exciting new method of problem solving called design thinking. The idea is that you will use this approach to

come up with solutions to existing problems or concerns as they relate to food in our particular community.

This statement communicated to students what the teaching team saw as the heart of the course—the DT for sustainability framework that EcoEthos brought to Wesleyan. We reinforced that message throughout the semester. For example, the course began with a two-hour DT crash course that took students through the whole DT process to introduce the steps and show the value of the course. In WISe 102, we explained that they would all be using DT, a process that requires collaboration, creativity, good communication, and empathy, all core skills seen as vital for a twenty-first-century education. WISe instructors would use sustainability as a framework for the course as a way of understanding how large systems function and interconnect. Sustainability is about the intersection of the triple bottom line: people, planet, and profit; or equity, ecology, and economics. Sustainability also helps all people understand how our individual actions relate to expanding circles from the local to the global. It helps us see how the present connects to future generations. It connects academic work directly with real-world problems. As the teaching team put it succinctly, sustainability in WISe 102 wasn't about tree hugging. Loving nature and environmental activism are great if students want to pursue them, and Wesleyan certainly does all it can to promote such agency among its students. Sustainability in WISe 102, though, was about learning how to understand systems and how to become active, creative, and collaborative problem solvers.

The DT project in the course started with a common design challenge that faculty developed based on the theme of the class and connected to an issue on Wesleyan's campus. We asked our students, working in groups of about six, to find their own area within the challenge, identify and interview users related to the problem, then to come up with a solution based on their empathetic insights before prototyping their solution and testing it with users. At the end of semester, each group wrote a presentation that shared their solution and DT journeys with their classmates. The best presentation from each section presented to the whole first-year class, and the best overall presentation (as chosen by the WISe 102 faculty) received a commitment from the college to fund the solution.

INTEGRATING DESIGN THINKING WITH WRITING

In addition to the challenge of incorporating DT into WISe 102, our teaching team was also tasked with ensuring that the course remained dedicated to providing thorough writing instruction, particularly in the area of research writing, so that our students would be well prepared to enter coursework for their majors. The amount of class time already devoted to introducing and conducting a DT project meant that we had to be creative when it came to integrating writing into other parts of the course to avoid feeling a disconnect between its priorities, both for the sake of the students and the professors. Moreover, the flexibility of the course, which was a boon for professors as it allowed them to create sections within their own areas of expertise, proved challenging when it came to creating writing assignments that could be shared across all sections. In a given semester, for example, there might be a course on fire ecology taught by a biology professor; a course on the sustainability of tea production taught by an environmental studies professor; a course on the global food distribution network and hunger as a metaphor in literature taught by an English professor; a course on the design of food packaging taught by an art professor; a course on global perspectives on food, history, and political thought taught by a political science professor; and a course on experiential learning as it relates to the communal preparation and consumption of food taught by an education professor. The diversity of section topics in a given term was great for the students in terms of making it more likely that they could find something that interested them, but it proved daunting for creating assignments that could work for all of WISe 102. The goal of creating shared writing assignments was one the teaching team considered critical to the overall success of the course, though, so we spent a lot of time and effort developing tasks and instructions that could be adapted to specific section needs while maintaining a consistency across all classes that would ensure a similar experience for students across the course.

As a starting point, then, the teaching team decided to develop the "WISe 102 Writing Memofesto" (too short to be a manifesto and too important to be a memo, this light-hearted title also inserted some levity into the lengthy process of planning the course). The memofesto was written to be both faculty- and student-facing so that all stakeholders in WISe102 could know the writing goals of the course when planning, revising, or discussing assignments. The memofesto reads as follows:

WISe 102 Writing Memofesto

Because writing is a fundamental component that is critical to student success both within and beyond Wesleyan, and because WISe 102 is, for many of our students, the last formal writing instruction they will receive in their academic careers, the faculty of this course recognize the critical importance of and our role in writing instruction. As a result, all writing assignments in the course will adhere to the following goals:

Student Writing in WISe 102 Will Require Focus on and Promote Growth in the Following Areas:

1. Purpose: Writing in this course will require a clear focus (e.g., a thesis statement) that will guide both the organization and the content of the piece.
2. Organization: Assignments will allow students the opportunity to explore and use different organizational structures in their writing and will encourage students to identify and understand the role of organization in writing.
3. Evidence: When evidence is needed (i.e., when a student has made a claim that she needs to support), assignments will necessitate that students know a) how to find evidence; b) how to evaluate what they find; and c) how to smoothly and effectively integrate it into their own prose.
4. Clarity: Writing projects in WISe 102 will encourage students to write clear, concise prose.
5. Complexity: Writing tasks will emphasize that the desire to be clear does not erase the need for exploration of the complexity of ideas, their implications, and their relationship to each other.

With these goals agreed upon, creating individual assignments that could be shared across all sections was a much easier task.

In order to facilitate a connection between WISe 102's DT component and its writing instruction mandate, we developed three main writing assignments that would be included in all sections. In addition to these, section professors were expected to develop their own low-stakes writing assignments such as journal entries or discussion board posts so that students would have ample opportunities to get their thoughts written or typed before being asked to compose a major assignment. The three shared assignments were an ethnography, a research paper, and a reflective portfolio.

The ethnography was perhaps the best alignment of DT and writing instruction in the course. We designed this assignment to help with the Empathy stage of DT so that students could get to know potential users through interviews and then record and compile information about their interviewees to find the best possible user for each group. We developed a template for a single set of instructions for all our professors to use, and we organized it in the form of a student-facing letter that included a sample work plan for completing the assignment:

Ethnography Writing Assignment Instructions

Hello, students,

For this assignment, you will write a 3–4 page, thesis-driven essay in which you will summarize, analyze, and reflect upon the empathy work you have completed for your Design Thinking project (for a brief description of the differences between summary and analysis, see pgs. 76–9 of *RfW*). This paper will be due on ___ and must be formatted according to ___ guidelines. Please direct any questions to me at ___@wesleyancollege.edu.

Successful completion of this assignment will require organization, thoughtful reflection, and careful revision; following a schedule such as the one below is strongly advised:

1. Begin by taking thorough notes on all interview sessions during the Empathy work phase of your DT project. Even though you will be working with a partner (or partners) to conduct your interviews, you will need your own notes and your own impressions to successfully complete your Ethnography paper. If possible, and if you have permission from your interviewee, record each interview so that you can review it later.
2. After the interviews have been completed and your group has met to discuss them, look over your notes carefully, paying special attention to two questions: 1) What did you hope to learn from your group's interviews and 2) What did you actually learn in your interviews? You should also make sure that you have enough details to summarize and analyze at least two of your group's sessions in the Ethnography.
3. Develop a thesis statement based upon your answers to the two questions in #2. Once your thesis is ready, construct an outline that will map-out both how you will complete all three phases of the essay (summary, analysis, and reflection) and how you will transition from one section to another. (Note: there are many ways that this paper can be organized effectively; if you have any questions or doubts about your plan, let me know *before* you begin drafting.)
4. After outlining, write a draft of your paper. Aim to have your first draft completed by ___. (Note: this draft should absolutely *not* be what you turn in for a grade. Instead, it should be the first of at least two versions of your paper that will be revised before you turn it in for a grade.)
5. The final draft of your essay should be completed at least twenty-four hours prior to the due date on ___. That way you will have some time away from it before completing a last read-through/edit prior to submitting your work for a grade. Make sure to submit your work on time as all late penalties mentioned in the syllabus will apply to this assignment.

Good luck, and please let me know if you have any questions!

Dr. ___[12]

The *RfW* text mentioned in the prompt is Diana Hacker's *Rules for Writers*, which was the shared writing handbook used in all sections of the course. Having a shared text and a single prompt for all major writing assignments allowed us to maintain a consistency in our writing instruction in ways that would not have been possible otherwise.

In addition to the ethnography, which connected directly to the DT project, we also asked students to write a more traditional academic research paper. This assignment served two purposes. First, it helped achieve the goal of preparing students for more rigorous research assignments in upper-division courses, a need that the Wesleyan faculty expressed a concern about when we began redesigning WISe 102. Second, it helped establish a baseline of knowledge in the section's subject matter that the first-year students taking it might not otherwise have had. One of the biggest challenges we experienced with the entire DT project was helping our students generate enough expertise in their section's subject to feel confident enough to design a solution based on a user's problem in that subject area. Just because a first-year student shows interest in and signs up for a course on water conservation, for example, that does not mean that she knows anything about it, especially compared to what she might know later as a senior environmental studies major. The research paper was situated in the early- to middle-part of the course so that students could benefit from what they learned before finalizing their DT projects. As with the ethnography, we provided a detailed prompt and broke the assignment into smaller parts so that students who had never completed an assignment like this would have some help getting started and organizing their thoughts:

> In order to increase the likelihood of success on this project, there are several assignments beyond the essay itself that you will be expected to complete, all of which will add up to the 20% of the course grade that is devoted to the Research Project (see your syllabus for details on grade breakdowns):
>
> 1. Rely on the chapters on argument from your *Rules for Writers* textbook; once again, do not begin planning your essay until you have carefully read chapters 5–7 of *RfW*. Before beginning work on the essay itself, you will submit a research proposal. This document will only be one-page long, but it will state what topic you plan to research, why you are interested, and what questions you plan to answer. This assignment is due on Wednesday, 1/21, so you need to get started on it right away.
> 2. Once your research proposal has been approved by your professor, your next task is to construct and submit an annotated bibliography (see pgs. 448–456 of *RfW* for advice on maintaining a working bibliography and avoiding plagiarism). This assignment will include 7 sources you've found in your research with a 150-word description of what you learned from that source that you'll use in your paper. This assignment is due on Wednesday, 2/4.

3. Once your research is finished, your next task is to begin drafting your essay. This process will involve much more than simply sitting down to your computer and typing, and you should expect to complete multiple drafts of this paper before submitting it for a grade. In fact, before you turn in your final paper, you will submit a complete draft to your professor on Monday, 2/16, which can be used in any revision workshops or activities your professor asks you to complete. Remember, too, that you will be expected to adhere to the style sheet (MLA, Chicago, etc.) that is being used in your section, so make sure you know what your professor expects of you in that regard.
4. Within your paper itself, make sure to do the following: at the end of your introduction, include a *claim* (which will appear in your thesis statement) that directly asserts your overall opinion on the issue you have chosen (this will be written in third-person even though you are expressing your opinion as this is a formal academic paper). Remember, your goal is to convince your readers to agree with you, and your thesis has to be about an arguable or debatable issue. If you do not have a strong thesis statement, then you will not do well on this project.
5. After you have written your initial rough draft, it is a good idea to do an *audience profile* for this essay. To whom are you writing? How does this impact your choice of language and examples? Being careful of your audience is vital to the success of an argument paper; if your language is in any way offensive, you run the risk of alienating your reader (i.e., your readers will simply stop reading). Reread your rough draft and rewrite or eliminate any potentially offensive language that might lead your reader to disregard your opinion.
6. If you have any questions about this assignment, please let your professor know. You are encouraged to ask anything about the assignment you want to in class, but you may also e-mail, meet your professor during office hours, or schedule an appointment.
7. The final version of this project is due on Wednesday, 3/11. Good luck![13]

The final shared writing assignment across all WISe 102 sections was a reflective portfolio. In addition to revisions of DT-related assignments such as the ethnography and the script for the student's group presentation of its DT project to the class, the most important element of this assignment, from our perspective, was an initial reflective essay in which the student would think back on and write about what went well and what didn't in the DT process. We asked each student to:

[Write a] 3–4 page reflective essay (written according to the formatting rules your professor prefers) that will sum up your experience with DT as a whole— this is your opportunity to discuss what this entire process was like for you as an individual. What went well? What were the parts where you felt like you were "in your element" and making positive contributions to your group? Conversely, what didn't go well? When you discuss this aspect (the challenges you faced), be sure to make some suggestions about how things might be improved in future iterations of the course, and be careful with your tone here. Remember, this reflective essay is the "first impression" you will give to your reader, so do all that you can to ensure that your writing will come across as both thoughtful and constructive. Also, make sure that your thoughts are organized; pick a pattern of development (chronological, for example) and stick to it so that your reader doesn't get confused. One last thing—keep in mind that this reflective essay is the most important element of your portfolio; both of the elements matter, but this one will have the most weight in terms of determining your grade on the assignment.[14]

This last, summative writing task in the DT project gave students the opportunity to assess and argue for what they had learned about both the sustainability-themed topic of their section and the DT experience as a whole, which we felt was important to give them some closure on an undertaking that took up a great deal of their time in WISe 102.

In addition to shared writing prompts on major assignments and a shared handbook in *Rules for Writers*, the last effort we made to streamline our writing instruction across all sections of the course was to create shared rubrics for the ethnography, research paper, and reflective portfolio. The rubrics were holistic so that professors who were not used to grading papers or providing writing instruction could avoid feeling like they had to count grammatical mistakes to determine a score. Evaluation of papers was broken down into three categories: "Thesis & Organization," "Content & Support," and "Mechanics, Style, & Formatting."[15] Within each category there were five to six criteria that helped illuminate, both for student writers and faculty graders, what we were looking for in a successful paper. For example, under "Thesis & Organization," one criterion reads, "Orders ideas logically, and any pattern suggested in the thesis is mirrored using parallel structure," and under "Mechanics, Style, & Formatting" one states, "Varies sentence structure and vocabulary and uses an appropriate level of register for the assignment."[16] Each criterion was then evaluated on a five-point scale according to the following classifications: "Unacceptable U, Needs Work NW, Acceptable +, Good ++, Exceptional +++."[17] Finally, professors would finish their evaluations by writing a note to the student on the rubric using a "plus/delta" system to tell students what they did well and what they should work to change on the next assignment. Once all papers were evaluated and scored, we would finish up grading a major assignment by meeting together for a grade-norming session to make sure we were all on the same page in terms of what we were seeing in the papers and how the students performed.

FUNCTIONING OF THE COURSE

A crucial part of our WISe 102 was faculty willingness to work together to develop and implement the course's shared components. Our faculty team met together with Dr. Chu during the spring of 2013 to develop the initial semester's framework and theme. We worked through how to integrate our own subject content with the larger theme of the course and how to incorporate the DT project into the course. Dr. Lease led us in developing core principles for writing in the course and common assignments and rubrics we all would use. We knew that we would need the same kind of collaboration, creativity, communication, and empathy we would require of our students. Fortunately, our faculty team rose to the occasion and worked together beautifully.

In addition, during each semester we taught the course, faculty held weekly lunch meetings to discuss the past week, prepare for the coming one, and stay in sync with our common purpose and assignments. During a typical meeting, Dr. Martin would facilitate a discussion on what had worked well and not as well during the past week, what potential problems we saw coming, and what common messages we needed to communicate to students. Dr. Chu, in the semesters that she was helping us, would then "tee up" our DT work for the coming week to help us understand our activities and the rationale behind them. Following the model of WISe 101, which features weekly student-facilitated discussions each Friday, we initially decided to have DT Fridays which would space the project throughout the semester and give a predictable rhythm to the course. In later iterations of WISe 102, however, we moved DT into a larger unit closer to the end of the course so that section professors would have more time to introduce content related to their themes before the project work began. Both calendar methods had their advantages and drawbacks. For example, the DT Friday option gave students more time to complete different steps of the DT process, but the attenuation of the project over the course of the entire semester made momentum and energy hard to maintain. Conversely, grouping the project together at the end seemed to give students lots of energy as they worked quickly to complete the task well, but it also left them less time within the steps for work such as setting up and conducting interviews with potential users. Ultimately, we decided that the more compact method worked better for us so that our first-year students could have more time to learn about their section topics before diving into their DT work.

On weeks when writing assignments were approaching or due, Dr. Lease would lead a discussion to give us a common grounding for writing instruction in the class. We talked about how to introduce writing assignments to the students by helping them understand the common prompts. When we were getting ready to grade writing assignments, we talked through the purpose and function of our shared rubrics. In the grade-norming sessions, we also talked about and shared examples of what we saw as good, medium, and poor papers to develop a shared sense of student performance and how we should evaluate it in the major writing assignments.

HOW DID IT GO? HOW HAS IT EVOLVED?

At the end of each semester of WISe 102, faculty held a final longer meeting to celebrate the conclusion of WISe 102 and to debrief about how to make it better for the next year. The consensus, overall, was that the course was a success and had great potential as an introduction to problem-based learning for our students. Each semester we worked to streamline the course and made appropriate changes, such as the decision to concentrate the DT project toward the end of the semester instead of spaced evenly throughout.

Unfortunately, WISe 102 was eliminated during a revision of Wesleyan College's general education curriculum in 2016. Those of us teaching the course regretted this action. We felt the course was becoming more successful as we refined it and that it provided a strong foundation for our first-year students as they started their Wesleyan education. Staffing two required first-year seminars for all traditional students became unsustainable (forgive the pun) for the college, however, and faculty decided to eliminate this required course and give students more options in fulfilling our curricular goals.

Fortunately, the idea of a course built on DT for sustainability and writing continues at Wesleyan College. In 2016, Dr. Martin worked with Dr. Barbara Donovan (a political scientist and a core member of the WISe 102 team) and Dr. Barry Rhoades (a biologist and also a veteran WISe 102 faculty member) to adapt the core concepts of WISe 102 into a capstone course for our dual-degree students from Guangzhou University. These students spent an intense calendar at Wesleyan College earning sixty credit hours over two summer semesters, a fall semester, and a spring semester. Their course of study started with a summer course, WISe 201, an adaptation of WISe 101, and culminated with WISe 301, our adaptation of WISe 102. Called Interpretations of Land and Nature, the course used insights from political theory, history, literature, and environmental science to explore Wesleyan College's campus as a natural and constructed environment. Students' DT projects focus on how to redesign part of campus to meet human needs in a sustainable way. Recently, Dr. Martin, Dr. Donovan, and Dr. Rhoades have adapted the course as a synthesis (the culminating category in our current general education curriculum for traditional students) course during a fifteen-week semester and there are plans to use this revised class as part of a leadership certificate program the college is developing. As our DT for sustainability courses continue to evolve, faculty will work closely with Dr. Lease to ensure that the writing assignments and instruction in them continue to meet the needs of the college, the course, and our students.

NOTES

1. "About Wesleyan," Wesleyan College, accessed August 27, 2016, http://www.wesleyancollege.edu/about/index.cfm.

2. "Statement of Vision, Mission, and Values, Wesleyan College, accessed August 27, 2016, http://www.wesleyancolege.edu/about/missionstatement.cfm.

3. "Sustainability," Wesleyan College, accessed August 28, 2016, http://www.wesleyancollege.edu/about/Sustainability.cfm.

4. Derek Owens, *Composition and Sustainability: Teaching for a Threatened Generation* (Urbana: National Council of Teachers of English, 2001), 5.

5. Sidney I. Dobrin, "Writing Takes Place," in *Ecocomposition: Theoretical and Pedagogical Approaches*, eds. Christian R. Weisser and Sidney I. Dobrin (Albany: State University of New York Press, 2001), 18.

6. Jeanie K. Allen, "The Tensions of Creating a Good First-Year Experience Program: The Alpha Seminar," *About Campus* 8, no. 6 (January 2004): 25.

7. Daniel Västfjäll et al., "Compassion Fade: Affect and Charity are Greatest for a Single Child in Need," *PLoS One* 9(6): e100115, 1, https://doi.org/10.1371/journal.pone.0100115.

8. Deborah A. Small and George Loewenstein, "Helping *a* Victim or Helping *the* Victim: Altruism and Identifiability," *Journal of Risk and Uncertainty* 26, no. 1 (January 2003): 5, https://doi.org/10.1023/A:1022299422219.

9. "Our Point of View," Stanford University, accessed September 10, 2016, https://d.school.stanford.edu/our-point-of-view/#design-thinking.

10. "Use Our Methods," Stanford University, accessed September 10, 2016, https://d.school.stanford.edu/use-our-methods/.

11. "Resources," Stanford University, accessed July 21, 2019, https://dschool.stanford.edu/resources.

12. Joseph R. Lease, "Ethnography Writing Assignment Instructions" (class assignment, WISe 102, Wesleyan College, Macon, GA, March 9, 2015).

13. Joseph R. Lease, "Research Paper Prompt" (class assignment, WISe 102, Wesleyan College, Macon, GA, January 14, 2015).

14. Joseph R. Lease, "Portfolio Instructions" (class assignment, WISe 102, Wesleyan College, Macon, GA, March 13, 2015).

15. Joseph R. Lease, "WISe 102 2015 Research Paper Instructions" (class handout, WISe 102, Wesleyan College, Macon, GA, January 14, 2015).

16. Lease, "Research Paper Instructions."

17. Lease, "Research Paper Instructions."

Chapter Six

Creating Sustainability through Creativity

Using Creative Writing to Reframe and Build Connections

Lesley Hawkes

Creative writing degrees are popular in universities around the world, and many of these degrees now incorporate some environmental studies. Implementing ideas of sustainability through creativity is a growing area, and many universities are now teaching how skills from one can impact and work with the other. Iowa State University, for instance, offers an MFA in creative writing and environment, and the University of Delaware offers a minor in environmental humanities. Greg Garrard writes, "teaching undergraduate students environmental theories and literatures is the central kind of 'activism' to which many busy humanities academies can aspire, and arguably the most effective too."[1] Yet for all the teaching of these units, there is still little scholarly work on the pedagogy of ecocriticism in literary studies. Frederick Waage's *Teaching Environmental Literature* (1985), Sidney Dobrin and Christian Weisser's *Natural Discourse: Toward Ecocomposition* (2002), Laird Christensen, Mark Long and Frederick Waage's *Teaching North American Environmental Literature* (2008), and Greg Garrard's *Teaching Ecocriticism and Green Cultural Studies* (2011) are four key texts to date with a pedagogical framework. These four works are a beginning but there is still much work to be done in this area.

One method for addressing the work still to be done in this area is to examine specific courses being taught at universities. In the Creative Writing and Literary Studies Discipline at Queensland University of Technology (Brisbane, Qld, Australia), one of the compulsory units for all the creative writing students is "Introduction to Literary Studies." This subject introduces mainly first-year students to different theoretical frameworks they may encounter throughout their writing degree. This unit is also one of the first times many students are introduced to environmental concerns. Most universities that teach the humanities offer excellent introductory theoretical units, but this unit differs in its approach to assessment as there is a creative choice for the major assessment project. This assessment allows students to combine their theoretical knowledge with practical application of environmental concerns.

The assessment requires students to pick a local site, place, or space and write a creative piece motivated by a theory or theories they have encountered throughout the unit. They write a 500-word rationale to accompany the 2,500 word creative work (this may be a short story, a suite of poems, a personal essay, or a graphic novel) where they explain their aims, goals, and motivations. The aim of the assessment project is to discuss, explore, and reimagine their chosen site in relation to specific cultural and literary studies theories. The focus is on practical application through a creative form of the concepts they have studied and a consideration on how their chosen place is practiced. This means students have to observe how the space they have chosen is lived, imagined, and related to other spaces around it. The theories the students study are varied, and the unit is an introductory one where students are introduced to the key concepts and ideas behind each theory. However, each week the students are asked to understand and explain the connections between the different theoretical lenses and notice how these different lenses work with or against other theories. Students study theories such as formalism, structuralism, semiotics, consumerism, gender, postcolonialism, indigenous knowledges, spatial theory, and ecocriticism. Each week they reflect on past weeks and how the knowledge from each theory is having an impact upon their understanding of other theories. In this way the students are always engaging in the active meaning-making processes of knowledge building.

BIOREGION

Students have to choose a local site for their assessment piece and this addresses notions of bioregion. Buell writes, "So far the new environmental criticism's most distinctive contribution to the taxonomy of place-scale may be the concept of bioregion."[2] The advantage of a bioregion approach is it is "neither a species of environmental determinism nor of cultural constructionism, but an attempt to integrate ecological and cultural affiliations within the framework of a place-based sensibility."[3] This is not to suggest that each locale is not related to the next locale or that networks do not reach out and have an impact upon other regions. Rather it is appreciation that "regions remain permeable to shock waves potentially extending worldwide."[4] The stories students are writing may be local stories but they are not produced, consumed, or read in isolation. The choosing of a local lived site is also a way to allow students to engage with their environment without feeling they are being judged in any way. Adrienne Cassel writes, "There is room for critical thinking about local place" to occur "without the shaming that is often associated with asking students to engage in an ecological assessment of any aspect of their lives."[5] Students have agency in this project as they pick a site that is relevant to their lives and this leads to a sense of engagement from the beginning of the project to the final writing up stage.

One of the most popular theories students choose to creatively respond to is "ecocriticism." In many ways, all the students have to address ecocriticism to some extent because the site has to be a physical lived space of their choosing. Students are eager to apply in a creative manner the concepts they encounter through learning about "ecocriticism." In many ways this is not surprising as Cheryll Glotfelty defines ecocriticism as "the study of the relationship between literature and the physical environment [which] negotiates between the human and the nonhuman."[6] Students are mostly creative writing students (although there are also literary studies, law, and education students), and they are interested in how creative writing and the ideas associated with ecocriticism inform each other. The imagined spaces of fictional writing become potential sites for allowing students to think differently, to "know about the 'other,'" and to motivate them "to contemplate different spatial and social orders that would otherwise remain concealed or suppressed."[7] These spatial and social orders have, in part, remained concealed or suppressed because the tools to recognize them are not known. Timothy Clark finds that "language is, rather, a kind of decisive environment out of which we define ourselves. This is an environment that, especially in the West, expresses the overwhelming and often oppressive weight of centuries of anthropocentric modes of thought and perception but that still contains hidden resources and inventive possibilities for those writers and thinkers able to discern and exploit them."[8] Through practice, consideration, and engagement it is hoped that students will begin to unlock some of these hidden resources and inventive possibilities and consider the complexities that lay beneath their creative choices.

CREATIVE WRITING AND ECOCRITICISM

Lawrence Buell writes, "Environmental criticism strives to move the notion of environment from abstraction to a tangible concern."[9] Buell pushes for realism as the most legitimate form to write about the environment as he believes it is only in realist writing that truths can be seen. However, Buell also recognizes the limitations of realist writing, "Realism can heighten the divide between narrative consciousness and the text's represented world even as it purports to serve as a bridge."[10] However, all creative writing gives students some practical tangible techniques to apply to their reading and writing and brings their ideas and concerns about the environment from abstraction to application. It is hoped that during the unit students will move beyond conventional reading and writing framings by thinking and imagining place and nonhumans in different ways and in different contexts. In their assessment projects, students attempt to write place and the nonhuman in diverse and active contexts. Through discussion, reading, and writing, students begin to understand how the environment and the nonhuman have their own agency and legitimacy, which is not dependant on human power structures, and this includes human narrative structures.

Students begin to notice that the environment does not have to be a backdrop, plot-driver, or a mood builder in stories, but rather it is an interactive, changing, and connected process in action. Some excellent creative work is produced as well as an opening up of dialogue around sustainability. Students also begin to explore their connection in wider networks and consider how their writing choices have an impact upon meaning formations. Graham Huggan and Helen Tiffin find literature is a space that enables thinking beyond standard boundaries and borders.[11] However, students need to be able to discuss and enter into the dialogues around these conceptual categories before they can subvert or move beyond them. Wendy Steiner asserts, "We cannot read without interpreting, and the more we learn about the structures that shape and express literary meaning, the more sophisticated our interpretations become."[12] Learning about reading and writing structures enables the students to enter into a dialogue around sustainable reading and writing.

SUSTAINABILITY, EXPECTATIONS, AND EXPERIENCE

It becomes clear from early in the semester that students want to engage with and explore notions of sustainable writing. Buell defines sustainability as a "mode or subsistence and more specifically a rate of agricultural or crop-yield that can be maintained without detriment to the ecosystem."[13] Sustainable creative writing can therefore be defined as creative writing that is not detrimental to the ecosystem. It could be implied that all creative writing is sustainable as it does not directly have an impact on the ecosystem. However, stories have a huge cultural, historical, social, political, and imaginative impact upon how people respond to, perceive, and engage with the environment. The choices embedded in creative narratives can shape the way the environment is known and lived in societies. Students are pushed to explore whether it is possible to write from a nonhuman perspective and whether their stories can have environmental concerns that move beyond mere description and move into a more intersubjective space. They are asked to explore the processes involved in shared-meaning making.

JOURNAL QUESTIONS

Each week students write responses to questions. These journal questions are intended to stimulate tutorial discussion and further reading around the area. The journal questions for the week on ecocriticism are: Do you think it is possible, as a creative writer, to write from outside a human-centred perspective? And is the environment something you consider when you read a work of fiction?

These two questions are meant to allow students to begin round table discussions of how the nonhuman environment can move past a mere framing device for the human characters in their stories. The first question they have to consider is, "What is a human-centred perspective?" They are asked to consider whether the conventional reading and writing strategies they know and use can be shifted in such a way to reveal the active voice of the environment and whether this voice can become entwined so intricately in the narrative that it cannot be removed from the story.

In order for these shifting in reading and writing boundaries to begin to be broken down students are introduced to notions of green consciousness, and they ask themselves the question, "Can the nonhuman imagine?" and what ethical considerations come with this answer. If the reply to this question is "no," then the students need to ask "Why not?" If they answer "yes," then, again, they must consider what this means for their writing. This question then feeds into a wider one of, "Can the human imagination incorporate a nonhuman consciousness?" The notion of a green consciousness is often a new concept for students, and it takes a number of exercises and readings for them to recognize the possibilities that may occur when stories move beyond structures of binaries. M. H. Abrams and Geoffrey Galt Harpham find that one of the most important modes of analysis that an ecocritic must undertake is "a critique of binaries."[14] Instead of finding meaning through binaries, an emphasis should be placed on the interconnectedness of things and also the way things are "mutually constitutive."[15] In many ways binary constructions have been implemented so as to read ourselves against what we are not and these binary structures teach us to fear the "other."

Australian ecofeminist Val Plumwood, along the same line, puts forward the idea that there is an underlying assumption in Western thought that only human activity really matters. She goes further and finds that even when humans conserve and fight for natural reserves it is driven by human utility and the impact it will have for future human generations. She argues that divisions remain between humanity and nature even when humans seek to look after the environment. Plumwood finds that in Western knowledge-based systems humans have built their identity of binaries, and one of the biggest binaries in human construction is human/nonhuman. Plumwood promotes the need for an "ethic of nature." One that hasn't "polarised understanding and in which the human and nonhuman spheres correspond to two quite different substances or orders of being in the world."[16] There is no hierarchy in these orders, and one is not better than the other but merely different. They are all involved in intersubjective, meaning making processes. The question then remains of how this "ethic of nature" can begin to be produced. Is it possible to write with an ethos of sustainability? As previously stated, one of the starting points to doing this may indeed be the shifting of the boundaries around the construction of narratives, and specifically fictional narratives.

Lawrence Buell reminds us that language is "the instrument through which we acquire knowledge about the environment and through which we acquire or change attitudes towards it."[17] Fiction is where language can be pushed, experimented, and explored. Literary devices and using language differently remain the foremost techniques of fiction writing. However, Buell also reminds us that we must take a critical stance on the "narrative conventions that shape environmental discourse."[18] It is not enough to write stories about the environment if they follow the same narrative pattern as previous stories. Literary devices may be experimental and push boundaries, but the structures that encode these devices and the reading of these literary devices also need to allow for differences. Reading and writing frameworks of knowledge need to be shifted and altered so these processes are not only subjective but become intersubjective. If shifts in narrative structures occur then fictional writing may play a vital role in shaping and managing our future understandings of place and identity.

Helen Tiffin writes, "What is probably most needed is not the capacity to think beyond the human, but the courage to imagine new ways in which human and non-human societies, understood as being ecologically connected, can be creatively transformed."[19] It is the practice and processes of creatively transforming that students want to explore. They begin to recognize that they can be active participants in this process and their writing may make a difference to how landscape is known. Buell finds that there may be a way to move forward and transform our understandings, but it requires a shift in the way we actually read a text. This may sound like a simple task; to read differently. However, as Buell, makes clear, our reading strategies are based on long-standing literary traditions. According to Alfred K. Siewers, Buell finds there must be an "upending (of) a traditional quasi-Aristotelian fourfold framework for reading literature (plot, characterisation, theme and setting)," and there is a need to refocus our frameworks of reading around setting, the element most often neglected in Western criticism.[20] Studying ecocriticism and creative writing may be a way to stop the neglect of setting and open new dialogue around place.

Lawrence Buell sets out four principles for shifting boundaries of reading and writing:

1. The nonhuman environment is present not merely as a framing device but as a presence that begins to suggest that human history is implicated in natural history.
2. The human interest is not understood to be the only legitimate interest.
3. Human accountability to the environment is part of the text's ethical orientation.
4. Some sense of the environment as a process rather than as a constant or a given is at least implicit in the text.[21]

These four principles become ways in which students can work through their own writing and that of other authors. They will keep returning to these four principles throughout their creative reading and writing exercises.

TUTORIAL EXERCISES: READING STRATEGIES

As stated earlier, at the beginning of the tutorial students discuss some of the key points in relation to ecocriticism: What is Human? What is Nonhuman? What is Landscape? How is setting represented in novels they know and read? Also, they are asked to consider "how" they read for setting in these novels. Students come up with some insightful evaluations of their own reading practices and points that correlate closely with Buell's four-point plan. Students identify they were more interested in plot and character than place, or more specifically they had read the novels within a framing of plot and character and even theme, but setting was a belated secondary consideration. When they read novels they immediately placed the human as the most important subject in the story and they read the plot to see what would happen to and with each human character. Students did not read for any presence other than the human and they were mostly interested in human interactions with other humans. When they did come across sections where humans were absent, they skim read to get to the sections where the human character reenters the story.

Students were following, because of convention and training, reading patterns according to Aristotle's framework. This was even the case for readers and writers of fantasy. The secondary world building, which fantasy is well-known for, is still only built to place the human or to carry out the plot. Many students admitted they read these descriptions quickly to get to the "real" plot. Students were surprised by the structures they applied around their reading, especially as many saw themselves as having a strong green ethic. However, as Yi-Fu Tuan argues in his book *Topophilia: A Study of Environmental Perception, Attitudes and Values* (2013, 1972), a love and understanding of place is not an instinctual response for humans. In order to make meaning, students are searching out what they know, and it is not easy for them to consider a shift in their conceptual knowledge base.

As stated, even work that is underpinned by an ethos of environmentalism is human centered. Claire Bradford, Kerry Mallan, John Stephens, and Robyn McCallum after analyzing young adult and children's literature found, "The ecopoietic children's literature of the last 15 years has not sought to address anthropocentrism, apart from a few exceptions."[22] Environmental children's and young adult fiction is often didactic and "teaches" children lessons they can apply in a practical sense, but the narrative structure of the work still follows conventional modes. So while much contemporary work offers valuable lessons to follow in a practical sense, in the physical world the building blocks of the imagined world are still quite conventional. It is not only content that is important but also the narrative structure of that content.

TUTORIAL ACTIVITIES

When students begin to understand they are reading through a conventional reading framework, they become open to alternative readings and especially open to trying new ways of writing. Creative writing can become a way for conventions of narrative to be pushed, subverted, or challenged by thinking past the traditional fourfold way of approaching story. This is not to suggest that all stories have to be read by pushing through conventional boundaries but more that alternative readings are possible, and these alternatives should also be considered when meaning making. These activities and exercises provide theoretically informed guidance on how to read for difference and possibilities through an ecocritical lens.

ACTIVITY ON READING

During tutorials, students read through a number of different chapter beginnings from different novels. These novels span different authors, times, styles, and countries. It does not matter that these works are not all contemporary. In fact, for these exercises it is important for the students to see the continued cycle of the way setting is written and read. Students may have read these works in their entirety, but for this exercise it is not important (however, most students will be required to read and study all or some of these novels for other units as they progress through their writing degree). What is important is the manner in which the narratives frame the environment and the nonhuman and the way the students read the environment and the nonhuman. Some of the novels for study are *Tess of the d'Urbervilles*, by Thomas Hardy (1891), *Plains of Promise*, by Australian indigenous author Alexis Wright (1997), and the travel memoir *Eat, Pray, Love*, by Elizabeth Gilbert (2006). Students are also able to choose any novel they are reading at the moment for these activities. Before students look at the passages from the chapters, they are given a number of narrative strategies to consider throughout their readings. Students are reminded at all stages of their analysis that there is no one singular framework for an ecocritical approach. However, underlying all the differences in approaches is the need for a shift in perception in understanding and representation of the environment. During their reading and analysis, they are reminded to consider Buell's four point strategy (above) or Kate Soper's three key ways of writing nature.

In her 1995 book *What is Nature? Culture, Politics and the Non-Human* Kate Soper identifies three ways that nature is conventionally written about in works of fiction. The first way is that nature is written as metaphysical concept. Characters may consider the big philosophical questions: "What does it mean to be human?" and in order to work through this question binaries are applied and they begin to build their identity based on everything they are not. Everything that is not human becomes nonhuman. In order to find their "essence" the characters look inward and self-reflect. During their reading students look for the binaries in the work and consider how these binaries are setting up oppositions between human and nonhuman. The second way that nature has been looked at according to Soper is as a realist concept. The structure and processes of nature are explored, and the causes and effects of these are processed and reflected. Cycles, seasons, the laws of nature are all examined but always as a means to discover how humans fit into this natural world and how if need be the human can change it. For instance, these may be stories of the hardships of flood or drought and how human characters endured and produced the means to change these things for the better. During their readings students look for moments when nature is categorized and how humans fit into this categorization. The third way nature is written is as a lay or surface concept. The observable features of nature are written about. All the noticeable features are described. Much creative writing falls into this third way. Authors may describe in detail all the features that a character may pass or notice. This technique, in part, is used to place the story. The reader feels a sense of recognition and can map the story and therefore follow the story.[23]

These three approaches to world building have strengths and work to create a vision of the world in which the story is taking place. However, as Soper reminds us, all three approaches place humans at the center of the narrative. The human retains the power and agency in these approaches and remains the central figure around which everything else revolves. The story is a human story, and the human may form a close connection with the environment, but this connection is always on the changes it has made to the human.

ANALYSIS OF THE CHOSEN WORKS

Next, students can choose to work through the passages from the chapters using any or all of the reading strategies and to consider how the authors have framed the landscape in their stories. In *Tess*, students notice that Hardy gives detailed descriptions of the landscape. It is also easy to place this location onto a physical map. The center is given as London and the countryside is read against this location. There is also an indication that the "real" story has yet to begin. The landscape becomes a backdrop onto which the "real" story will take place. The beginning of chapter 2 starts:

> The village of Marlott lay amid the north-eastern undulations of the beautiful Vale of Blakemoor aforesaid, an engirdled and secluded region, for the most part untrodden as yet by tourist or landscape-painter, though within a four hours' journey from London.
>
> It is vale whose acquaintance is best made by viewing it from the summits of the hills that surround it—except perhaps during the droughts of summer. An unguided ramble into its recesses in bad weather is apt to engender dissatisfaction with its narrow, tortuous, and miry ways.
>
> This fertile and sheltered tract of country, in which the fields are never brown and the springs never dry, is bounded on the south by the bold chalk ridge the embraces the prominences of Hambledon Hill, Bulbarrow, Nettlecombe-Tout, Dogbury, High Stoy, and Bubb Down. The traveller from the coast, who after plodding northward for a score of miles over calcareous downs and corn-lands suddenly reaches the verge of one of these escapements, is surprised and delighted to behold, extended like a map beneath him, a country differing absolutely from that which he has passed through.[24]

When analyzing this piece of writing it becomes clear that the place is being located through markers on a map: "four hours' journey from London." The vale becomes known through the known places that surround it, and the writing describes how a human would first observe and encounter the site. All the names of other prominences allow readers to situate themselves and prepare for the story. The landscape may be "beautiful" but in a very traditional, pastoral manner. The setting remains uneventful until the human story enters the narrative and a tension arises between the human and the nonhuman. Nature is set up as belonging to the past, and it is beginning a process of erosion.

Students have come or will come across the term "pastoral" in their studies in works of poetry and fiction. The pastoral, as Leo Marx alerts us in his best known work *The Machine in the Garden* (1964), is a complex term. Marx found there are two types of pastoral: The idealistic pastoral and the complex pastoral. The idyll pastoral presents an innocent past that is often in danger because of encroaching technology. The passage from Hardy can be seen as an idyll pastoral as it presents an image of an unspoilt landscape with a sense of approaching danger. Marx also found that there is a complex pastoral where the environment and human have a more complicated relationship than a simple binary one. A complex pastoral can be found in the next novel that students read. The text that students found to push the conventional modes of writing strategies the most is Alexis Wright's *The Plains of Promise*. The beginning of chapter 2 reads:

> Up North the clouds of night split fast at dawn. A dark-red dawn that crawls with increasing brightness over fresh green growth breaking through the burnt stubble roots of a claypan fire. A claypan covered in cobweb mist. And here they come. Through the track that splits the stubble, a track packed down hard from travelling feet. The so-called mindless ones walk on. They walk on the cutting edge between reality and beyond, placing new footprints in the thin layer of moist earth. They come separately, about five or six old ones, taking their routine walk.
>
> No one cuts the white matted hair on head or face. Their long limbs of dry, sagging black skin are covered with dust. They are naked. Their chewing tobacco in its moist little lump behind the left ear or rolling in mouths with clicking tongues. Except for Old Eddie, who pushes bicycle handles-bars attached to a pole fixed on tricycle wheels, they walk unaided. Their faces are mapped by the deep gorges of great wisdom and knowledge of their traditional homelands. Their eyes stare downward into an earth eagerly expecting their return.[25]

This indigenous text takes a different approach to narrative structure. From the beginning, the readers of this story cannot locate the conventional binaries to begin to build conventional oppositional meaning. Wright's work is intersubjective, mingling different narratives, points of view, and time periods. The conventional structural markers are dismantled, and in their place the story becomes far more interconnected. There is a map, but it is not the official map of cities, directions, and length. Rather it is an engrained map where it is the land itself that has a memory. The land remembers the stories and enacts this memory onto the people who pass over it. The land has a consciousness.

If Buell's four principles for shifting narratives of reading and writing are applied to these two texts, it can be seen that it is only Wright's novel that incorporates all four. This may be because Wright's story, although written in English and for a mainly Western audience, is not entrenched in Western epistemologies. Her knowledge and lived experience of indigenous cultures free the text from presupposed monolithic structures and allow multiple narratives to emerge. There is a tendency to see indigenous frameworks as belonging to the past, but as Clare Archer-Lean asserts, "Indigenous Knowledges is not only an explicating of the past," it can also be read as "a future *way* in which we might unite epistemologies to know our present condition."[26] As previously stated, the students have already had a lecture on indigenous knowledges (by Dr Sandra Phillips), and they are aware of the new meanings and understandings that a knowledge base other than a Western epistemological one may bring. Ecocriticism allows the students to consider the rich possibilities for future discourse that indigenous knowledges may bring to readings. Scott Hess calls for a "sustainable pastoral," but defines it in general terms as a call "to action and participation, rather than escapism."[27] Students cannot read Wright's novel as a form of escapism, but rather they recognize there is a different framework surrounding this novel and one that is destabilizing their understanding of meaning making. Wright's novel is sustainable writing as it reveals the active processes of a lived and imagined environment.

Students are also asked to consider the travel memoir of *Eat, Pray, Love*. Chapter 2 begins:

> And since I am already down there in supplication on the floor, let me hold that position as I reach back in time three years earlier to the moment when this entire story began—a moment which also found me in this exact same posture: on my knees, on a floor, praying.
>
> Everything else about the three-years-ago scene was different, though. That time I was not in Rome but in the upstairs bathroom of the big house in the suburbs of New York which I'd recently purchased with my husband. It was a cold November, around three o'clock in the morning. My husband was sleeping in our bed. I was hiding in the bathroom for something like the forty-seventh consecutive night, and—just as during those nights before—I was sobbing. Sobbing so hard, in fact, that a great ocean of tears and snot was spreading before me on the bathroom tiles, a veritable lake Inferior (if you will) of all my shame and fear and confusion and grief.[28]

Gilbert's work uses Soper's three modes of writing about nature in her story. It certainly is used in a metaphysical sense as the female protagonist struggles to find her meaning in life. The author uses metaphors to create a sense of character unease and anxiety. For instance, the ocean is used as a metaphor to develop the wide gulf the protagonist feels with her surroundings. The names of places are given but only as a way for readers to locate the protagonist. The second way is as a Realist concept where the seasons of nature are used to correspond with an awakening in the character. It is a cold November night and the character is also emotionally frozen, unable to find her way. The surface details of the physical environment are also carefully defined. These three uses build to a character-based story (even though this is a travel memoir, it is far more about character than any of the landscapes the protagonist travels through). This story reinforces Soper's identification of the way nature is "used" in construction of narratives. Works of fiction that focus on the linear progression of the narrative, or the protagonist having an epiphany or reaching maturity (e.g., a bildungsroman) remain human focused. The characters move through events and setting in order to find their place in the world. Of course Gilbert's work is popular fiction, and it was written to have wide appeal to a broad audience. However, this is the point of this exercise. Students begin to notice that narrative structure is important in any story formation and narrative choices have an impact upon the way meaning is made in each story. Any work of fiction can be used for these exercises. There will be no one definitive analysis of each work, but students will begin to pay attention to how setting is written and why it is written in a particular manner.

TUTORIAL EXERCISE: WRITING

Students are not only given reading exercises but also writing exercises. Dobrin finds in relation to ecocriticism and literature courses the "teaching of writing is often lost in favour of critical inquiry of the subject matter at hand."[29] Reading and writing exercises are both needed to allow students to consider the frameworks that surround their own writing choices. Students may begin to read from an ecocritical framework, but they also need to consider how and why they write the environment. These writing exercises are used as a way for students to begin to understand their own patterns of writing and where these patterns come from as well as how easy or difficult it is to shift these conventions.

In *Modern Criticism and Theory* (2008), David Lodge and Nigel Wood put forward three categories of how conventional descriptions of place occur: "preparing the location for the following scenes, dramatic intensification, and symbolic."[30] Students are given sentences and then asked to consider whether they fall into any one of the categories. For instance, the sentence: "The dirty winding streets of London only gave a hint of what was to come" implies the important story is yet to occur. The landscape and setting is described but only for the action that will begin to take place. It is taken for granted that the more important story will begin once the protagonist (a human) enters this setting. It is also suggested that place cannot understand all that is to come. In some ways it is suggested the human condition is too complex to be fully represented through an analogy of place. Humans may understand place but place does not have the rational or logical thought to understand the human.

The second manner in which place is written is dramatic intensification: "The owl hooted and then flew away." The nonhuman is used to create mood and atmosphere rather than having agency and a story of its own to tell. The description of the nonhuman is there to intensify the tone and mood of the work. An owl signifies a feeling of intensity and this intensity will then be transferred to the human character's arrival. The language of the owl is momentary heard but it is gone before any interpretation is needed. The human will enter this story and begin the "real" dialogue through a "real" language.

The third manner is symbolic doubling: "The night was dark and gloomy just like Ben's heart." The setting is described in a way that alerts the readers to the feeling of the human character. The reader is not reading about place to learn about it but rather she or he is reading place in order to know the human. All these approaches to writing are valid ways to begin a story; however, they all place the environment in a lesser role than the human. The environment becomes a backdrop onto which the "real" story will take place. The "real" story is the one that will involve the human. Students are then asked to write their own introduction to a story and to notice how they write setting. They are to consider whether their opening sentences fall into any of the above categories or whether they are pushing or subverting these approaches. They are also asked whether they attempted to push or subvert the conventions but found they could not. If they tried but could not, what does this suggest about these conventions? Cato and Myers write, "Our knowing of the world is informed by practices which organise knowledge and meaning."[31] Students begin to think about what happens when these organizing categories are questioned.

TUTORIAL EXERCISE ON READING AND WRITING PLACE

Students are also asked to consider the role of place in the stories they write. Authors may give names to places in their stories or give brief descriptive passages but only as a way to get into the more important story about the human characters, or if setting is described it is used as the backdrop for the human action to occur. Setting may also be used in a thematic sense, but once again it is used to explain character development or motivation. The emphasis of the story remains character, plot, and theme, and setting is added to accommodate and accentuate these dominant three. Many writers and readers have not yet incorporated a green consciousness into their narrative making processes—the idea that the environment can be part of our imaginings. Our imagination needs to undertake a process of regeneration. Eudora Welty in her essay "Place in Fiction" finds "place is one of the lesser angels that watch over the racing hand of fiction."[32] Welty is not saying that writers purposely neglect place but more that plot, character, and theme are what guide most authors through the planning processes of their stories. On first impressions place seems simplistic to define, but its complexity is revealed when a clear definition is sought. Yi-Fu Tuan finds place "is not only a fact to be explained in the broader frame of space, but it is also a reality to be clarified and understood from the perspectives of the people who have given it meaning."[33] This definition is further complicated when one considers the imaginative construction of place.

Of course, it is easy to apply a named locale to the story, but eco-writing is more than labelling a site with a name. Places are more than the name that has been applied to them. Places are the processes, lived experiences, stories, and memories that are called into being all at the same time. Named places can also highlight the hierarchy that has been applied to certain areas—both real and imagined. Huggan and Tiffin find that certain landscapes are usually written about in negative terms while other landscapes are given prominence in the imagination. For instance, mangroves, desert landscapes, mud, and swamps are all represented as negatives while water, forests, and the ability to look out across the land are represented in positive terminology. There is a definite hierarchy of landscape, and the landscapes that do not fit this image are placed on the margins of the story or are seen as hazards to overcome. This may be considered a small and unimportant matter in narrative construction, but it highlights the point that how we write place can have a direct influence upon our understanding and conception of certain areas.

In Edward O. Wilson's *Biophilia* (1984), he writes about how humans shape a taste for landscape: "It seems that whenever people are given a free choice they move to open tree-studded land on prominences overlooking water."[34] These landscapes are valued and sought, while other landscapes further down the hierarchy of landscape are neglected. When writing these negative landscapes in a fictional story, they become associated with the villain or are seen as working against the hero making his/her journey more difficult.

One only has to think of all the settings where the villain lives in a devalued landscape to understand how this construction works. Making meaning through binaries builds on this negativity of certain places and devalues their existence in the real and imagined worlds. An ecocritical approach demands "an interrogation of the nature/culture binary as a step towards dismantling the other binarisms."[35] These negative stereotypes of landscapes need to be dismantled and other creative options sought.

Seeing things differently and expanding the notion of community so that it becomes situated within the ecological community as well as the human community are just some ways that creative writers can begin to engage with eco-writing strategies. Students already understand creative writing is a process and they understand the building blocks that are part of this process. They are used to reading for and writing plot, characterization, theme, and setting, but they are not used to considering alternatives to these building blocks.

Other Possibilities

David Abram in *The Spell of the Sensuous* offers a different view on how language is constructed. He purports that just "As nonhumans, animals, plants, and even inanimate rivers once spoke to our tribal ancestors, so the 'inert' letters on the page now speak to us! This is a form of animism that we take for granted, but it is animism nonetheless—as mysterious as a talking stone."[36] In Abram's view, language is not the exclusive property of humans, and humans need to learn how to read the other networks of meaning making processes. Language is not based on binaries but rather on intersubjectivity. To consider language a human-centered activity is to disregard all the other possible language systems that may exist. Timothy Clark writes there is the assumption that only humans have a language and language "is a mere tool for humans to represent and manipulate the world."[37] Clark finds the danger with this assumption is that it locks knowledge in a human prison and does not allow for other possibilities of meanings to be acknowledged.

Cary Wolfe, according to Clark, finds, "Human language is only one of the vast networks of signifying possibilities across species."[38] Humans cannot fully understand language, and there are still many properties opaque to human understanding and certainly not a matter of instrumental control. Students begin to question the possibility of other meaning-making systems. The ability to step outside of a human-centered understanding is difficult one and the structures that are behind such understanding are complex and deeply embedded. However, students begin to think seriously about why and how they privilege the human above all other species. They also experiment through their writing ways to dismantle this privilege. For instance students are asked to write a passage where they describe the environment without using similes. This simple exercise pushes students to stop thinking of the landscape in terms of what it is like and to understand it for what it is. Timo Maran and Kalevi Kull find that, "all living systems can be seen as meaning-making systems."[39] Students engage in ecosemiotics and consider how reordering the relational signs they read and make meaning through can lead to a reordering in other structures as well. One student who chose to write a suite of poems from the perspective of a huge Moreton Bay fig wrote in the rationale that accompanied her creative work that "I didn't just want to sound like a human pretending to be a tree." She went on to write, "I originally intended to write a short story but what came out was closer to poetry than prose." A section of one of her poems includes, "Our life blood drips from varicose veins and into our Mother/Mourn for us."[40] This student identifies that trying to communicate in the voice of the "other" forced her to change her chosen form and structure.

Ecocriticism is not carried out in isolation, and the structures that limit narrative discourse are often the same structures that limit and constrain other voices. Shifting narrative structures will not only give rise to the environment and the nonhuman telling their stories but also those "others" who have been neglected or rejected. The stories may be filtered through the human perspective, but if writers are more aware of the plurality of possibilities of different voices they can open up the spaces in which we read and write. As Cary Wolfe reminds us:

> It is not simply a question of giving language back to the animal, but rather of showing how the difference in kind between human and animal that humanism constitutes on the site of language may instead be thought as difference in degree on a continuum of signifying processes disseminated in a field of materiality, technicity and contingency, of which 'human' 'language' is a specific (albeit highly refined instance).[41]

CONCLUSION

Examples of students' works indicate that many still struggle with the notions of a nonhuman voice and point of view. As stated earlier, one of the questions the students are asked to consider in their journals is whether it is possible to write from a nonhuman perspective. This is a difficult question because how is a definitive answer ever to be known. Most students recognize the difficulty involved in trying to move past the human point of view, but a number of students attempt to experiment with point of view and voice in their creative project. There are some excellent projects where the students push through narrative structures and attempt a reimagining of the chosen place through other narrative modes and styles. One student wrote about the act of writing when viewed from a nonhuman perspective. The work is titled "Calligraphy" and begins with "Scribbling scuttles,/Woven filaments and Devoured Dreams./Pictures drawn in sand. Graffiti."[42]

However, a number of the student projects also reveal the difficulty involved in the process and merely become an imposed voice onto a nonhuman being. The story may be about a talking plant, but it is a plant that follows the same speech patterns as a human. It becomes the voice of a human in disguise. In other words, the student is merely applying a human language and consciousness onto the nonhuman. Their writing remains anthropocentric in its frame of reference. In "Children as Ecocitizens: Ecocriticism and Environmental Texts," Geraldine Massey and Clare Bradford find "the possibility of texts presenting an ecocentric position is problematic. The environment has no ability to speak for itself. . . . All environmental discourses are constituted by humans who speak on behalf of the environment, which means humans always have the potential to adopt a patronizing, custodial approach."[43] The environment has no ability to speak for itself through a Western human language system, but other knowledge systems may provide a possible space for voices of difference to be heard. Creative writing activities encourage students to engage in embedded environmentality through creative writing, narrative scholarship, and lived everyday experiences.

Students are genuinely interested in learning and applying concepts of ecocriticism to their reading and writing strategies. They are interested in the notion of sustainable writing. It may not be possible for them to move totally beyond the frameworks of conventional reading and writing strategies, but their engagement with and writing of these concerns and concepts reveal these imposed boundaries can be shifted, and once shifted an awareness of engagement emerges. Michael Payne writes, "The developing field of ecocriticism highlights the potential both for further reassessment of Western intellectual and social history in a global context, and for new coalitions on environmental and related issues between different non-modern worldviews globally."[44] Of course it is extremely difficult to measure the "success" of the students' assessment when it comes to outcomes. Their stories can be assessed based on conventional criteria, but it is harder to determine the actual eco-outcomes of these tasks. It is hoped students will become more ecological aware; however, it is difficult to measure this outcome. In future, quantitative as well as qualitative measures need to be developed to provide tangible evidence on the success of these writing programs. This is especially the case considering how much weight is given to quantitative research at formal institutions. Criteria for grading the assessment items may also need to be altered to incorporate stronger ideas of ecocritical practice. However, at this stage it is possible to ascertain that creative writing is a space of fertile possibilities and alternatives that allow for voices of difference to be heard.

NOTES

1. Greg Garrard, "Introduction," *Teaching Ecocriticism and Green Cultural Studies*, ed. Greg Garrard (Houndmills, Basingstate: Palgrave, 2011), 1.
2. Lawrence Buell, *The Future of Environmental Criticism: Environmental Crisis and Literary Imagination* (Oxford: Wiley-Blackwell, 2005), 83.
3. Buell, *Future of Environmental Criticism*, 83.
4. Buell, *Future of Environmental Criticism*, 88.
5. Adrienne Cassel, "Walking in the Weathered World," in *Teaching Ecocriticism*, ed. Garrard, 29.
6. Cheryll Glotfelty, "Introduction: Literary Studies in an Age of Environmental Crisis," in *The Ecocriticism Reader: Landmarks in Literary Ecology*, ed. Cheryll Glotfelty and Harold Fromm (Athens: University of Georgia Press, 1996), xviii–xix.
7. Angharad Saunders, "Literary Geography: Reforging the Connections." *Progress in Human Geography* 34, no. 4 (2009): 441.
8. Timothy Clark, *The Cambridge Introduction to Literature and the Environment* (Cambridge: Cambridge University Press, 2010), 54.
9. Buell, *Future of Environmental Criticism*, 29.
10. Buell, *Future of Environmental Criticism*, 40.
11. Graham Huggan and Helen Tiffin, *Postcolonial Ecocriticism: Literature, Animals, Environment* (New York: Routledge, 2010), 7.
12. Wendy Steiner, *Literature as Meaning* (New York: Penguin, 2005), 37.
13. Buell, *Future of Environmental Criticism*, 148.
14. M. H. Abrams and Geoffrey Galt Harpham, *A Glossary of Literary Terms* (Boston: Wadsworth Cengage Learning, 2012), 98.
15. Abrams and Harpham, *Glossary of Literary Terms*, 98.
16. Val Plumwood, "Decolonizing Relationships with Nature," in *Decolonizing Nature: Strategies for Conservation in a Post-Colonial Era*, ed. William M. Adams and Martin Mulligan (London: Earthscan, 2003), 55.
17. Buell, *Future of Environmental Criticism*, 45.
18. Buell, *Future of Environmental Criticism*, 45.
19. Huggan and Tiffin, *Postcolonial Ecocriticism*, 215.
20. Alfred K. Siewers, "Ecocriticism," in *A Dictionary of Cultural and Critical Theory*, 2nd ed., ed. Michael Payne and Jessica Rae Barbera (Malden and Oxford: Wiley-Blackwell, 2010), 206.

21. Buell, *Future of Environmental Criticism*, 7–8.
22. Clare Bradford et al., *New World Orders in Contemporary Children's Literature* (Houndmills, Basingstate: Palgrave, 2011), 82.
23. Kate Soper, *What Is Nature? Culture, Politics and the Nonhuman* (Malden, MA: Blackwell, 1995).
24. Thomas Hardy, *Tess of the d'Urbervilles* (1891; repr., London: HarperCollins, 2010), 9.
25. Alexis Wright, *Plains of Promise* (St. Lucia, Brisbane: University of Queensland Press, 1997), 19.
26. Clare Archer-Lean, Susan J. Carson, and Lesley Hawkes, "Fiction as a Form of Change: An Overview of a Literature Panel Discussion," in *Future Nature, Future Cultures*, ed. Susan Davis (Noosa, QLD.: Noosa Biosphere Limited & CQUniversity, 2013), 30.
27. Scott Hess, "Postmodern Pastoral, Advertising, and the Masque of Technology," *ISLE: Interdisciplinary Studies in Literature and Environment* 11, no. 1 (2004): 95, quoted in Gordon Sayre, "The Oxymoron of American Pastoralism," *Arizona Quarterly* 69, no. 4 (2013), 17.
28. Elizabeth Gilbert, *Eat, Pray, Love* (London: Bloomsbury, 2006), 10.
29. Sidney Dobrin and Christian Weisser, *Natural Discourse: Toward Ecocomposition* (New York: State University of New York Press, 2002), 120.
30. Nigel Wood and David Lodge, *Modern Criticism and Theory: A Reader*, 3rd ed. (New York: Pearson Education Limited, 2008), 668.
31. Molly Scott Cato and Jan Myers, "Education as Re-Embedding: Stroud Communiversity, Walking the Land and the Enduring Spell of the Sensuous," *Sustainability* 3, no. 1 (2011): 51–68.
32. Eudora Welty, "Place in Fiction," in *On Writing* (1978; repr., London: Random House, 2002), 39.
33. Yi-Fu Tuan, *Topophilia: A Study of Environmental Perception, Attitudes and Values*, rev. ed. (1972; repr., New York: Columbia University Press, 2013), 387.
34. Edward O. Wilson, *Biophilia* (Cambridge, MA: Harvard University Press, 1984), 110.
35. Bradford et al., *New World Orders*, 85.
36. David Abram, *The Spell of the Sensuous: Perception and Language in a More-Than-Human World* (New York: Vintage Books, 1997), 131.
37. Timothy Clark, *The Cambridge Introduction to Literature and the Environment* (Cambridge: Cambridge University Press, 2010), 46.
38. Clark, *Cambridge Introduction*, 53.
39. Timo Maran and Kalevi Kull, "Ecosemiotics: Main Principles and Current Developments," *Human Geography* 96, no. 1 (2014): 41.
40. These extracts are taken with permission from a student assignment submitted in 2013. The student's name has been withheld by mutual agreement.
41. Cary Wolfe, "In the Shadow of Wittgenstein's Lion," in *Zoontologies*, ed. Cary Wolfe (Minneapolis: University of Minnesota Press, 2003), 35, quoted in Clark, *Cambridge Introduction*, 53.

42. This extract is taken with permission from a student assignment submitted in 2013. The student's name has been withheld by mutual agreement.
43. Bradford et al., *New World Orders*, 114.
44. Siewers, "Ecocriticism," 209.

Chapter Seven

East to West

The Interconnectedness of All Things Created

Pamela Herron

Wanwu 万物 in Chinese literally means the ten thousand things, but wanwu is more often translated as the myriad things, all things created, or all things on earth, implying the inclusion of animals, plants, and humans. Wanwu would also include mountains, waters, winds, and other natural elements. From China's earliest written records of the *Dao De Jing*, Chinese thought has not placed humans above or in domination over other creatures; rather Chinese philosophy emphasizes the constancy of change, of cycles and seasons, of birth, ripening, maturity, and eventual passing. Similarly, in both the *Dao De Jing* and the *Yijing* 易經 (*I-Ching*), an even more ancient text, recognition is placed upon balance and harmony and a productive generative cycle within all of nature. In our modern culture of capitalism and consumption, we seem to have lost our way. Climate change is now recognized as a real threat not only to humans as a species but to wanwu, or all things on Earth.

In spring 2015, the University of Texas at El Paso offered for the first time a course titled "Dao De Jing and the Environment," which used the *Dao De Jing* as the central text and included a variety of more modern environmental texts including essays, poetry, and nonfiction that explore the natural world, sustainability, and the human connection and influence.[1] Some modern works focused on parallels between American Indian/First Nations beliefs about nature and the natural world, while others were written by more traditional nature or environmental writers such as Rachel Carson, Terry Tempest Williams, Aldo Leopold, and others. The writing-intensive course required students to read and analyze a variety of written texts, maintain a nature journal throughout the course, engage in eco-criticism of both individual works and comparative analysis, and communicate their ideas and discoveries both orally and in written form. This course could fit into an English department literature section, but in this particular case the course grew out of the success of my "Confucianism and Daoism" course, which is taught under religious studies. We chose to cross-list the course with women's studies and Asian studies to further attract a wide range of students from different disciplines.

This chapter documents the process and pedagogy of developing and teaching this class. This was a new venture for my university and for my students as there were no courses available in environmental or nature writing, sustainability issues, or similar topics except for those focused on environmental science. At the time the course was developed, there were few opportunities to take a course with Asia or China content, and environmental literature or nature writing had not been a priority on the campus. This course offered an opportunity to pioneer a STEAM course, crossing the boundary of literary arts and the sciences. So-called STEAM courses include the arts along with science, technology, engineering, and math. This becomes essential when universities, colleges, and secondary schools are cutting back on liberal arts and humanities courses. I have found that my courses under liberal arts that recognize connections between the sciences and the arts tend to attract a broad range of students from multiple disciplines. Proposing and developing this course was a natural progression out of my development and teaching of "Confucianism and Daoism," "China Culture and Humanities," "Introduction to Asian Studies," "Revolutionary Women of China," "Asian Film and Culture," and other China- or Asia-related classes. "Daoism and the Environment" was the first effort to offer a writing-intensive course comparing Chinese literature with Western literature, and the first time to offer a course exploring both environmental and sustainable literature with environmental and sustainable writing. After my initial effort in teaching this class, I have noticed that across the United States there seemed to be a flowering of courses, or at least modules, pairing Chinese classics with environmental concerns, so perhaps the course was timely, especially considering the growing concern for climate-change issues and a growing interest in more sustainable living. Classic Chinese texts have long recognized the interconnectedness and interrelationality of humans, plants, animals, the elements, and all aspects of the natural world and the cosmos. In my opinion, what some may see as looking backward to the past is in reality a huge step forward in heightening awareness of sustainability and the peril of environmental degradation globally.

Classic Chinese texts emphasize working toward a harmony and balance with nature, without the assumption of humans set above plants, animals, mountains, water, and other aspects of nature; rather humanity is an integral part of this greater whole. This course challenges the view of human superiority or dominion over nature and explores specific references in the assigned texts that reinforce this idea of humans being simply part of the natural world. By comparing the *Dao De Jing* with more contemporary texts, students examine the possible influence or impact on contemporary, sustainable, environmentally responsible attitudes of Chinese or Eastern philosophical thinking; of traditional nature/environmental writers; and of the beliefs, poetry, and traditions of American Indian/First Peoples culture. They focus on the question, "Are ancient and modern concepts of interconnectedness and sustainability relevant to environmentalists, eco-critics, and the general public today?" This course has allowed students to interpret and respond to concepts within these texts that present relationships between humans and nature, man and woman, and humans and their governments, and to assess their significance in today's culture and society. The required reading list for the course included but is not limited to the following texts:

Roger T. Ames and David L. Hall, *Dao De Jing: Making This Life Significant: A Philosophical Translation* (New York: Ballantine, 2003).

Lorraine Anderson, *Sisters of the Earth: Women's Prose and Poetry about Nature* (New York: Vintage, 1991).

Jason Gardner, *The Sacred Earth: Writers on Nature & Spirit* (Novato, CA: New World Library, 1998).

Aldo Leopold, *A Sand County Almanac and Sketches Here and There* (New York: Oxford UP, 1987).

David T. Suzuki and Amanda McConnell, *The Sacred Balance: Rediscovering Our Place in Nature* (Amherst, NY: Prometheus, 1998).

In addition, the course included a number of films and other documents, including reviews, creative works, and essays. Relevant and timely articles were also posted on the course Blackboard site. These injected an even more contemporary element into the classroom and provided impetus for lively class discussions. Blackboard also served as the medium for class discussions. This generated more interaction between students than is possible in a traditional method of turning in papers or critical analysis, which would only be between the instructor and the individual student. In our class discussion format, students learned to listen and be respectful of differing viewpoints among their peers, both online and face to face. This interaction helped many of them better articulate their arguments and opinions since they were not operating in a vacuum. Often students are required to submit papers with limited feedback from peers or the instructor, unless a course is set up workshop style. Throughout the duration of the semester, students had many opportunities to "test" their arguments in multiple settings, including in-class discussions, interaction on Blackboard through organized Discussion

Boards with specific parameters and guidelines, and small-group work. For many individuals, this gave an opportunity to experience immediate reactions to their comments or opinions. As the instructor, I observed that this led to students taking more care in communication with each other and ultimately in their research papers and oral presentations. They appeared to become more sensitive to differing or dissenting opinions and therefore crafted their written work and oral discussions more carefully. For a course such as this, and indeed in many literature or humanities classes, students learn that there may not be a definitive right or wrong answer; rather there may be several valid approaches worth consideration. Awareness of diverse opinions leads them to become more discerning in their writing and in their communication with others.

WHAT ARE DAOISM AND THE *DAO DE JING*?

The *Dao De Jing* 道德經 is the foundation of Daoism, while the *Lun Yu*, or the *Analects of Confucius*, is the central text for Confucianism or *Ruxue* 儒學. In addition to a heritage of more than two thousand years, *Dao De Jing* in particular has long been a popular text within the New Age spiritual movement in Western culture. Many different translations are applied to the *Dao De Jing*, and this is reflective of the interpretation and sometimes ambiguity of the entire text. Roger Ames and David Hall use the subtitle "Making this life significant,"[2] and that is certainly a reasonable interpretation. To break down the title, the word "dao" means the way, path, or direction, but in the case of this notably spiritual text most would refer to have it capitalized as "The Way" to imply a greater, more significant concept. "De" is often translated as virtue or even virtuosity, but there is a deeper implication of strength, integrity, and inherent power. The word "jing" refers to a book, in this case a classic text. To get the sense of the meaning of the title, one might also translate it as, "The classic text of seeking a virtuous method of being."

Both texts, or at least the men associated with them, Laozi and Confucius, have been somewhat conscripted by popular culture without most of the general public having read, studied, or understood either text. Both classic Chinese texts emphasize working toward a harmony with nature without the assumption of humans set above plants, animals, mountains, water, and other aspects of nature; rather humanity is a part of this greater whole. Both classic texts contain specific references that reinforce this idea of humans being simply part of the natural world. In particular, can these concepts influence contemporary sustainable environmentally responsible attitudes? Are the *Dao De Jing* and the *Analects of Confucius* relevant to environmentalists and eco-critics today? The concepts within these ancient texts examine the interconnectedness of the cosmos. Although they are ancient texts, such relationships still hold significance in today's culture and society.

We know that the *Dao De Jing* emerged during the period in China called the Warring States (c. 403–221 BCE). Confucius 孔子, also known as *K'ung fu tzu*, *Kong Fuzi*, and Master Kong, lived from 551–479 BCE.[3] The *Lun Yu* or *Analects of Confucius* were not actually written by Confucius himself; rather his students, or disciples as many call them, wrote them down after his death. Archaeology is a relatively new field and area of attention for Chinese scholars, and over the past few decades various manuscripts have been unearthed. Based on the text evidence, the *Analects of Confucius* may have been composed over the course of three centuries. Confucius not only taught students but also taught teachers who later went on to found and lead schools where they modeled and continued the style of teaching, love of the classics, and enormous respect for education and literature that have been carried down and become part of the fabric of the cultures of the People's Republic of China, Hong Kong, Taiwan, Singapore, Japan, Korea, and Vietnam. This respect for learning and education continues to be a pervading influence, which explains why students from these countries so often excel over those from the United States and most European countries.

Certainly within our own times we have seen a push to include Chinese philosophy and spiritual thought in university communities worldwide. In the past, these same institutions centered their focus solely on Western thinkers as the standard, relegating Chinese writers and scholars to a brief reference if included at all. This is changing rapidly. Students eagerly seek courses with Chinese and Asian content and recognize the importance of learning to understand Asian cultures. Examining and studying the *Dao De Jing* or the *Analects*, especially in a literature-based writing-intensive course, is an excellent beginning.

Although the *Dao De Jing* emerged in the Warring States, many scholars believe that its origins are much earlier and that its content was perhaps transmitted through oral tradition, much as indigenous knowledge in various peoples have been transmitted for thousands of years. Although the documented texts of the *Dao De Jing* are dated after the time of Confucius, Confucius himself frequently referenced his efforts to "follow the Dao." This lifelong effort to discover and follow the Dao is most evident in his teachings to his students, which are documented in the *Analects* and in other classic Chinese texts, so it seems clear that knowledge of the Dao, or The Way, predates Confucius and his followers. Elements in the *Dao De Jing* hearken back to a much earlier Chinese classic text, the *Yijing*, sometimes translated as the Book of Changes or as I-Ching. The *Yijing* dates back at least 4,000–4,500 years and is the oldest of all the Chinese classic texts. The history of the *Yijing* has roots in divination, but this should by no means be reduced or simplified to "fortune-telling." The counterculture movement in the United States in the 1960s brought a renewed interest in both the *Dao De Jing* and the *Yijing* for their use as fortune-telling or divination devices, but many of the translations from this period are rather shallow and facile, ignoring the depths and complexities of both texts. The *Yijing* provides a thoughtful context in which to consider all aspects of the human condition, while the *Dao De Jing* provides a more inclusive look at our environment with guidance for our actions, self-cultivation, leadership, and governing, and—most significant in this chapter—it provides an ancient wisdom for our relationships with each other and with the environment.

A NOTE ABOUT TRANSLATED TEXTS

Translations are problematic at best. For those who are monolingual or not sufficiently fluent in another language, any time we read a translated text we rely on the expertise and knowledge of translators for interpreting those texts. Good translations open windows to other concepts, literatures, and cultures. Bad or inadequate translations may be better than no translation at all, but in many cases they can be responsible for misunderstandings and misinterpretations. For example, if two or three translations of the *Dao De Jing* are read side by side, the reader could be excused for thinking they are translations of entirely different texts. This is quite noticeable in earlier translations of ancient Chinese texts by religious scholars or missionaries who clearly felt a need to reconcile these foreign texts with a more Christian point of view. When educators make the choice to expose students to a foreign text, and in this case an ancient foreign text, both teacher and student are faced with appreciating and understanding the importance of sensitive translation, the difficulty of trying to capture the true meaning and intention of the original text, and the subjectivity of the entire task of translation and the holistic aspect of attempting to understand significant texts in another language for another culture. Language is embedded in culture and vice versa. Faithful translation and the teaching of a text cannot ignore or dismiss the importance of language choices and cultural implications.

Chinese is a concept-based language without an alphabet. Each character is freighted with meaning that can alter or be enhanced by its juxtaposition with other characters. Li-Hsiang Lisa Rosenlee, in her book *Confucianism and Women: A Philosophical Interpretation*, said, "In the same way, without a genuine understanding of Chinese culture, [this] reflects more the assumptions that Western observers have in organizing the world and in making the world of others intelligible to themselves than the reality."[4]

Aiwei Shi, a professional translator and faculty member at Xinzhou Teachers University, Shanxu China says:

> Translation is communication. When the translation causes trouble in understanding or results in zero communication, it is a failure. . . . What causes such failure: one is a misconception that translation is a word-for-word process whereas the other is the translator's blindness to cultural differences. Translation does not only happen intra-linguistically but inter-linguistically. It is natural that different languages entail different cultures behind it. Without such consciousness and appropriate cultural knowledge it would be no surprise that communication failed.[5]

Authors Kam-por Yu, Julia Tao, and Philip Ivanhoe in their book *Taking Confucian Ethics Seriously* point out that many studies of Confucianism strive to *learn about* a culture instead of approaching study with the intention to *learn from* the culture.[6] The model for this course is to *learn about* and to *learn from* the teachings of this ancient and revered text, the *Dao De Jing*. This is a subtle but significant difference. Examining, reading, discussing, and writing about these ancient Chinese classic texts does indeed help us in the West to know more about China, its history and its culture, but more significant is the fact that there is much to learn from the study of these ancient texts especially if we treat them as a documentation of ethics, a way of life, and appropriate behavior for all.

For educators who might feel hesitant to teach or discuss a classical Chinese text such as the *Dao De Jing*, or any other Chinese text, there are some excellent resources available to introduce students to the structural and linguistic differences inherent in Chinese texts. These resources also contribute to a feeling of confidence when introducing material that may be out of the educator's comfort zone. One such resource is *An Introduction to Chinese Culture through the Family*, which is part of the State University of New York Press (SUNY) series on Asian Studies Development edited by Roger T. Ames and Peter D. Hershock. The first chapter in their book, by Linda S. Pickle, is called "Written and Spoken Chinese: Expression of Culture and Heritage." Pickle's chapter is a well done discussion of how Chinese language works and how it developed. Another useful resource is an appendix included in Bryan Van Norden's *An Introduction to Classical Chinese Philosophy*. Van Norden's book also has a chapter on the *Dao De Jing* that uses excerpts but not the complete text.

If we choose to use a classical Chinese text in the classroom, it is imperative that we, and by extension our students, learn to understand Chinese culture and not judge it by Western standards or assumptions. This is particularly important when examining an ancient text such as the *Dao De Jing*. This ancient wisdom is available to us and has much to offer our contemporary culture, especially in these times of factionally divided countries, terrorism, religious differences, gender issues, and perilous environmental degradation. Although we may speak different languages and come from different cultures, we are all still people in this world and we are all connected.

STRUCTURE AND SCOPE OF THE COURSE

The course begins with a brief discussion of Daoism and its history but moves immediately into examining passages together as a class. My goal is to establish a community of learners who feel free to question and offer their own interpretation. In this way we learn together. Students read the introductory material in the Ames and Hall required text. This introduction gives an extensive lexicon of the kinds of terms that cannot be readily translated; for example, *tian* is not the equivalent of heaven especially under Western views, and *wuwei*, often translated as doing nothing, does not mean literally to do nothing. Because of the complexity of these terms, Ames and Hall often devote a page or more to a significant term. Roger Ames, David Hall, and Henry Rosemont Jr. (another philosopher focusing on Chinese texts), often use the term "concept clusters," which provide a set of related words instead of a single word translation. This gives students a glimpse into the complexities of Chinese language. A word may change its meaning depending on its context. The words preceding or following a particular character may alter the meaning, so one-word snap translations are misleading. My students are encouraged to start using the appropriate term in class rather than relying on a translation substitute. This seems to be highly effective, particularly for those who go on to other Asian content classes or pursue learning the Chinese language. We find that students who take one of these classes frequently are intrigued enough to take future classes.

These first sessions introduce the classical text and its significance in Chinese and contemporary culture. The first meeting also provides information and a discussion of the history of the environmental movement in the United States and current environmental issues. Students discuss course expectations and possibilities for their final project. It is important to note that this course relies on critical thinking, commentary and criticism by the students, active participation in class discussions both online and face to face, research, and comparative skills. The course does not include any quizzes or exams, and the students' grades depend solely on their written work and their contributions and participation in class discussions. Many students are happy to see no quizzes or exams, but they are expected to write between 1,000 to 1,500 words each week, and those assignments must show evidence of reflection and engagement with the reading texts.

The course relies heavily on the Blackboard Discussion Board tool. After reading the introduction, which in addition to the glossary of terms has information on the authors' approach to translating this text and some general comments on how Chinese culture is based on relationships with others and less on autonomous individuality, students then post questions and commentary on the Discussion Board. This assignment is quite open and flexible. They may ask questions about concepts they didn't understand, cultural differences, the structure of the text, or other concerns they may have. They are expected to post at least one question of reasonable complexity and then respond to two of their classmates' questions. This initiates the kind of query and commentary style that will be followed throughout the semester. The Blackboard questions and commentary are then explored further in the face-to-face classroom. My observation and experience is that students today are less skilled in critical thinking and formation of arguments. Too many years have been spent teaching to the test instead of teaching to learn. This question-and-commentary approach can be unfamiliar and perhaps intimidating to some students at the beginning. The purpose of these initial assignments is to create a safe and respectful community where each student feels their voice is valuable and their contribution to the class is essential.

The second major assignment is to read the *Dao De Jing*. The Ames and Hall book includes "Translation and Commentary" for each chapter of the *Dao De Jing* along with "Notes to the 'Translation and Commentary'" in the back of the book. I offer students the choice of reading the *Dao De Jing* straight through without the commentary and then rereading it with the accompanying commentary and notes, or they may choose to go through each passage with all the support material. This approach acknowledges that there are different reading and learning styles; the important point is that they read to achieve a level of understanding of the text. After they have read the *Dao De Jing*, the second written assignment requires that they choose passages in which they identify environmental themes. They should discuss how those environmental themes are presented, how they might apply to Chinese philosophical thinking, and how they, as students, understand them. Again they are expected to present their own views and then respond to their classmates. The original format of the class required individual reflection papers on the same material. I have since found it much more effective to use an interactive discussion technique both virtually and online. Students often find it easiest to discuss and write about a concept they feel they understand or with which they agree. It becomes more challenging to address a concept or passage they glossed over because it didn't appeal to them or didn't make sense. For this assignment, students first choose the passages that resonated most for them. The second part requires them to address passages they did not choose. Often, hearing another classmate discuss what the passage meant to them can enhance understanding for the class as a whole. Students' understanding and engagement with the texts is increased by their dynamic interaction with each other.

After the students have demonstrated an adequate understanding of the *Dao De Jing* and its inherent themes and concepts, we move to examining more contemporary literature. In turn, they read selections from each of the required texts: first, the anthology *Sacred Earth: Writers on Nature and Spirit* edited by John Gardner; second, the anthology *Sisters of the Earth* edited by Loraine Anderson; and finally, *The Sacred Balance: Rediscovering our Place in Nature* by David Suzuki. Occasionally it can be difficult to get sufficient copies of *Sacred Earth* for a class. *Sustainability: A Bedford Spotlight Reader*, edited by Christian Weisser, is a suitable substitute. *Sacred Earth* covers a wide range of some of the most significant environmental and nature writers in the genre, but it is rather unbalanced with a majority of male writers. The anthology *Sisters of the Earth* contains collected works by only women nature writers, many of whom are American Indian or have connections to American Indian culture. This collection appeals to students pursuing a major or minor in women and gender studies. David Suzuki's work is more scientific and data driven. His book makes a compelling case for the serious need for environmental activism and change in personal lifestyle. He is particularly appealing since he is currently a strong activist and advocate in Canada for environmental issues globally. Regular updates from his foundation website are often of interest to the class too.

For each of these texts, the students read selected works in the anthologies and then compare them with what they have learned about Daoist principles and values. Each of these is a separate Discussion Board on Blackboard. Blackboard is a particularly effective medium that hones student communication skills. Blackboard Guidelines are posted that delineate what is expected in a Discussion Board. Most important is that students must read and comprehend not only the assigned texts but also their classmates' assessments and analyses of those texts. In Blackboard, there is no sitting quietly in the back of the class. Everyone participates actively and dynamically. Crafting a well argued Discussion Board post is a different task from casual conversation or even open face-to-face class discussion. Students learn to be clear and concise to communicate their points. They are expected to build and expand on each other's comments. All of this combined makes them stronger, more deliberate writers, and that is evident in their work as the semester progresses and in their final projects.

The assignments may vary depending on the class members. I may assign some specific sections, but there is also the option to choose among the works included in the anthologies. I prefer that students examine fewer works in depth rather than skim over too many authors and works and never achieve any depth of discussion. The Suzuki book we read in its entirety. It usually requires more class discussion time because it is a different type of work with an obvious "call to action," and it is more scientifically based than most of the other works. Interspersed with these assignments are timely news articles, films and documentaries, and, if opportunity presents, relevant local public speakers. These assignments lead up to their final project. The final project counts in lieu of a final exam and is weighted heavier than the earlier assignments. Students research an environmental or nature writer of their choice approved by the instructor. These writers may author one of the assigned texts, or they may be others we have not covered. Students read and analyze three works by their chosen writer, two if their usual genre is a longer book or novel. Then students prepare a critical literary analysis of these works focusing on environmental themes or concepts. The final project must compare the chosen writer's work with the *Dao De Jing*, specifically using text citations from the contemporary writer and the *Dao De Jing*. The project consists of both the researched critical analysis and comparison with an oral presentation to the class using a PowerPoint, Prezi, Keynote, or other tool highlighting the chosen selected passages. Presentations also include some biographical information about the writer, his or her most notable works, and the significance of the writer and works within the greater body of environmental and nature writing. To highlight these connections, students present in order chronologically according to their writer's most significant works. This presentation order made evident to the students how earlier writers influenced later nature writing and how later writers built upon and expanded themes or approaches pioneered by earlier authors. This technique enhanced and made obvious that our present-day knowledge and concern about sustainability and environmentally conscious living is not new; rather we see a continuum from these principles in the *Dao De Jing*, written thousands of years ago, that spans the years so that the principles are still a relevant concern today. Writers chosen for final projects ranged from classic and well-known writers such as Emerson and Thoreau to newer writers like Rachel Carson and Edward Abbey. Certain writers we chose to discuss in class such as Aldo Leopold and Wendell Berry, both of whom have been a huge influence on my own writing. I encouraged students to look at publications such as the *Journal of Sustainability Education* and *Orion Journal*, both of which are available online.

Students brought in news or resources on writers or environmental actions to share with the class. Films, both short and long, became a refreshing break from close text readings and writing. Cinema is another medium artists, documentarians, and news organizations use for focusing on sustainability and environmental issues. Some of the films were screened during class time, while others were recommended or links were provided. The students responded enthusiastically to the occasional film and found ways of weaving what they had learned about the *Dao De Jing* and sustainability into their discussions of the films too. Films provided a unique window into a culture, a point of view, or a timely issue and gave the students additional points of discussion to connect to the assigned texts. Students who might find it difficult to analyze and discuss a literary work could wax eloquent on a film. The weaving of films throughout the semester captured the attention of less strong writers and gave them confidence to develop their comments and opinions in discussions and writing assignments. In this way, the use of film is not a distraction but can be an enhancement to a writing-intensive class.[7]

SOME ADDITIONAL CONTEXT ON TEACHING THE DAO

Regarding translations, the class begins with a discussion of various translations of selected chapters in the *Dao De Jing*. Below is chapter 1 using the Ames and Hall translation, but the students also examine translations of the same chapters by authors such as John C. H. Wu, Wing-tsit Chen, and others. The Chinese Text project (ctext.org) is readily available online and often uses James Legge's translations, which are now in the public domain. Providing students with even three or four examples of translated chapters enables them to see how problematic translations can be. Some authors strive for the meaning truest to their interpretation of the original text, while others may make choices that result in a more poetic, lyrical text pleasing to the Western ear. James Legge, a nineteenth-century missionary from Scotland, translated many of the Chinese classics, but some of these translations seem to attempt to force a Christian corollary that is difficult and inaccurate since certain concepts in Chinese spirituality or cosmology do not have a parallel in Western faith-based ideas.

> Chapter 1
> Way-making (dao) that can be put into words is not really way-making.
> And naming (ming) that can assign fixed reference to things is not really naming.
> The nameless (wuming) is the fetal beginnings of everything that is happening (wanwu),
> while that which is named is their mother.

Thus, to be really objectless in one's desires (wuyu) is how one observes the mysteries of all things,
while really having desires is how one observes their boundaries.
These two—the nameless and what it names—emerge from the same source yet are referred to differently.
Together they are called obscure.
The obscurest of the obscure,
They are the swinging gateway of the manifold mysteries.[8]

The reading and comparison of these various translations sets the tone for the beginning of the course and opens the discussion on a brief history of Daoism. It should be noted that I do not teach or use the *Dao De Jing* as a religious text, but it is important that students be made aware of the context of the text. For the purposes of this course, we treat it as environmental literature but with respect to the fact of a long and influential history in China. The *Dao De Jing* was the foundation text for Daoism in China. The concept of Dao predates the life of Confucius or Kong Fuzi and so is well over 2,500 years old. The religion of Daoism developed much later. The concept of the Dao profoundly influenced all of Eastern Asia. Many see Daoism as a possible precursor and a great influence on Shinto in Japan and perhaps on other nature-based, animistic, or spiritual practices in other parts of Asia. It should be noted there are many parallels and similarities between various American Indian spiritual beliefs and Daoism. Considering the transmission of legends and beliefs through oral tradition, it is entirely possible that they may spring from the same source. The *Dao De Jing*, as in the belief of many American Indian or First Peoples, promotes a recognition of the inseparable relationships of all things, both living and nonliving. Humans, animals, plants, and the planet are part of a web of life. The *Dao De Jing* presents a world that is impersonal to humans and a world that they cannot control. All Chinese cosmology has at its center the belief that the only constant is change. It emphasizes the cyclical nature of all things: we are born, we live, we die, we return to nurture others. The *Dao De Jing* springs from a primarily agrarian people who lived close to the earth and its cycles.

The *Dao De Jing* is often considered to be ambiguous and open to multiple interpretations. Students reading the *Dao De Jing* for the first time may have completely conflicting views on the meaning of a particular text. Perhaps due to its ambiguity, the *Dao De Jing* became popular among many of the New Age movement. Some translations of the *Dao De Jing* are lyrical and appealing, more like reading poetry than other spiritual texts.

Many elements of Daoism are evident in popular culture. With the rise in popularity of tattoos, many people request Daoist elements such as the yin/yang symbol or the bagua and trigrams of the *Yijing*. We see them as decals in car windows or inked on skin, but do those fascinated with these images and symbols understand any of the deeper meaning or philosophy behind the Dao? Or is it that Asian symbols and characters have achieved a level of "coolness" and that is sufficient? Too often, characters are written incorrectly or even completely reversed. Chinese is not a language that can be translated literally word for word, so people put together strange combinations that don't really say anything meaningful. Far too many times, students have lifted a sleeve or unbuttoned a shirt to ask an Asian person if what they have permanently inked on their skin actually says what they think it says. It is difficult to believe that someone would take the step of getting a permanent tattoo without confirming the actual meaning. In my experience, students have a romanticized fascination with Eastern Asian culture with very little knowledge or understanding, but that curiosity or fascination often brings them to my courses and they leave with a greater understanding and appreciation of why a text like the *Dao De Jing* has endured for more than two thousand years.

The ultimate goal of Daoism is to establish harmony with the Dao or "The Way." Chinese legend attributes the *Dao De Jing* to Lao Zi (c. 500 BCE). One story says that when Lao Zi died, before he was allowed to pass into the spiritual realm, he was required to stay on earth long enough to write down his wisdom; the result was the *Dao De Jing*. In reality, elements of the *Dao De Jing* were most likely in existence as oral tradition long before it was codified into a written document. Confucius and his followers refer many times to the Dao and their efforts to follow the Dao. Aside from the *Dao De Jing*, one of the most enjoyable ways to explore the Dao is through the writings of *Zhuangzi* (c. fourth century BCE), one of the definitive texts of Daoism. The work of *Zhuangzi* is perhaps even more circuitous and ambiguous than the *Dao De Jing* as it illuminates elements of the Dao through vignettes or anecdotes. Many scholars who strive for meaning within the *Dao De Jing* find the *Zhuangzi* a deceptively easier read, almost playful at times. *Zhuangzi* toys with our inflated perceptions of our own self. One of the best known stories is that of the man and the butterfly in which the subject dreams he is a butterfly but then finds himself questioning whether he dreamed himself as the butterfly or is the butterfly now dreaming he is a man. All of this is perhaps to puncture our sense of hubris and school ourselves to step back and question our perception of any given event or concept. This Daoist concept becomes of even greater importance in an egocentric individualistic Western society.

The Three Treasures of Daoism are compassion, moderation, and humility. These virtues continue to be reflected in the teachings of Confucius and later Mencius or Mengzi. Although there are passages in the *Dao De Jing* that specifically deal with governing, war, and other issues, the underlying theme throughout is associated with harmony with nature and the ultimate interconnectedness of all things. These basic elements of the Dao also form the foundation for the *Yijing* (The Book of Changes) and the practice of *taijiquan*, qi-gong, feng shui, and traditional Chinese medicine.

Certain terminology is difficult to translate into Western concepts. Philosophers and Asianists Roger Ames, David Hall, and Henry Rosemont Jr. choose not to translate certain terms; rather they have developed what Henry Rosemont calls "concept clusters." My students in examining and discussing the *Dao De Jing* are encouraged to embrace the Chinese word for these concepts rather than an ineffective single English word that poorly represents a complex idea. Among these are 萬物 wanwu, or the ten thousand things, that we might roughly translate to all of nature or perhaps Mother Nature. One concept frequently misunderstood is 無為 wuwei. The English translation of "no action" is extremely misleading; better to think of it as letting nature take its course or as noncoercive action. *Wuzhi* 無知, meaning no knowledge or no wisdom, is better understood as accepting all things and events or 萬物 wanwu as they are. These *wu*-forms appear throughout the text of the Dao De Jing and should be understood not as doing nothing but rather as an effort not to be coercive in actions or deeds. This concept is essential to understanding many passages, so it is worth spending some time discussing the wu terms so that students comprehend their use. Here is an example:

> Chapter 29
> If someone wants to rule the world, and goes about trying to do so,
> I foresee that they simply will not succeed.
> The world is a sacred vessel,
> and is not something which can be ruled.
> Those who would rule it ruin it;
> Those who would control it lose it.
> In the way of things:
> Some move ahead while others follow behind;
> Some breathe to warm themselves while others breathe to cool themselves down;
> Some are strong while others are disadvantaged;
> Some accumulate while others collapse.
> It is for this reason that the sages eschew the excessive, the superlative, and the extravagant.[9]

In Elizabeth Kolbert's book, *The Sixth Extinction*, she compares human impact on the planet to the asteroid believed to have caused the extinction of the dinosaurs. We as a species are that devastating. In a National Public Radio interview with Terry Gross on *Fresh Air* she said:

> We are effectively undoing the beauty and the variety and the richness of the world which has taken tens of millions of years to reach. . . . We're sort of

unraveling that. . . . We're doing, it's often said, a massive experiment on the planet, and we really don't know what the end point is going to be.

Amphibians have the dubious distinction of being the world's most endangered class of animals. . . . But also heading toward extinction are one-third of all reef-building corals, a third of all fresh-water mollusks, a third of sharks and rays, a quarter of all mammals, a fifth of all reptiles and sixth of all birds.

The definition [of mass extinction], I suppose, would be many, many organisms across many, many different groups. And that is, really, what we are seeing and that is what makes scientists fear . . . that we're in a mass extinction. . . . About a quarter of all mammals are considered endangered. . . . About 40 percent of all amphibians are considered endangered. But we're also seeing organisms, invertebrates, for example, are endangered . . . many species of reef-building corals are now considered very, very endangered.

So you're seeing extinctions across a wide variety of groups, and that, I think, would have to be one of the defining characteristics of a mass extinction.[10]

Headlines around the world in recent years are evidence of alarming trends of severe weather, freak storms, and an increase of wholly preventable ecological disasters. Many people are old enough to remember the Exxon Valdez oil spill twenty-five years ago in 1989 that was considered to be one of the worst manmade disasters ever to occur. Our country and our earth now have these types of disasters on a regular basis, perhaps so regular that we have become immune to being concerned about the devastation. Fracking is now causing earthquakes in areas that were never prone to them before. Island and coastal nations or settlements are now disappearing under rising seas. This tragic consequence is not just occurring in faraway countries. In spring 2016, an entire community of Americans Indian in Louisiana had to be relocated from their coastal home, leaving the ancestral grounds they had settled generations ago. The *New York Times* called them the "First Climate Refugees."[11] How sad to see a group of our First Peoples become the first American victims of climate change and rising coastlines. And what does this herald for the future? In this case it would appear that the people who attempt to live lightly on the land are suffering for the misdeeds and neglect of generations of others.

The opening section of chapter 79 of the *Dao De Jing* as translated by John C. H. Wu reminds us:

When a great wound is healed,
There will remain a scar.
Can this be a desirable state of affairs?[12]

The same chapter 79 as translated by Ames and Hall ends with this:

The way of tian (heaven) shows no partiality;
It is really on the side of people who are good in their relationships.[13]

We were warned much more recently, too, by Chief Sealth, more commonly known as Chief Seattle, who was chief of the Dwamish and Suquamish tribes of the Puget Sound area. Indeed he is said to be one of the first to see the white men who arrived in this region that is now in Washington State. In accounts of his best known speeches and writings, he addressed the interconnectedness of all of nature similar to passages in the *Dao De Jing*. Perhaps this is not surprising when more and more evidence points to the First Peoples' descent from those who crossed the Asian land bridge into the Americas generations ago. With the American Indian respect for the land and all that is in it, along with respect for oral tradition, perhaps it was easier for their peoples to remember the ancient lessons learned. Some of the wisdom attributed to Chief Seattle includes the following:

> The whites, too, shall pass—perhaps sooner than other tribes. Continue to contaminate your own bed, and you might suffocate in your own waste.
> Humankind has not woven the web of life. We are but one thread within it. Whatever we do to the web, we do to ourselves. All things are bound together. All things connect.
> There is no quiet place in the white man's cities, no place to hear the leaves of spring or the rustle of insects' wings. Perhaps it is because I am a savage and do not understand, but the clatter only seems to insult the ears.
> What is man without the beasts? If all the beasts were gone, man would die from a great loneliness of spirit. For whatever happens to the beasts, soon happens to man. All things are connected.
> The earth does not belong to man, man belongs to the earth. All things are connected like the blood that unites us all. Man did not weave the web of life, he is merely a strand in it. Whatever he does to the web, he does to himself.
> All things share the same breath—the beast, the tree, the man . . . the air shares its spirit with all the life it supports.[14]

This embodies the Hawai'ian peoples' concept of aloha. When we breathe the same air, we are inseparably connected. And perhaps the most significant statement of all attributed to Chief Seattle is this: "We do not inherit the earth from our ancestors; we borrow it from our children."[15]

In recent years, it has been called into question whether Chief Seattle actually said these things. The only reliable documentation of his words is a translated version of a speech made in 1854, twelve years before his death. Sources point to a television script written by Texas screenwriter Ted Perry in the early 1970s for a show called *Home* produced by the Southern Baptist Radio and Television Commission. Perry may have been inspired by the text of Chief Seattle's speech and other American Indian beliefs, but he intended the script as fiction. Many of the quotes now attributed to Chief Seattle seemed to have passed into the popular canon within the past forty-five years.[16] Some have said, though, that the sentiments certainly reflect a closer bond with nature and an attempt to articulate the importance of the natural world within Americans Indians' and First Peoples' spiritual beliefs and practices.

Chapter 54 of the *Dao De Jing* is a distant echo from an earlier time:

> What has been well-planted cannot be uprooted;
> What is embraced tightly will not escape one's grasp;
> With one's children and grandchildren performing the customary rites
> The autumnal sacrifice will never be interrupted.[17]

Or, as John C. H. Wu's alternative translation gives us, "for generations without end." The Ames and Hall translation continues:

> Cultivate it in your person, and the character you develop will be genuine;
> Cultivate it in your family, and its character will be abundant;
> Cultivate it in your village, and its character will be enduring;
> Cultivate it in the state, and its character will flourish;
> Cultivate it in the world, and its character will be all-pervading.[18]

Clearly we have lost sight of this practice of examining ourselves first. We cannot expect to change the world unless the change begins within each of us. Then we will become an influence on our families and our communities, and the shift in attitude will spread.

Since the time of the Industrial Revolution, or perhaps even predating that time, we as humans have separated ourselves from the natural world. In the Abrahamic religions, this is often interpreted as man having dominion over the earth, but even in the Bible man speaks of the importance of good stewardship. In the first chapter of Ecclesiastes, which teaches that "all is vanity," it also says, "one generation passeth away, and another generation cometh: but the earth abideth forever."[19]

If we consider human impact on the earth and on the natural world, we must ask whether we as humans have been good stewards of the earth. What legacy do we leave for our children and the generations to come after? When the focus is on getting, gaining, and acquiring, how much consideration is given to leaving the planet in the same or better condition than before human footsteps? The generations to follow us become our judge and jury for our stewardship. John C. H. Wu's translation is even more to the point as chapter 54 continues:

> Cultivate Virtue in your own person, and it becomes a genuine part of you.
> Cultivate it in the family, and it will abide.
> Cultivate it in the community, and it will live and grow.
> Cultivate it in the state, and it will flourish abundantly.

Cultivate it in the world, and it will become universal.
Hence, a person must be judged as person;
A family as family;
A community as community;
A state as state:
The world as world.
How do I know this about the world?
By what is within me.[20]

One of the students of Confucius asked the Master for advice: "Analect 15.24—Zigong asked, 'Is there one expression that can be acted upon until the end of one's days?' The Master replied, 'There is shu 恕: do not impose on others what you yourself do not want.'"[21] This term *shu* 恕 also translates to forgiveness, pardon, or excuse. This passage and others are often referred to as the Rule of Reciprocity, or the Silver Rule, and predate the more familiar Golden Rule attributed to Jesus in the Bible. In some ways, the Rule of Reciprocity is perhaps a stronger and more complex command. It not only tells us how to treat others but also exhorts us not to impose upon others actions or results we would not wish for ourselves.

What have we imposed upon the world? If we each examine ourselves honestly, how do we measure? Confucius in another passage gives guidance to becoming *junzi* 君子, or an exemplary person:

Analects 1.4—Master Zeng said, "Daily I examine my person on three counts. In my undertakings on behalf of other people, have I failed to do my utmost zhong? In my interactions with colleagues and friends, have I failed to make good on my word xin? In what has been passed on to me, have I failed to carry it into practice?[22]

Analects 14.27—The Master said, "Exemplary persons would feel shame if their words were better than their deeds."[23]

Perhaps *Zhuangzi* explains it in simpler terms:

On cyclical nature of thing—All existing things are really one. We regard those that are beautiful and rare as valuable, and those that are ugly as foul and rotten. The foul and rotten may come to be transformed into what is rare and valuable, and the rare and valuable into what is foul and rotten. Life comes from the earth and life returns to the earth.

On wúwéi 無為—Flow with whatever may happen and let your mind be free. Stay centered by accepting whatever you are doing. This is the ultimate.

On wisdom *zhi* 知—Men honor what lies within the sphere of their knowledge, but do not realize how dependent they are on what lies beyond it.[24]

Ultimately we are all connected, not just to each other but to the earth and its every element or, as the Chinese would say, to the 萬物 wanwu or the myriad things. The *Dao De Jing* describes a peaceful, pastoral world without wars:

> Chapter 46
> When way-making (dao) prevails in the world,
> The finest racing steeds are used to provide manure for the fields.
> But when way-making does not prevail in the world,
> Warhorses are bred just outside the city walls.
> There is no crime more onerous than greed,
> No misfortune more devastating that avarice.
> And no calamity that brings with it more grief than insatiability.
> Thus, knowing when enough is enough
> is really satisfying.[25]

Although the Dao is visible and evident in popular culture, the teachings of Daoism have so much more to offer. Rather than wearing the Dao on an arm or car window, we would find it much more effective to apply the principles in the *Dao De Jing* to our own lives. Do we examine ourselves daily? Do we consider carefully the consequences of our actions? Even on an individual basis, we have the ability to choose. We have the ability to make a positive impact. When will we realize that enough is enough?

CONCLUSION

All my courses are interdisciplinary in their content and nature. By combining an ancient text with more contemporary texts and by examining cultures of East, West, and Native or indigenous peoples, this course expands cultural and literary horizons for the participating students. Expectations for the course are explicit in the syllabus with a clearly stated requirement of writing a minimum of 1,000 to 1,500 words every week. Although this may take many forms, from formal papers to online discussions to participation in group wikis, the amount of reading and writing can be daunting for students who do not consider themselves to be strong writers. Many of my students are English language learners with Spanish as their first language, so writing and class discussion in English does not come easily for them, and most have not encountered ancient Chinese philosophical texts before my class.

Experienced writers will agree that writing is a practice, and inspiration along with clarity come with a constant honing of one's craft. My students have stated that my writing expectations have cured them of "writer's block." After a course where they are expected and required to read and analyze challenging, diverse texts and then produce quality writing products throughout the semester from the first week, they no longer fear sitting in front of a blank screen wondering what to write. This type of intensive practice helps train their minds to process the material, organize their thoughts, and communicate their interpretations to their classmates and their instructor. Many instructors may prefer quizzes or short writing assignments with a longer research product at the end of the course. In my opinion, that works best with students who already possess strong reading, research, and writing skills. The final grade for a long research paper is given when the semester is over, so for students who struggle, where is the opportunity to improve or to correct mistakes? Those who are lacking get left behind, and as educators we cannot afford to let those students fail.

In this course, the early assignments aren't perfect. With immediate and consistent feedback from their classmates and from their instructor, student writing improves dramatically. Often students give tentative responses to the literature at the beginning, but the dynamic interactive nature of the class and the opportunity to experiment with various formal and informal writing and discussion modules help them build confidence in their abilities. Our university has an excellent writing center, and students are encouraged to utilize it for grammar and organization, but engagement with the texts is of primary importance for me. It is essential to me that they realize they have a voice. Reading and digesting complex texts such as the *Dao De Jing*, poetry, fiction, essays, scientific justifications, and more exposes students to a broad range of literature that they might not ordinarily experience in one course. The texts and the writing assignments in this course provide them with an opportunity to discover a shared concern for the environment and a continuity of purpose that is woven throughout our various world cultures and has sustained humanity for more than two thousand years.

Words matter, and students discover the impact and meaning a well-written text can have long after the words are composed. They realize the sharing of these texts is far more than just a class assignment. The people who wrote these words believed passionately in the importance of nature, the environment, and the interconnectedness of all of us who share this planet. My students leave the class believing their words matter too. They see the impact and the connections among the readings. The texts illuminate the fact that words—good communication—can effect change. I have students who, aside from the impact on their writing, decided to make small changes in their lives. One started a garden. Some began buying local produce or buying organic. One is now working for a national park. Some are teachers. Sustainability happens one step at a time. One step for my students is my course on Daoism and the Environment.

NOTES

1. This chapter and the related course emerged and developed out of an eco-critical presentation called "Ecological Issues: A Daoist Confucian Perspective" at the Southwest Popular/American Culture Association, February 20, 2014, Albuquerque, New Mexico. I would also like to acknowledge the contribution and support of the Asian Studies Development Program at East-West Center, University of Hawai'i at Manoa, for their encouragement of my continued research and exploration of Confucianism and Daoism.

2. Roger T. Ames and David L. Hall, *Dao De Jing "Making this life significant": A Philosophical Translation* (New York: Ballantine, 2003). Roger T. Ames in the preface states that he and David Hall developed a "self-consciously interpretive translation." Ames and Hall make an effort to create an understandable translation that does not compromise the meaning or philosophy of the text.

3. Roger T. Ames and Henry Rosemont, Jr., *The Analects of Confucius: A Philosophical Translation* (New York: Ballantine, 1999). In the introduction, Ames and Rosemont provide information commonly known about the life of Confucius.

4. Li-Hsiang Lisa Rosenlee, *Confucianism and Women: A Philosophical Interpretation (SUNY Series in Chinese Philosophy and Culture)* (New York: SUNY Press, 2007, E-book).

5. Aiwei Shi, "Causes of Failure in Translation and Strategies," *Translation Directory*, http://www.translationdirectory.com/article129.htm.

6. Kam-por Yu, Julia Lai Po-Wah Tao, and P. J. Ivanhoe, *Taking Confucian Ethics Seriously: Contemporary Theories and Applications* (Albany: State University of New York Press, 2010). The authors emphasize "learn about" and "learn from" to highlight the difference in seeing the material solely as something only relevant to East Asian culture rather than being open to its relevance to human ethics and contemporary society.

7. There is additional scope for scholarly research on connecting film with sustainability-centered courses. Documentaries, fiction, and anime all are readily available and provide an essential resource for presenting sustainable options to students.

8. Ames and Hall, *Dao De Jing*, 77.

9. Ames and Hall, *Dao De Jing*, 122.

10. Elizabeth Kolbert, "In the World's 'Sixth Extinction,' Are Humans the Asteroid?" interview by Terry Gross, *Fresh Air*, NPR, February 2, 2014, https://www.npr.org/2014/02/12/275885377/in-the-worlds-sixth-extinction-are-humans-the-asteroid?utm_medium=Email&utm_campaign=20140213&utm_source=books.

11. Coral Davenport and Campbell Robertson, "Resettling the First American 'Climate Refugees,'" *New York Times*, May 3, 2016, accessed July 17, 2016, http://www.nytimes.com/2016/05/03/us/resettling-the-first-american-climate-refugees.html?_r=0.

12. John C. H. Wu, *Lao Tzu: Tao Teh Ching* (New York: St. John's University Press, 1961), 161.

13. Ames and Hall, *Dao De Jing*, 199.

14. These quotations have no original source and were found at the quotation compilation web page, "Top 15 Chief Seattle Quotes," *Seattle's Travels*, http://seattlestravels.com/chief-seattle-quotes/.

15. Chief Seattle, "Chief Seattle Speech: Chief Seattle's 1854 Oration," ver. 1., Suquamish Tribe website, accessed February 2, 2014, https://suquamish.nsn.us/home/about-us/chief-seattle-speech/.

16. John Scull, "Chief Seattle, er, Professor Perry Speaks: Inventing Indigenous Solutions to the Environmental Problem," accessed February 2, 2014, http://www.ecopsychology.org/journal/gatherings2/scull.htm.

17. Ames and Hall, *Dao De Jing*, 190.

18. Ames and Hall, *Dao De Jing*, 190.

19. *The Holy Bible* (authorized King James version) (New York: The World Publishing Company, 1980).

20. Wu, *Lao Tzu: Tao Teh Ching*, 111.

21. Ames and Rosemont, *Analects of Confucius*, 189.

22. Ames and Rosemont, *Analects of Confucius*, 72.

23. Ames and Rosemont, *Analects of Confucius*, 178.

24. *Zhuangzi Says*, Wise Men Talking Series (Beijing: Sinolingua, 2006).

25. Ames and Hall, *Dao De Jing*, 149.

Chapter Eight

"Against Sustainability"

And Other Provocations for a First-Year Writing-Intensive Seminar

Abby L. Goode

It was the third week of the semester at Rice University and the students of "Sustainability in America" came to class alarmed. As part of their first year, these students were required to enroll in a themed First-Year Writing-Intensive Seminar (FWIS), and they had selected "Sustainability in America" as one of their top two choices.[1] They registered for the class expecting to encounter arguments about how we should live more sustainably—how we should, as the UN's Brundtland Report (1987) puts it, "meet the needs of the present generation without compromising the ability of future generations to meet their own needs."[2] Yet what they found instead not only challenged their expectations of the course, but also revealed the limitations and contradictions of sustainability discourses. By the third week of class, these students had read three articles, two of which were pithily entitled "Against Sustainability," and the other, "How Sustainable is the Idea of Sustainability?"[3] I began class by asking the students to provide a verb that described how these readings impacted their conceptions of sustainability, partly to catalogue their intense reactions to the readings but also to highlight how arguments actively *do* things. Among the many verbs that surfaced in discussion—"narrowed," "complicated," "shifted,"—one stood out as particularly powerful: "ruined."

Although the verb "ruined" evokes destruction and defeat, my goal in designing "Sustainability in America" was not to transform ambitious first-years into deflated pessimists. Rather, I sought to expose the students to a dynamic, surging debate about sustainability, one that questions its very viability as a concept, one that they could enter, transform, and ultimately, lead. To be clear, the student who declared that the readings "ruined" his conception of sustainability was far from cynical. In fact, he was more energetic than ever, having realized that the planetary crises of climate change and environmental devastation are much more complex and massive than we think, and that sustainability discourses urging us to carpool and buy local have failed to resolve these crises, perhaps even exacerbated them. It was precisely this kind of energy that I was hoping to provoke with these critiques, an energy that would nourish the creation of innovative, student-led endeavors that extended far beyond the classroom and my own expertise.

Surely none of the scholars who promote sustainability-focused writing instruction would endorse "ruin[ing]" a student's conception of sustainability. Indeed, in the past two decades, the concept of sustainability has motivated reassessments and new theories of writing-intensive pedagogy, none of which advocate assigning readings that argue "against sustainability."[4] Rooted in sustainability's capacity to transform the classroom, these theories tend to emphasize the following: (1) a democratic educational environment in which students contribute knowledge and shape class agendas; (2) various forms of service learning, activism, and civic engagement that transcend the classroom and connect students with their local surroundings; and (3) process-based and post-process-based pedagogical techniques that focus on "the coconstitutive existence of writing and environment."[5] Diverse works such as Christian R. Weisser and Sidney I. Dobrin's *Ecocomposition: Theoretical and Pedagogical Approaches* (2001), Derek Owens's *Composition and Sustainability: Teaching for a Threatened Generation* (2001), and, more recently, Robert Yagelski's *Writing as a Way of Being: Writing Instruction, Nonduality, and the Crisis of Sustainability* (2011) argue for a fusion of writing-intensive and environmentally sound instruction that cultivates students' ecological awareness and responsibility. Focused on teaching for a "just and sustainable future," this scholarly corpus has been slow to critique discourses of sustainability and environmentalism, let alone discuss ways to encourage these critiques among students.[6] Meanwhile, in disciplines such as philosophy, architecture, and literature, the concept of sustainability has come under intense fire; scholars argue that the term is nothing more than a meaningless buzzword used to buttress corporate marketing campaigns and green consumerism.[7] Others contend that sustainability is anthropocentric and too narrowly focused on "future generations" at the expense of nonhumans.[8] How might we introduce these and other hard-hitting critiques to students, particularly those in their first year, who often approach the classroom optimistic and ready to engage in environmental practice? How might we reconcile the wide-ranging and diverse takedowns of sustainability with the equally valuable calls for sincere engagement in sustainability-oriented writing pedagogies?

In this chapter, I propose that we embrace the possibility of critique in the sustainability-focused writing-intensive classroom, that we provide opportunities for students to discover and address the thorny ambiguities, inconsistencies, and unexamined histories of sustainability—even if that means temporarily "ruin[ing]" their understanding of the concept. Following a brief overview of sustainability in composition studies, I examine the framework and outcomes of "Sustainability in America" as a case study of this *pedagogy of critique*. The first sustainability-themed FWIS at Rice, this course required students to design and propose an original sustainability initiative to be implemented on their campus and pitch their idea to a panel of university administrators and staff. Having examined sustainability's rhetorical patterns, as well as the concept's historical entanglement with colonialism, racism, sexism, and eugenics, students conceived of their initiatives as a response to a problem or gap in sustainability discourses. By questioning and exploring the limitations of sustainability, students became empowered not only to engage in current debates about sustainability, but also to change the way we think about the concept.

In an era focused on addressing climate change and global environmental crises, this pedagogical approach may seem wildly counterintuitive, especially for educators who want to engage students in the work of environmental activism and practice.[9] However, a writing-intensive pedagogy that fosters a critical interrogation of sustainability ultimately *deepens* students' engagement in environmental issues and emboldens them as thinkers and writers; it challenges students' expectations of the class—indeed, of sustainability discourse itself. It invites them to join a real-time, unfinished conversation and provokes creative and sophisticated projects that transcend the first-year writing-intensive classroom. This pedagogical approach, which renders concepts such as "sustainability" vulnerable to critique, allows us to engage students in unsolved, pressing environmental issues and thereby work toward an interconnected and community-based model of writing education. More broadly, as students encounter critiques of seemingly stable or innocuous concepts, particularly early in the semester, they become more motivated to embark on an authentic, inquiry-based, interdisciplinary learning experience, one championed by scholars such as Cathy Davidson, Joshua Eyler, and Paul Hanstedt, one where I, the professor, do not know the answer beforehand.[10]

SUSTAINABILITY AND THEORIES OF WRITING-INTENSIVE PEDAGOGY

While the concepts of sustainability, ecology, and environmentalism have occasioned new and productive theories of writing-intensive pedagogy, the terms themselves have remained relatively unquestioned and stable in composition studies. Especially in the last fifteen years, with the emergence of "ecocomposition," scholars have devoted their energies to demonstrating that the writing-intensive classroom provides a range of unique opportunities for responding to our current environmental crises. Derek Owens, a leading voice in sustainability and composition studies, argues that "the cross-disciplinary permeability of the composition classroom" renders it an ideal and flexible site for pedagogical experimentation and differentiated learning.[11] Owens suggests, moreover, that writing and communication programs can function as platforms for disseminating sustainability and environmental studies across the curriculum: "Because of our extensive contact with first-year undergraduates, composition faculty can create environments that serve as filters through which students might apply a growing sense of sustainable awareness to the goals implicit within their chosen majors."[12] Highlighting the benefits of combining environmental and writing-intensive education, scholars such as Owens tend to focus on defining and promoting an ecological model of composition pedagogy.[13] In so doing, they spend less time problematizing the dominant paradigms of environmental studies—paradigms that have come under fire in other scholarly arenas—and often assume a consensus regarding the acceptability and durability of terms such as "nature," "place," and, of course, "sustainability." Yet it is precisely this problematizing that brings us closer to realizing the very pedagogy that these scholars envision.

Before sustainability became a critical term for composition studies, it emerged as a paradigm for rethinking higher education writ large. Some scholars have gone so far as to suggest that our current environmental crises are largely the result of an educational system that prioritizes industrial and economic development over the natural world. For instance, David Orr contends that university research and knowledge production has long been "motivated by the fantasy of making an end run around constraints of time, space, nature, and human nature. It is, in short, part of the old project of dominating nature at whatever cost."[14] Proposing a different model of education inspired by the values of sustainability, Orr recommends a curriculum that draws substantially on the humanities (since the problems of sustainability are "rooted in the human condition"), encourages ecological competence across the disciplines, and facilitates community engagement.[15] A central figure for scholars interested in sustainability and writing-intensive pedagogy, Orr champions a "connective" understanding of education that focuses on collaboration, interdisciplinarity, and the cultivation of a community that "includes future generations"—a phrase that perhaps intentionally echoes the Brundtland Report.[16]

Writing at a moment when a theory of sustainability in higher education was sorely needed, Orr reproduces and affirms the dominant definition of sustainability as "meet[ing] the needs of the present generation without compromising the ability of future generations to meet their own needs."[17]

Yet in the past decade, literary critics and humanists more broadly have been less than satisfied with this definition, critiquing sustainability to the point of advocating that we abandon it altogether. These scholars argue that sustainability is not radical enough to produce environmentalist change, that it advocates maintaining an anthropocentric and less-than-ecologically-aware status quo, that it has been absorbed into corporate marketing campaigns of green consumerism, that it is rooted in vague and empty language, and that its version of history is too narrow to encompass geological timescales.[18] Moreover, critics such as John P. O'Grady, Karen Pinkus, Allan Stoekl, and Stacy Alaimo have raised questions about sustainability's definition in the Brundtland Report: What exactly are we trying to sustain? Who are these "future generations" and what does it mean to "meet [their] needs"? Does sustainability account for nonhumans or does it invoke, as Alaimo puts it, "an environmentalism without an environment"?[19] These critiques have identified a range of unresolved contradictions associated with the concept, and the writing-intensive classroom is an ideal site for inviting students to unpack the ambiguities and limitations of sustainability.

While the Brundtland Report's version of sustainability has indeed become a major facet of higher education in the past few decades, with the establishment of various research centers, curriculum enhancement programs, and the Association for the Advancement of Sustainability in Higher Education, its precise role in composition studies and writing-intensive curricula is less clear, in part because it often functions as a synonym for environmentalism. With the exception of Owens and Yagelski, who claim the term in the titles of their works, composition studies scholars have tended to encounter sustainability indirectly, under the rubric of "ecocomposition." An ecological theory of writing instruction, ecocomposition seeks to reframe composition studies around the notions of place, community, and our relationship with the nonhuman world. Influenced by Richard M. Coe's "Eco-Logic for the Composition Classroom" (1975), and later, Marilyn M. Cooper's essay, "The Ecology of Writing," (1986), ecocompositionists draw on broad, often amorphous ecological concepts—sustainability being just one of them—to understand writing as part of a larger social system, a dynamic milieu of writers, readers, texts, and environments.[20]

This concept of interconnectedness underpins ecocomposition theory. Consequently, terms vaguely associated with interconnectedness such as "nature," "place," and, less often, "sustainability" populate the pages of ecocomposition scholarship but remain murky and undefined. Dobrin and Weisser emphasize interconnectedness by making two central claims about ecocomposition—that human discourse constructs and defines the natural world, and that the natural world shapes discourse and the writing process.

Even as environmentalist commitments seem to motivate ecocomposition, Dobrin and Weisser insist that ecocomposition pedagogy must focus centrally on writing; they distinguish between ecological literacy—the teaching of environmental texts and the fostering of ecological consciousness—and what they call "discursive ecology," which asks students to see their writing as part of an interactive system.[21] Yet the distinction here remains relatively ambiguous. Ecocomposition scholarship tends to enact a slippage between (a) environment and ecology as contexts and relational systems and (b) environment and ecology as the stuff of rocks, mushrooms, and frogs. To be sure, Dobrin and Weisser contend that "ecocomposition is not 'writing about trees'; ecocomposition is the study of written discourse and its relationships to the places in which it is situated and situates."[22] Yet their *positive* definition of ecocomposition appears to invoke "writing about trees" in spite of itself: "Ecocomposition inquires as to what effects discourse has in mapping, constructing, shaping, defining, and understanding nature, place, and environment; and in turn, what effects nature, place, and environment have on discourse."[23] Without a critical interrogation of the meaning of these opaque terms, the difference between "writing about trees" and understanding the relationship between writing and "nature" is uncertain. And although Dobrin and Weisser do not list "sustainability" here, the term tends to function similarly in ecocomposition scholarship to the term "nature"—as an unexamined code word vaguely related to environmental education. Responding to the vagueness of environmental vocabulary, ecocritics in literary studies have vigorously critiqued the terms "nature" and "green," just as they have interrogated the meaning of "sustainability."[24] These critiques are useful for scholars and teachers working to rigorously define and broaden ecocomposition beyond "writing about trees"—to encompass active learning and engaged citizenship. Such critiques, moreover, provide opportunities to engage students in the ongoing process of revising, redefining, and renovating these concepts, without instructors knowing the answer beforehand.

Ecocomposition's focus on interconnectedness gains clarity when scholars detach it from the language of "nature" and talk about it as a classroom practice. In this context, ecocomposition resonates with Owens's and Yagelski's seemingly distinct theories of sustainability and composition: both emphasize an integrated learning environment where students and teachers collaborate in the process of learning and knowledge production. Articulating this form of interconnected pedagogy, Dobrin and Weisser describe the current state of composition studies as fundamentally ecological: "After all, composition studies in its post-cognitive, post-process, post-expressivist incarnation is also a study of relationships: relationships between individual writers and their surrounding environments, relationships between writers and texts, relationships between texts and culture, between ideology and discourse, between language and the world."[25] Working against the notion of the student as "a disembodied intellect," this interconnected pedagogy is rooted in a collaborative and democratic educational environment that values community engagement, local knowledge, and writing that transcends the classroom.[26]

Interconnected pedagogy invites students to participate in the process of knowledge production and curation. Such an approach to writing instruction challenges underlying assumptions about knowledge dissemination and aspires to enact Paulo Freire's theory of liberatory pedagogy—to inspire "not pseudo-participation, but committed involvement."[27] Endorsing this liberatory pedagogy, Yagelski critiques the typical physical arrangement of a classroom, in which students face the teacher rather than each other. This arrangement undermines students' valuable positions as knowers. Instead, they come to see themselves as "knowledge-*receivers*" in a "banking" form of education, as Freire describes it, "receiving, filing, and storing the deposits" of course material and instructor expertise.[28] In her work on sustainability and ecocomposition pedagogy, Annie Merrill Ingram suggests that we adhere to "ecology's central principle of interrelatedness" in our pedagogy, fostering an environment where students and instructors share in the responsibility of collective learning, course progress, and community involvement.[29] Given the cracks and fissures in sustainability, the concept lends itself to a more democratic form of pedagogy, or what some scholars might call *open pedagogy*, where students contribute knowledge and help to shape class agendas.[30] We have not yet solved the problems of sustainability, and doing so involves interrogating, even fundamentally rethinking the concept. Who better than students to tackle this challenge and lead the charge?

Championing this democratic form of education, ecocompositionists and other scholars of sustainability-focused pedagogy argue for the centrality of local knowledge in the writing classroom. Owens, for instance, proposes assignments such as oral history preservation projects, service-learning projects, and eutopia essays that ask students to imagine a "good" future of a familiar place. These assignments integrate what Owens describes as "*lower* learning":

> As educators we pride ourselves on teaching something called critical thinking but often at the cost of promoting local thinking. "Higher" learning aims upward, away from the mundane, the everyday, the provincial. . . . What we need more of is *lower* learning, thinking that keeps bringing us back to the local conditions of the communities that we and our students return to once we leave the classroom.[31]

Valued by other composition scholars such as Julie Drew, Steven Marx, and Bradley John Monsma, the cultivation of students' preexisting and local knowledge of their particular place and time enlivens and bolsters a democratic classroom in which students become empowered collaborators in a collective learning environment.[32] One of the challenges of this approach, however, is meaningfully integrating "higher" and "lower" learning, so that students are connecting the issues they confront in texts with their community knowledge. This is a question I encountered while discussing my own teaching experiences with a colleague. She asked: How does the close reading of a novel or essay [a central method in my own field of literary studies] impact how students design sustainability initiatives in their community? Since critical reading is an assumed but often overlooked component of the writing-intensive classroom, we as writing instructors will likely grapple with this question as we design assignments and courses that include forms of community engagement, service learning, and writing beyond the classroom.

As a central tenant of this local and democratic pedagogy, engaged learning is an essential avenue for teaching sustainability in a writing-intensive classroom. As Dobrin proclaims, "[E]cocomposition is a participatory discipline; it requires hands-on living."[33] In Ingram's related discussion of service learning in ecocomposition courses, she emphasizes that service learning dovetails with ecological theories of an integrated and collaborative classroom, deepening student engagement and instructor knowledge "outside the institutional walls."[34] Ingram follows a "read—do—reflect—write model" of service learning, where students read about issues pertaining to their organization or project (such as environmental justice or land ethics debates), engage in their project, reflect on their experience in discussion and writing, and write a paper that synthesizes all three forms of learning.[35] This model works toward integrating what Owens describes as "higher" and "lower" knowledge, and aims to inspire a sense of writing that moves beyond the classroom.

This democratic, local, and engaged pedagogy draws on and converges with post-process theory, which holds that writing is public, interpretive, and situated. Challenging the long-held notion of writing as a generalizable process, post-process theorists understand writing as an interchange within a larger system of readers and contexts. Since this system is always changing, the writing process itself is necessarily dynamic and situated, focused on interpreting "our [specific] readers, our situations, our and other people's motivations, the appropriate genres to employ in specific circumstances, and so forth."[36] Ecocompositionists and sustainability-focused writing instructors enact this theory by offering students opportunities for publishing their writing in online newsletters and other forums, or publically presenting their ideas for rethinking sustainability. These opportunities encourage students to take matters into their own hands, to follow through on their proposals and arguments long after the class is over and capture the attention of other community members, faculty, and administrators.

We can foster these pedagogical goals of democratic education, local knowledge, and engaged learning by rendering sustainability vulnerable to critique and renovation in the writing-intensive classroom and in composition studies writ large. Scholars interested in fusing environmental and writing-intensive education have left the concepts related to the "eco" in ecocomposition relatively unquestioned, and largely free from critique. Many of these scholars, such as Orr and Owens, are rightly invested in reimagining higher education through the lens of sustainability and thus focus on creating a space for environmental issues across the curriculum. Now that sustainability has become a veritable buzzword across college campuses, I propose a form of sustainability-focused writing-intensive pedagogy that begins with *critique* as a provocation, a pathway for students to come to critical consciousness about our ecological crises. This pedagogy, I argue, enriches and works toward pedagogical goals developed by Dobrin and Weisser, Owens, Yagelski, and others—goals of establishing community and interconnectedness beyond the classroom walls.

"SUSTAINABILITY IN AMERICA": A CASE STUDY

Rather than approach my FWIS by explaining to students why sustainability matters, I developed assignments that I hoped would motivate students to cultivate their own investments in ecological issues. Students came to the class with the expectation that this seminar would promote a certain kind of progressive, environmental politics, and introduce them to a mainstream tradition of environmentalist thought, but what they encountered was a rigorous inquiry into one of the most foundational and oft-used terms of contemporary culture. This inquiry propelled us into the major project of the course—the original sustainability initiative proposal—and brought surprising results that linked our course and its goals to the broader campus community.

As a FWIS at Rice, "Sustainability in America" is the first course of its kind to embrace the term "sustainability," although it joins a range of other courses focused on ecological themes. Inaugurated in 2012, FWIS courses expose first-year students to diverse fields of intellectual inquiry in the context of small, discussion-based seminars. In these courses, students grapple with the complex ideas and learn to construct written and oral arguments through extensive practice and substantive feedback.[37] Capped at fifteen students, these required seminars are designed to support interactive activities and close teacher-student relationships. Ranging from advanced graduate students to senior faculty, FWIS instructors design activities such as field trips to local museums, interviews, and creative projects, often moving beyond the confines of the traditional college essay assignment. In these ways, the FWIS program seeks to enhance the place of writing and communication in students' educational environment and daily life.

The FWIS program offered a particularly fertile and supportive venue for implementing "Sustainability in America," as it provided both pedagogical structure and freedom. FWIS courses are designed to achieve core learning outcomes related to writing and communication, as well as content- and skill-based outcomes, which are specific to each course. The FWIS program encourages and enables instructors to design their own project- and inquiry-based courses that draw on multidisciplinary material and strengthen analytical and communication skills. For "Sustainability in America," I designed the initiative proposal as a highly scaffolded project that included time and space for students to cultivate their proposals throughout the semester—an ambition that might prove more challenging in an English literature survey course. As Owens writes, "[T]he composition instructor enjoys a kind of contextual freedom and disciplinary flexibility unknown to many of his or her colleagues. This is composition's little secret."[38] The structure of the FWIS program, moreover, dovetails easily with the goals of ecocomposition: its flexible, supportive, and pedagogically rigorous context encourages the implementation of democratic education, civic engagement, and post-process pedagogies. The program also introduces first-years to academic life more broadly, encouraging them to enact an "environmental studies" of their college life and develop a connection with their campus community.

"Sustainability in America," like the other FWIS courses, included learning outcomes related to writing and communication, as well as content and debates that emerge from my disciplinary background in American literary studies and my research area in sustainability. While I avoided teaching my own scholarship, I developed the course with two underlying assumptions in mind, the same ones that drove and shaped my research questions: (1) Sustainability has a longer literary and cultural history than we think; the term did not emerge out of thin air in 1987 with the Brundtland Report. In fact, the Brundtland Report is an inheritor of a long-running textual history that extends at least back to the time of Thomas Jefferson. (2) Sustainability is full of ambiguities and contradictions. It is entangled with histories of colonialism, sexism, racism, and economic exploitation. And as it stands, the concept is not adequate for addressing our current ecological crises.

Our task was not only to explore this textual history and these entanglements, but also to begin to offer some answers that fundamentally reframe how we conceptualize and approach sustainability. My goal was to use the course material as a launching pad to provoke students into innovative proposals. With this ambition in mind, I designed the class to include four major and interrelated phases: (1) an introduction to sustainability, its complexity, haziness, and shortcomings; (2) a brief American literary and cultural history of sustainability (here students are confronted with the question of, "Just how *American* is sustainability, and what are the implications of this Americanness?"); (3) contemporary controversies attending sustainability such as population control and immigration; and (4) studio time, presentation workshops, and the final initiative proposal in group presentation and individually written forms. Since my own research focuses on the history and contradictions of sustainability in literature, I could not offer solutions for how to "fix" sustainability. I did not know the answer beforehand. My hope was that the course content and debates would invite students to take an active role in an unresolved and ongoing conversation about pressing global issues.

The first three weeks of "Sustainability in America" immediately engaged students in a range of short writing and presentation exercises, exercises that enabled them to come to understand sustainability as a problematic and difficult-to-define term. The course, in short, began by facilitating a critique of sustainability and the discourses and concepts that attend it. Whereas Owens opens *Composition and Sustainability* by paraphrasing the Brundtland Report's definition, I approached these first weeks from a different angle. I asked myself: What if we tackled sustainability and its definition not as a given but rather a contemporary intellectual problem that students could endeavor to solve?

This process began with a short writing assignment—the sustainability primer. A primer is a short, clear, and informative introduction to a subject of study. Beyond functioning as a writing assessment, the purpose of the assignment was to encourage students to access their preexisting knowledge and assumptions about a seemingly unfamiliar subject. Before students read a word, listened to a lecture, and obtain any information about the grounding concepts of sustainability, I asked them to write their own answers to the question, "What is sustainability?" I cautioned them not to consult any outside sources, including Google and Wikipedia. I advised them to think about what they already know about sustainability and identify examples of where and how the concept appears (perhaps considering, in this regard, the patterns that emerge across multiple examples). I encouraged them to be unconventional in their definitions, but also as lucid as possible in their language (I asked: "If you use broad terms such as 'social' or 'economic,' what do you mean by these terms?). Students submitted this assignment in the following class, during which they each gave a one-minute presentation of their primer. Practice for their final proposal presentation had already begun.

While many students wondered how they would define a vague concept about which they knew little, they were surprised at the breadth of their preexisting knowledge and assumptions, which ranged from architectural concepts to indigenous practices to the stewardship of their own chicken coops. With these primers, students began to shape the broader class trajectory, collectively building a foundation of ideas and narratives that they would expand, challenge, and revise throughout the semester. The primer assignment set the tone that we were all in this together, and that we offered a multiplicity of productive interpretations of sustainability. But given the challenging complexity of the assignment—How does one even begin to define sustainability in specific terms?—and the breadth of responses, it soon became clear to us that *we do not really know what we mean when we speak of sustainability.* After writing their primers, students read excerpts of the Brundtland Report itself; they continued to grapple with the murkiness of sustainability and began to confront the question of how we might make this concept more powerful or effective.

The following week, students began working on developing their sustainability initiatives in groups. But since the project asked them to identify a problem or gap in sustainability discourses, summarize debates surrounding this aspect, and propose a response to this problem or gap, they were not yet at the point of brainstorming ideas for their initiatives. They were in the preliminary research phase. As part of this phase, students read the introduction to Cedric Cullingford's *The Sustainability Curriculum* (2004). In class, they worked with their groups on a structured research exercise. Here students examined four sustainability initiatives in higher education, not just to identify their aims and successes but also to locate their underlying assumptions, analyze how they define sustainability, and discover what might be missing in sustainability initiatives in higher education today. They answered questions such as: What kinds of questions or problems motivate this initiative? How does it treat and use the concept of sustainability? What might have been overlooked here? Rather than simply use these initiatives as models, students approached them as part of a broader and not-yet-refined discourse in need of their interventions.

As a follow-up to their research, students presented their findings to the class as a whole, addressing the following questions: What kinds of trends or tendencies do you notice across all four initiatives? Based on your findings, how would you describe the current role of sustainability in higher education? What do these sustainability initiatives tend to assume? What kinds of goals do they tend to have? Where do they tend to focus their attention? Finally, and perhaps most importantly, what gaps, problems, or inconsistencies do you notice? What ground has not yet been covered? Here students began to be more critical of the discourse of sustainability, approaching it as a form of rhetoric that can be highly deceptive. One student even called a friend at another school to learn that the level of food waste in dining halls was particularly high, despite the school's website's self-congratulatory claim to sustainable facilities management.

Having confronted the complexity of sustainability, we turned to the critiques of sustainability mentioned in the very first paragraph of this essay—two of which bear the provocative title of "Against Sustainability." The readings implicated sustainability in anthropocentric understandings of the environment and false marketing campaigns for environmentally friendly products. They questioned the term's meaning and its adequacy for addressing environmental crises on the geological scale—not just for "future generations" but for the planet writ large. After reading these articles, many students experienced a challenging level of pessimism regarding the magnitude of our climatological and environmental crises, crises that composting toilets alone could not solve. My colleagues who teach environmental studies courses have also noted that their students experience this pessimism, but that it is a necessary stage of critical consciousness—a precursor to intellectual innovation and action. As Orr writes, "[T]he study of environmental problems is an exercise in despair unless it is regarded as only a preface to the study, design, and implementation of solutions."[39] Following Orr, I attempted to maintain the class's liveliness, even in the face of disheartening critiques.

To avoid a collapse into cynicism, I followed these readings up with an in-class debate that I hoped would harness students' critical energy. Each student wrote a précis of one critical article, its major claims and rhetorical maneuvers, and brought it to class. Using their crisp summaries of these arguments, students worked in teams to prepare statements for or against sustainability, strengthening their positions by employing the argumentative techniques of Gerald Graff and Cathy Birkinstein's *"They Say/ I Say"* (2006). Scaffolding the rhetorical and presentation skills necessary for their final proposals, the debate required students to collaborate in small groups, synthesize and talk across a range of readings, and join a relevant conversation about global issues. Moreover, since one of the groups was charged with the task of defending the concept, even in light of the reading, this debate recovered the value of sustainability after a series of harsh critiques (Just what exactly are we sustaining, anyway?). The critiques challenged students to resist rehashing the "future generations" argument and develop a revised definition of sustainability in light of those critical readings.

Moving from the general concept of sustainability to its more specific role in historical and literary texts, students employed literary analysis in the following weeks to identify and examine early, implicit forms of sustainability. Readings ranged from J. Hector St. Jean de Crèvecoeur's early American epistolary novel *Letters from an American Farmer* (1782) to Henry David Thoreau's canonical work of nature writing *Walden* (1854) to Charlotte Perkins Gilman's feminist utopian novel *Herland* (1915). Students also read Theodore Roosevelt's presidential speeches on the importance of rural life and American population fertility, as well as excerpts from Gifford Pinchot's *The Fight for Conservation* (1910) and Liberty Hyde Bailey's *The Country Life Movement* (1911). These readings collectively exposed students to a longer history of sustainability rooted in agrarian and conservation ideals, one that also dovetailed with histories of colonialism in the Americas and the sexism and racism that attended the rise of US eugenics. During these weeks, students also wrote regularly for the course blog, posting Thoreauvian manifestoes and analyses of Crèvecoeurian, small farming images in recent Monsanto advertisements, and they met with their groups to begin brainstorming initiative ideas. During these weeks, students also completed a multiphased process that culminated in a critical essay. This process included (1) a discussion of how to develop arguments and organize information for a critical essay, (2) a thesis development paper—a working thesis, topic sentences, and pieces of evidence—and (3) a full draft and intensive peer review process. Essays engaged a range of topics and considered how early representations of sustainability shape notions of land use, resource consumption, feminism, and democracy. This process engaged students in discourse analysis, a method necessary for critiquing and renovating sustainability. It also prepared students for the similarly multiphased process of proposal drafting and presentation practice that they would enter in the second half of the semester.

After delving into the history of sustainability, we returned to more contemporary accounts of related topics: population control, US immigration, and local and transnational environmental justice movements. Students analyzed and discussed excerpts from Paul Ehrlich's *The Population Bomb* (1968) and Lester Brown's *Beyond Malthus* (1995), encountering these texts as discourses with particular grounding representations—such as Ehrlich's opening description of a crowded Delhi—and assumptions about overpopulation's relationship to poverty, sexual behavior, and developing countries. We analyzed Julia Alvarez's modern sustainability fable, *A Cafecito Story* (2001), which narrates the struggle of an organic coffee farm against big agribusiness in the Dominican Republic, and the subsequent establishment of a multicultural agrarian community. Alvarez's story provoked students to question the tacit "Americanness" of sustainability, an inquiry that proved equally relevant in a distinct but related reading: Lisa Sun-Hee Park's and David Naguib Pellow's *The Slums of Aspen* (2011), a study of the xenophobic underpinnings of sustainability rhetoric in the wealthy community of Aspen, Colorado. These readings compelled us to struggle with the power and contradictoriness of sustainability rhetoric as it emerged in disparate contexts.

At this point in the semester, "Sustainability in America" students had grown into outspoken and challenging thinkers, comfortable with taking adversarial and skeptical positions toward even the most benign-seeming subject matter. For instance, after discussing Mark Kitchell's documentary, *A Fierce Green Fire: The Battle for a Living Planet* (2011), some of the students went so far as to critique the film's appeal to the beauty of the Grand Canyon and the monstrosity of whale harpooning, arguing that we have become desensitized to this environmentalist imagery. Extending these critiques, one student interpreted these overly familiar images as cold, hard, evidence that we need a new environmentalist discourse, one that speaks to a perhaps more pessimistic audience, but that continues to address our massively damaging practices. During these weeks, students worked periodically on their initiatives, reading examples, posting sections of their individually written proposals on the blog, and responding to comments on their work. As students became more accustomed to critiquing sustainability discourses, they were also tasked with improving and contributing to this conversation.

The final weeks of class included guest speakers, oral presentation workshops, studio time to work on initiatives in groups, peer review sessions, and formal, videotaped, presentation rehearsals. During this time, I met with the director of Rice's Center for Sustainability and Energy Management to discuss the students' ideas and the possibility of implementing them in the coming years. He was enthusiastic and spoke of specific ways that the students could approach their initiatives and highlighted previous undergraduate work in their areas of interest. This meeting was not entirely preplanned on my part. I was so impressed by the groups' concepts for the initiatives—for food waste management programs, rooftop gardens, and cardboard furniture installations—that I wanted to explore the on-campus resources for supporting these endeavors. After the meeting, as students were drafting their proposals, I suggested to them that we turn these presentations into a reality—that students present their initiatives not just to me, but to a panel of staff and administrators who can offer institutional information, insight, and next steps should they decide to move forward with the initiative. My hope was that this panel would motivate them beyond their grade on the presentation, and enable them to interact with other members of the campus community who have vital knowledge about environmental efforts, student activities, and facilities operations. The final presentation proved to be a proud moment for all of us, as our guest panel provided authentic and encouraging feedback such as "Hey! Let's do this" or "Here's how this might work moving forward." Despite the critical stance that we inhabited throughout the semester, students ended this class on a hopeful note about improving our environmental futures.

In fact, this critical stance ultimately facilitated a pedagogy of interconnectedness in "Sustainability in America," one that drew on ecocomposition principles of democratic education, local knowledge and civic engagement, and writing beyond the classroom. Assignments that focused on collaborative and active learning—peer review sessions, group presentations, and debates—aimed to empower students as knowers and escape what Cooper calls the "tyranny" of "the solitary author."[40] With the initiatives in particular, I tried to avoid constructing them as a "right answer" assignment and made clear to students that I myself did not know how to "fix" sustainability. I sought to integrate students into the knowledge-building process, giving them authority over what counts as knowledge and encouraging them to function collectively as knowers within their community and institution. Although we as instructors tend to structure and scaffold our assignments, projects like the initiatives lend themselves to a more organic development, particularly as they extend beyond the classroom and create new, uncharted paths that move outside the scope of our instruction and expertise. As Mark C. Long writes, "The greatest risk for a course in ecocomposition is to determine the continuity between coursework and the work of life in advance. For if we simply model 'correct' relations in terms of civic action, we miss the fact that these models and relations are inspiring precisely because they are creative *attempts* to formulate and develop a plan for action."[41] After the semester ended, some students met with me about next steps for implementing their initiatives, convening group meetings, and contacting community members. But ultimately, the futures of these projects belonged to the students who conceived of them.

Incorporating but also moving beyond the course material, the initiatives promoted civic engagement and various forms of local knowledge; they required us to observe and interact with the campus more broadly. While students developed their plans, they performed institutional research, conducted student surveys, investigated similar initiatives and past programs, and located resources that would support their endeavors. Moreover, as I designed and facilitated students' completion of this project, I learned from the students, the greater campus community, and pedagogical resources. For instance, to show students the range of perspectives on sustainability, I invited a faculty member from the anthropology department to share her research on wind power development and indigenous communities in Mexico with us. Rather than see myself as "alone" in teaching this course, I drew support from the Center for Written, Oral and Visual Communication (CWOVC), which is deeply integrated with the FWIS program. Before the semester began, I shared and revised my syllabus with the CWOVC's professional staff, all of whom had experience teaching FWIS courses and providing pedagogical training for FWIS faculty. I invited the writing program director to lead a public speaking workshop with my students, and an undergraduate communication consultant from CWOVC joined me in providing feedback on students' oral presentation rehearsals. The initiatives also enabled me to connect with sustainability management staff and learn about the projects that undergraduates had already undertaken, enhancing my own knowledge of sustainability as a community and multifaceted effort beyond the specialized contours of my scholarship in literary studies. Overall, the course helped me avoid becoming detached from the university's social ecosystem. For as Eric Zencey points out, "Professors tend to be rootless [and] systematically ignorant of a key aspect of an integrated life, the life that is, after all, a primary goal of a good liberal arts education. They are woefully ignorant of the values of connectedness to place."[42] The initiative assignment encouraged students to make connections between their education and their campus community. And as I sought to guide them, I, too, was compelled to move beyond the classroom, learning more about my institutional surroundings than I would have otherwise.

Our work on the initiatives throughout the semester allowed us to attend to what might happen after writing—to understand writing as part of a larger context, undertaken for specific purposes and audiences. Just as scholars of ecocomposition and writing pedagogy more generally seek to transform authors (people who have produced texts) into writers (people engaged in writing), so, too, do they seek to transform a general audience into real readers. Paul Heiker argues that "[w]riting teachers need to relocate the *where* of composition instruction outside the academic classroom because the classroom does not and cannot offer students real rhetorical situations in which to understand writing as social action."[43] While students in "Sustainability in America" proposed their initiatives to me—the instructor with knowledge of our course journey—they also presented their ideas to each other and an outside panel who would evaluate their initiative as a real possibility for their institution. This prospect encouraged them to take ownership of their initiatives, which in turn gave their communication goals exigency and purpose. More broadly, this external audience hopefully strengthened students' sense of themselves as researchers, writers, speakers, and pioneers in their community.

CONCLUSION: TOWARD A PEDAGOGY OF CRITIQUE

Rather than try to convince students outright that we should all save the environment, "Sustainability in America" focused on the limitations of sustainability discourses, the problems, gaps, unexamined histories, and opportunities for critique, revision, and reinvention. This pedagogy of critique, which invites students to interrogate the contradictions of sustainability, provoked students into designing their own paths to environmental action and thought—initiatives that remodel sustainability discourse and practice. Encouraging an afterlife of the seminar, the course design may very well have suggested to students that the inquiry of sustainability is a vital intellectual process that leads to productive action.

The connection between critique and action, however, remains unclear—an ambiguity that I have continued to investigate in subsequent classes. As one colleague asked me, How did the students' analysis of eugenics and sustainability in novels and historical documents shape how they conceived of their rooftop garden projects? What was the connection between critique, discourse analysis, and innovative design? To be sure, the students approached their projects from a critical standpoint; they critiqued the practice of recycling and promoted the repurposing of campus cardboard into furniture as an alternative. As this group wrote in their initial description, "[B]y exposing the hidden structural value in the things we consider garbage, we can change our perception of 'waste' and the way we recycle." Another group told the story of how our systems of agriculture, food production, and dining halls are connected in a way that fosters food waste, and presented a comprehensive program for countering that waste at Rice. The final group in the class outlined an architectural and economic plan for a rooftop garden by proposing that we reimagine agrarianism in an urban context. Since this first class, students have drawn on intellectual history to bolster their projects; one group, for instance, proposed transparent trash cans to make waste visible on campus. They saw this project as a response to what they called "aesthetic environmentalism"—a form of environmentalism focused on beauty, cleanliness, and purity. Each group drew on course materials to argue for the urgency of their initiative, and each endeavored to question an underlying assumption about sustainability. But the relationship of literary and cultural analysis to design is still murky; How did examining a novel or film help them develop these initiatives? The answer to this question, I believe, could have profound implications for interdisciplinary and project-based learning.

To engage students in debates about the very viability of sustainability is to contemplate a plethora of perspectives and against-the-grain arguments in the writing classroom, a practice that Weisser and Dobrin highlight in their introduction to *Ecocomposition*. A reviewer of the collection, they wrote, had cautioned against presenting a "totalizing narrative" of "ecological thinking, activist pedagogies, and benevolent teaching of ecological discourses" without any form of "critical attention."[44] David Thomas Sumner offers an important point of departure in this regard, offering a "stasis theory" of pedagogy focused on arriving at "points of stasis" in class discussion, or "real questions-at-issue" that "cannot be determined ahead of time."[45] These "points of stasis" provide occasions for writing beyond the classroom and entering unfinished conversations. One of the dangers of assuming that we in the academy all agree on sustainability is that it gives the impression that we as teachers know the answer beforehand, the right way to be and live in the world. This impression minimizes the far-reaching potential of students' work. In all its haziness and complexity, "sustainability" offers students the opportunity to use writing to change how others think—to tackle an unsolved, complex problem with massively high stakes. But we as educators must take care to present it to them as such, rather than an assignment to be completed, a university requirement to be fulfilled.

NOTES

1. I would like to thank Tracy Volz and Jennifer Shade Wilson for their support of this seminar and their feedback on earlier versions of this chapter. I am also very grateful to the students of my sustainability-themed writing-intensive courses past, present, and future.

2. World Commission on Environment and Development, *Our Common Future* (Oxford: Oxford University Press, 1987), 8.

3. John May, "Against Sustainability," *I.D.* (January/February 2010): 20–21; John P. O'Grady, "How Sustainable Is the Idea of Sustainability?" *ISLE* 10, no. 1 (February 2003): 1–10; Ben Hill, "Against Sustainability," *Community College Moment* 6 (Spring 2006): 61–65.

4. As I show elsewhere in this chapter, the concept of sustainability has also inspired broader reassessments of the purpose of higher education. David Orr argues in his seminal work, *Ecological Literacy: Education and the Transition to a Postmodern World*, that if environmental education "is to become a significant force for a sustainable and humane world, it must be woven throughout the entire curriculum and through all of the operations of the institution, and not confined to a few scattered courses. This will require a serious effort to rethink the substance and process of education, the purposes and use of research, the definition of knowledge, and the relationship of institutions of higher education to human survival" (Albany: State University Press of New York, 1992, p. 152).

5. Christian R. Weisser and Sidney I. Dobrin, "Breaking New Grond: An Introduction," in *Ecocomposition: Theoretical and Pedagogical Approaches*, eds. Christian R. Weisser and Sidney I. Dobrin (Albany: State University Press of New York, 2001), 2.

6. Robert P. Yagelski, *Writing as a Way of Being: Writing Instruction, Nonduality, and the Crisis of Sustainability* (New York: Hampton Press, 2011), 8.

7. For an example of this kind of critique, see May, "Against Sustainability."

8. For an example of this critique, see Stacy Alaimo, *Exposed: Environmental Politics and Pleasures in Posthuman Times* (Minneapolis: University of Minnesota Press, 2016), 169–88.

9. Karen Kilcup is one such educator who engages her students in the work of environmental practice and activism. As she writes, the "challenge for literary studies is to make an environmental perspective fundamental far beyond the discipline, to avoid making ecocriticism merely another interpretive system" ("Fresh Leaves: Practicing Environmental Criticism," *PMLA* 124, no. 3 [May 2009]: 847).

10. Davidson's work reveals the importance of teaching learners how to learn, which is particularly essential in a constantly evolving and technologically enhanced world. Eyler promotes "authentic" teaching in the classroom, such as engaging students in the work of scholarly research. Hanstedt makes the case for teaching students to become "authorities"—enabling them to practice working as leaders, practitioners, and scholars. This practice better prepares them to become agents of change in their world. See Cathy Davidson, *The New Education: How to Revolutionize the University to Prepare Students for a World in Flux* (New York: Basic Books, 2017); Joshua R. Eyler, *How Humans Learn: The Science and Stories Behind Effective College Teaching* (Morgantown: West Virginia University Press, 2018); and Paul Hanstedt, *Creating Wicked Students: Designing Courses for a Complex World* (Sterling: Stylus, 2018).

11. Owens, "Sustainable Composition," in *Ecocomposition*, ed. Weisser and Dobrin, 29.

12. Owens, "Sustainable Composition," in *Ecocomposition*, ed. Weisser and Dobrin, 29.

13. Composition studies scholars are not entirely in agreement on this issue. Dobrin and Weisser challenge Owens's assertions in their book, *Natural Discourse: Toward Ecocomposition*. While they hesitate to embrace a cynical position, Dobrin and Weisser remind us that composition "sits at the bottom of the food chain—an uncomfortable position to occupy, and a difficult place from which to initiate anything." They also emphasize that ecocomposition must focus on writing: "Our classrooms cannot be just about the politics of environmental crisis, they must be about writing." See Sidney I. Dobrin and Christian R. Weisser, *Natural Discourse: Toward Ecocomposition* (Albany: State University Press of New York, 2002), 137, 158.

14. Orr, *Ecological Literacy*, xi.

15. Orr, *Ecological Literacy*, 84.

16. Orr, *Ecological Literacy*, 138.

17. World Commission on Environment and Development, *Our Common Future*, 8.

18. May, "Against Sustainability"; Robert Markley, "Time: Time, History, Sustainability," in *Telemorphosis: Theory in the Era of Climate Change*, vol 1., ed. Tom Cohen (Ann Arbor, MI: Open Humanities Press, 2012), 43–65; Steve Mentz, "After Sustainability," *PMLA* 127, no. 3 (2012): 586–92.; O'Grady, "How Sustainable Is the Idea of Sustainability?"; Karen Pinkus, "The Risk of Sustainability," in *Criticism*,

Crisis, and Contemporary Narrative Textual Horizons in an Age of Global Risk, ed. Paul Crosthwaite (London: Routledge, 2011), 62–80; Haun Saussy, "Sustainability," in *Impasses of the Post-Global: Theory in the Era of Climate Change*, vol. 2., ed. Henry Sussman (Ann Arbor, MI: Open Humanities Press, 2012), 212–16.

19. Alaimo, *Exposed*, 176; Jeremy Butman, "Against 'Sustainability,'" *New York Times*, August 8, 2016; O'Grady, "How Sustainable Is the Idea of Sustainability?"; Pinkus, "The Risk of Sustainability"; Allan Stoekl, "'After the Sublime,' after the Apocalypse: Two Versions of Sustainability in Light of Climate Change," *diacritics* 40, no. 3 (2013): 40–57.

20. Richard M. Coe, "Eco-Logic for the Composition Classroom," *College Composition and Communication* 26, no. 3 (1975): 232–37; Marilyn M. Cooper, "The Ecology of Writing," *College English* 48, no. 4 (1986): 364–75.

21. Dobrin and Weisser, *Natural Discourse*, 116.

22. Dobrin and Weisser, *Natural Discourse*, 10.

23. Dobrin and Weisser, *Natural Discourse*, 9.

24. For examples of this kind of ecocritical scholarship, see Jeffrey Jerome Cohen, ed., *Prismatic Ecology: Ecotheory Beyond Green* (Minneapolis: University of Minnesota Press, 2013) and Timothy Morton, *Ecology without Nature: Rethinking Environmental Aesthetics* (Cambridge: Harvard University Press, 2007).

25. Dobrin and Weisser, *Natural Discourse*, 9.

26. Yagelski, *Writing as a Way of Being*, 18.

27. Paulo Freire, *Pedagogy of the Oppressed*, trans. Myra Bergman Ramos (1970; repr., New York: Continuum Publishing Company, 1997), 51.

28. Yagelski, *Writing as a Way of Being*, 19; Freire, *Pedagogy*, 58.

29. Annie Merrill Ingram, "Service Learning and Ecocomposition: Developing Sustainable Practices through Inter- and Extradisciplinarity," in *Ecocomposition*, ed. Weisser and Dobrin, 211.

30. Open pedagogy is an access-oriented form of teaching and learning that encourages us to see students as contributors rather than just consumers of knowledge. See Robin DeRosa and Rajiv Jhangiani, "Open Pedagogy," *Open Pedagogy Notebook*, http://openpedagogy.org/open-pedagogy/; Abby Goode, "Against 'Product-Based Learning': Open Texts are Never Finished," *Open Pedagogy Notebook*, http://openpedagogy.org/course-level/against-product-based-learning-open-texts-are-never-finished/.

31. Derek Owens, *Composition and Sustainability: Teaching for a Threatened Generation* (Urbana, IL: National Council of Teachers of English, 2001), 75.

32. Julie Drew, "The Politics of Place: Student Travelers and Pedagogical Maps," in *Ecocomposition*, ed. Weisser and Dobrin, 57–69; Steven Marx, "Think Global, Write Local: Sustainability and English Composition," *A Presentation to the UC/CSU/CCC Sustainability Conference*, http://digitalcommons.calpoly.edu/cgi/viewcontent.cgi?article=1122&context=susconf; Bradley John Monsma, "Writing Home: Composition, Campus Ecology, and Webbed Environments," in *Ecocomposition*, ed. Weisser and Dobrin, 281–91.

33. Sidney I. Dobrin, "Writing Takes Place," in *Ecocomposition*, ed. Weisser and Dobrin, 18.

34. Ingram, "Service Learning," 211.
35. Ingram, "Service Learning," 219.
36. Thomas Kent, "Introduction," in *Post-Process Theory: Beyond the Writing-Process Paradigm,* ed. Thomas Kent (Carbondale: Southern Illinois University Press, 1999), 2.
37. Tracy Volz, personal communication to author, December 13, 2015.
38. Owens, *Composition and Sustainability*, 5.
39. Orr, *Ecological Literacy*, 94.
40. Cooper, "Ecology," 366.
41. Mark C. Long, "Education and Environmental Literacy: Reflections on Teaching Ecocomposition in Keene State's Environmental House," in *Ecocomposition*, ed. Dobrin and Weisser, 142.
42. Eric Zencey, "The Rootless Professors," in *Rooted in The Land: Essays on Community and Place*, ed. Wes Jackson and William Vitek (New Haven, CT: Yale University Press, 1996), 16.
43. Paul Heiker, "Rhetoric Made Real: Civic Discourse and Writing Beyond the Curriculum," in *Writing the Community: Concepts and Models for Service-Learning in Composition*, ed. Linda Adler-Kassner, Robert Crooks, and Ann Watters (Urbana, IL: American Association for Higher Education, 1997), 71.
44. Weisser and Dobrin, *Ecocomposition*, 9.
45. David Thomas Sumner, "Don't Forget to Argue: Problems, Possibilities, and Ecocomposition," in *Ecocomposition*, ed. Weisser and Dobrin, 274.

Bibliography

Abbott, Porter H. *The Cambridge Introduction to Narrative*. Cambridge, UK: Cambridge UP, 2002.

"About Wesleyan." Wesleyan College. Accessed August 27, 2016. http://www.wesleyan college.edu/about/index.cfm.

Abram, David. *The Spell of the Sensuous: Perception and Language in a More-Than-Human World*. New York: Vintage Books, 1997.

Abrams, M. H., and Geoffrey Galt Harpham. *A Glossary of Literary Terms*. Boston: Wadsworth Cengage Learning, 2012.

Alaimo, Stacy. *Exposed: Environmental Politics and Pleasures in Posthuman Times*. Minneapolis: University of Minnesota Press, 2016.

Allan, Elizabeth G., and Dana Lynn Driscoll. "The Three-fold Benefit of Reflective Writing: Improving Program Assessment, Student Learning, and Faculty Professional Development." *Assessing Writing* 21 (2014): 37–55.

Allen, Jeanie K. "The Tensions of Creating a Good First-Year Experience Program: The Alpha Seminar." *About Campus* 8, no. 6 (January 2004): 24–27.

Ames, Roger T., and David L. Hall. *Dao De Jing "Making this life significant": A Philosophical Translation*. New York: Ballantine, 2003.

———, and Henry Rosemont, Jr. *The Analects of Confucius: A Philosophical Translation*. New York: Ballantine, 1999.

Anderson, Benedict R. *Imagined Communities: Reflections on the Origin and Spread of Nationalism*. Rev. ed., London/New York: Verso, 2006.

Anderson, Lorraine, and Thomas S. Edwards, eds. *At Home on This Earth: Two Centuries of U. S. Women's Nature Writing*. Hanover, NH: UP of New England, 2002.

Anderson, Paul, Chris Anson, Robert Gonyea, and Charles Paine. "The Contribution of Writing to Learning and Development: Results from a Large-Scale Multi-institutional Study." *Research in the Teaching of English* 50, no. 2 (November 2015): 199–239.

Andrews, Richard, ed. *Narrative and Argument*. Philadelphia: Open UP, 1989.

Archer-Lean, Clare, Susan J. Carson, and Lesley Hawkes. "Fiction as a Form of Change: An Overview of a Literature Panel Discussion." In *Future Nature, Future Cultures*, edited by Susan Davis, 29–36. Noosa, QLD: Noosa Biosphere Limited & CQUniversity, 2013.

"Basic Plots of Literature: Special Collections Created by IPL2." The I-School at Drexel College of Information Science and Technology, 2012. Accessed November 6, 2014. http://www.ipl.org/div/farq/plotFARQ.html.

Bates, Albert. "The Gospel of Chief Seattle: Written for Television?" *Natural Rights* (Spring 1990). Accessed May 28, 2014. http://www.thefarm.org/lifestyle/albert-bates/akbseattle.html.

Beavan, Colin. "Ten Ways to Overcome Futility (About Life, Climate Change, or Anything Else)." *Colin Beavan: aka No Impact Man*. Accessed December 16, 2015. http://colinbeavan.com/ten-ways-overcome-futility-life-climate-anything-else/.

Beavers, Mary Morgan. "Ecological Wonder in Annie Dillard's Pilgrim at Tinker Creek." *Graduate Student Theses, Dissertations, & Professional Papers*.11360, 2019. https://scholarworks.umt.edu/etd/11360.

Beitsch, Rebecca. "Cities, States Turn to Emergency Declarations to Tackle Homeless Crisis." Pew Charitable Trusts, November 11, 2015. http://www.pewtrusts.org/en/research-and-analysis/blogs/stateline/2015/11/11/cities-states-turn-to-emergency-declarations-to-tackle-homeless-crisis.

Berry, Wendell. Plenary Address. South Atlantic Modern Language Association, Atlanta, 2014. (Personal notes.)

———. "The Want of Peace." *The Selected Poems of Wendell Berry*. Washington, D.C.: Counterpoint, 1998.

Biggers, Jeff. "Iowa's Climate-Change Wisdom." *New York Times*, 20 November 2015. Accessed 22 November 2015. https://www.nytimes.com/2015/11/21/opinion/iowas-climate-change-wisdom.html.

Bizzell, Patricia. "William Perry and Liberal Education." *College English* 46, no. 55 (September 1984): 447–54.

Bourdieu, Pierre. "Distinction (English Translation 1984)." *English Studies in Canada* 41, no. 4 (1979): 12.

Bradford, Clare, Kerry Mallan, John Stephens, and Robyn McCallum. *New World Orders in Contemporary Children's Literature*. Houndmills, Basingstoke: Palgrave, 2008.

Bradway, Margi. *2015 Portland Traffic Safety Report*. Portland Bureau of Transportation, February 8, 2016. efiles.portlandoregon.gov/Record/8991354/File/Document.

Brosious, Emily G. "Marijuana Shops Now Outnumber Mcdonald's and Starbucks in Oregon." *Chicaco Sun-Times*, November 8, 2015. Accessed August 22, 2016. http://extract.suntimes.com/news/10/153/7281/more-marijuana-shops-oregon-than-mcdonalds-starbucks/.

Bruner, Jerome. "Research Currents: Life as Narrative." *Language Arts* 65, no. 6 (October 1988): 574–83.

Buell, Lawrence. *The Environmental Imagination: Thoreau, Nature Writing, and the Formation of American Culture*. Cambridge, MA: Belknap Press of Harvard University Press, 1996.

———. *The Future of Environmental Criticism: Environmental Crisis and Literary Imagination*. Oxford: Wiley-Blackwell, 2005.

Butman, Jeremy. "Against 'Sustainability.'" *New York Times*, August, 8, 2016.

Cassel, Adrienne. "Walking in the Weathered World." In *Teaching Ecocriticism and Green Cultural Studies*, edited by Greg Garrard, 27–37. Houndmills, Basingstoke: Palgrave, 2011.

Cato, Molly Scott, and Jan Myers. "Education as Re-Embedding: Stroud Communiversity, Walking the Land and the Enduring Spell of the Sensuous." *Sustainability* 3, no. 1 (2011): 51–68.

Cavallaro, Gabe. "Office of Sustainability Plans to Revitalize Lake Herrick for Recreational Use." *The Red and Black*, November 21, 2014. Accessed February 16, 2016. http://www.redandblack.com/uganews/office-of-sustainability-plans-to-revitalize-lake-herrick-for-recreational/article_e585bb62-70f7-11e4-ab5b-7b54c87a11c1.html.

Chan, Wing-tsit. *A Source Book in Chinese Philosophy*. Princeton, NJ: Princeton University Press, 1963.

Chief Seattle. "Chief Seattle Speech: Chief Seattle's 1854 Oration," ver. 1. Suquamish Tribe website. Accessed February 2, 2014. https://suquamish.nsn.us/home/about-us/chief-seattle-speech/.

———. "Quotes." *Goodreads*. https://www.goodreads.com/author/quotes/331799.Chief_Seattle.

———. "Top 15 Chief Seattle Quotes." *Seattle's Travels*. http://seattlestravels.com/chief-seattle-quotes/.

"Cholera in 1832." *Virtual New York*. Accessed August 30, 2016. http://www.virtualny.cuny.edu/cholera/1832/cholera_1832_set.html.

Christensen, Laird, Mark Long, and Frederick Waage, eds. *Teaching North American Environmental Literature*. New York: MLA, 2008.

City of Portland. "Frequently Asked Questions about Portland's Plastic Bag Ban." 2016. https://www.portlandoregon.gov/bps/article/402484.

Clark, Timothy. *The Cambridge Introduction to Literature and the Environment*. Cambridge: Cambridge University Press, 2010.

Coe, Richard M. "Eco-Logic for the Composition Classroom." *College Composition and Communication* 26, no. 3 (1975): 232–37.

Cohen, Jeffrey Jerome, ed. *Prismatic Ecology: Ecotheory Beyond Green*. Minneapolis: University of Minnesota Press, 2013.

Columb, Gregory G. "Franchising the Future." *College Composition and Communication* 62, no. 1 (September 2010): 11–30.

Cooper, Marilyn M. "The Ecology of Writing." *College English* 48, no. 4 (1986): 364–75.

Cox, Robert, and P. C. Pezzulo. *Environmental Communication and the Public Sphere*. 3rd ed. London: Sage Publications, 2013.

Craige, Betty Jean. *Eugene Odum: Ecosystem Ecologist and Environmentalist*. Athens, GA: University of Georgia Press, 2001.

Davenport, Coral, and Campbell Robertson. "Resettling the First American 'Climate Refugees.'" *New York Times*, May 3, 2016. Accessed July 17, 2016. http://www.nytimes.com/2016/05/03/us/resettling-the-first-american-climate-refugees.html?_r=0.

Davidson, Cathy. *The New Education: How to Revolutionize the University to Prepare Students for a World in Flux*. New York: Basic Books, 2017.

Davis, Ellen F. *Scripture, Culture, and Agriculture: An Agrarian Reading of the Bible*. Cambridge; New York: Cambridge University Press, 2009.

DeRosa, Robin, and Rajiv Jhangiani. "Open Pedagogy." *Open Pedagogy Notebook*. http://openpedagogy.org/open-pedagogy/.

Desmet, Christy et al. *A Guide to First-year Composition at University of Georgia*. Sweetwater, TX: Fountainhead, 2015.

Devlin-Glass, Frances. "A Politics of the Dreamtime: Destructive and Regenerative Rainbows in Alexis Wright's *Carpentaria*." *Australian Literary Studies* 23, no. 4 (2008): 392–407.

Dillard, Annie. *Pilgrim at Tinker Creek*. New York: Harper's Magazine Press, 1974. Repr., Harper Collins e-books, 2009, Kindle edition.

Dobrin, Sidney I., ed. *Ecology, Writing Theory, and New Media: Writing Ecology*. Routledge Studies in Rhetoric and Communication. Florence: Taylor and Francis, 2011.

———. *Saving Place: An Ecocomposition Reader*. New York: McGraw Hill, 2005.

———. "Writing Takes Place." In Weisser and Dobrin, eds., *Ecocomposition*, 11–25.

———, and Christian R. Weisser. *Natural Discourse: Toward Ecocomposition*. New York: State University of New York Press, 2002.

Donnelly, Paul, ed. "Sustainability and the Humanities: 86th Annual Conference." South Atlantic Modern Language Association, November 7–9, 2014, Atlanta Marriott Buckhead Hotel and Conference Center. Atlanta: Georgia State U, 2014.

Downs, Douglas, and Elizabeth Wardle. "Teaching about Writing, Righting Misconceptions: (Re)Envisioning 'First-Year Composition' as 'Introduction to Writing Studies.'" *College Composition and Communication* 58, no. 4 (June 2007): 552–84.

Drew, Julie. "The Politics of Place: Student Travelers and Pedagogical Maps." In Weisser and Dobrin, eds., *Ecocomposition*, 57–69.

Egan, Timothy. "Chief's Speech of 1854 Given New Meaning (and Words)." *New York Times*, April 22, 1992. http://www.nytimes.com/1992/04/21/us/chief-s-speech-of-1854-given-new-meaning-and-words.html?src=pm&pagewanted=1.

Eyler, Joshua R. *How Humans Learn: The Science and Stories Behind Effective College Teaching*. Morgantown: West Virginia University Press, 2018.

Farris, Christine. "Literature and Composition." *Guide to Composition Pedagogies*, edited by Gary Tate, Amy Rupiper, and Kurt Schick. New York: Oxford UP, 2014.

Felstiner, John. *Can Poetry Save the Earth: A Field Guide to Nature Poems*. New Haven CT: Yale UP, 2009.

Fisher-Wirth, Ann, and Laura-Gray Street, eds. *The Ecopoetry Anthology.* San Antonio, TX: Trinity UP, 2013.
Fox, Mem. *Reading Magic: Why Reading Aloud to Our Children Will Change Their Lives Forever.* New York: Harcourt, 2001.
Frost, Robert. "Mowing." *Poetry Foundation.* https://www.poetryfoundation.org/poems-and-poets/poems/detail/53001.
"Framework for Success in Postsecondary Writing." Council of Writing Program Administrators. Accessed 21 November 2015. http://wpacouncil.org/framework.
Freire, Paulo. *Pedagogy of the Oppressed*, translated by Myra Bergman Ramos. 1970; repr., New York: Continuum Publishing Company, 1997.
Fulkerson, Richard. "Composition at the Turn of the Twenty-First Century." *College Composition and Communication* 56, no. 4 (June 2005): 654–87.
———. "Four Philosophies of Composition." *Composition in Four Keys: Inquiring into the Field*, edited by Barbara Gleason, Louise Wetherbee Phelps, and Mark Wiley, 551–55. Mountain View, CA: Mayfield, 1996.
Gardner, Janet E. *Reading and Writing About Literature: A Portable Guide.* 3rd ed. Boston: Bedford/St. Martin's, 2013.
Garrard, Greg. "Introduction." In *Teaching Ecocriticism and Green Cultural Studies*, edited by Greg Garrard, 1–11. Houndmills, Basingstoke: Palgrave, 2011.
———. *Ecocriticism.* 2nd ed. New York: Routledge, 2012.
Gee, James Paul. *An Introduction to Discourse Analysis: Theory and Method.* 3rd ed. New York: Routledge, 2011.
———. *Social Linguistics and Literacies: Ideology in Discourses.* 4th ed. Abingdon, Oxon; New York: Routledge, 2012.
Gilbert, Elizabeth. *Eat, Pray, Love.* London: Bloomsbury, 2006.
Glotfelty, Cheryll. "Introduction: Literary Studies in an Age of Environmental Crisis." In *The Ecocriticism Reader: Landmarks in Literary Ecology*, edited by Cheryll Glotfelty and Harold Fromm, xv–xxxvii. Athens: University of Georgia Press, 1996.
Goode, Abby. "Against 'Product-Based Learning': Open Texts are Never Finished." *Open Pedagogy Notebook.* September 26, 2018. http://openpedagogy.org/course-level/against-product-based-learning-open-texts-are-never-finished/.
Gunn, Joshua. "Size Matters: Polytoning Rhetoric's Perverse Apocalypse." *Rhetoric Society Quarterly* 38, no. 1 (2008): 82–108.
Gustafson, Abel and Matthew Goldberg. "Even Americans Highly Concerned about Climate Change Dramatically Underestimate the Scientific Consensus." Yale Program on Climate Change Communication. Accessed July 29, 2019. https://climatecommunication.yale.edu/publications/even-americans-highly-concerned-about-climate-change-dramatically-underestimate-the-scientific-consensus/.
Hairston, Maxine. "Diversity, Ideology, and Teaching Writing." *College Composition and Communication* 43 (May 1992): 179–93.
Hanstedt, Paul. *Creating Wicked Students: Designing Courses for a Complex World.* Sterling: Stylus, 2018.
Hardy, Thomas. *Tess of the d'Urbervilles.* A facsimile of the manuscripts with related materials. 1891; repr., London: HarperCollins, 2010.

Haskell, David George. *The Forest Unseen: A Year's Watch in Nature*. New York: Penguin, 2013.
Heiker, Paul. "Rhetoric Made Real: Civic Discourse and Writing Beyond the Curriculum." In *Writing the Community: Concepts and Models for Service-Learning in Composition*, edited by Linda Adler-Kassner, Robert Crooks, and Ann Watters, 71–711. Urbana, IL: American Association for Higher Education, 1997.
Henshaw, Paul, Stephen Cervi, and Alex J. McCorquodale. "Simple Cost Estimator for Environmental Dredging in the Great Lakes." *Journal of Waterway, Port, Coastal and Ocean Engineering* 124, no. 5 (1999): 241–46.
Herndl, Carl G. *Sustainability: A Reader for Writers*. Oxford: Oxford University Press, 2014.
———, and Stuart Brown, eds. *Green Culture: Environmental Rhetoric in Contemporary America*. Madison: University of Wisconsin Press, 1996.
Hess, Scott. "Postmodern Pastoral, Advertising, and the Masque of Technology." *ISLE: Interdisciplinary Studies in Literature and Environment* 11, no. 1 (Winter 2004): 95. Quoted in Gordon Sayre, "The Oxymoron of American Pastoralism," *Arizona Quarterly* 69, no. 4 (2013): 17.
"High-Impact Educational Practices." *Association of American Colleges & Universities*. Accessed December 15, 2015. https://www.aacu.org/leap/hips.
Hill, Ben. "Against Sustainability." *Community College Moment* 6 (Spring 2006): 61–65.
Holy Bible (authorized King James version). New York: The World Publishing Company, 1980.
Hothem, Thomas. "Suburban Studies and College Writing Applying Ecocomposition." *Pedagogy: Critical Approaches to Teaching Literature, Language, Composition, and Culture* 9, no. 1 (2009): 35–59.
Huggan, Graham, and Helen Tiffin. *Postcolonial Ecocriticism: Literature, Animals, Environment*. New York: Routledge, 2010.
I AM. Documentary directed by Tom Shadyac. 2010; DVD Universal City, CA: Gaiam Entertainment, 2012.
Ingram, Annie Merrill. "Service Learning and Ecocomposition: Developing Sustainable Practices through Inter- and Extradisciplinarity." In Weisser and Dobrin, eds., *Ecocomposition*, 209–35.
Kareiva, Peter, Michelle Marvier, and Robert Lalasz. "Conservation in the Anthropocene: Beyond Solitude and Fragility." *The Breakthrough*. http://thebreakthrough.org/index.php/journal/past-issues/issue-2/conservation-in-the-anthropocene.
Kent, Thomas. "Introduction." In *Post-Process Theory: Beyond the Writing-Process Paradigm*, edited by Thomas Kent. Carbondale: Southern Illinois University Press, 1999.
Kerridge, Richard, and Neil Sammells, eds. *Writing the Environment: Ecocriticism and Literature*. London and New York: Zed Books Ltd, 1999.
Kidwell, Blair, and Robert Turrisi. "An Examination of College Student Money Management Tendencies." *Journal of Economic Psychology* 25, no. 5 (2004): 601–16.
Kilcup, Karen. "Fresh Leaves: Practicing Environmental Criticism." *PMLA* 124, no. 3 (May 2009): 847.

Killingsworth, M. Jimmie and Jacqueline S. Palmer. "The Discourse of 'environmentalist hysteria.'" *Quarterly Journal of Speech* 81.1 (195): 1–19. https://doi.org/10.1080/00335639509384094.

———. *Ecospeak: Rhetoric and Environmental Politics in America*. Carbondale, IL: Illinois UP, 1992.

———. "Millennial Ecology: The Apocalyptic Narrative from Silent Spring to Global Warming. In *Green Culture: Environmental Rhetoric in Contemporary America*, edited by Carl G. Herndl and Stuart C. Brown, 21–45. Madison: University of Wisconsin Press, 1996.

Kingsnorth, Paul. "Dark Ecology." *Orion Magazine*. https://orionmagazine.org/article/dark-ecology/.

Kolbert, Elizabeth. "In the World's 'Sixth Extinction,' Are Humans the Asteroid?" Interview by Terry Gross. *Fresh Air*, NPR, February 2, 2014. https://www.npr.org/2014/02/12/275885377/in-the-worlds-sixth-extinction-are-humans-the-asteroid?utm_medium=Email&utm_campaign=20140213&utm_source=books.

Lacan, Jacques, and Anthony Wilden. *The Language of the Self: The Function of Language in Psychoanalysis*, edited by Johns Hopkins Paperbacks. Baltimore: Johns Hopkins University Press, 1981.

Lang, James. "The Grounded Curriculum." *Chronicle of Higher Education*. July 3, 2012. Accessed November 6, 2014. https://www.chronicle.com/article/The-Grounded-Curriculum/132679.

Lease, Joseph R. "Ethnography Writing Assignment Instructions." Class assignment, WISe 102, Wesleyan College, Macon, GA, March 9, 2015.

———. "Portfolio Instructions." Class assignment, WISe 102, Wesleyan College, Macon, GA, March 13, 2015.

———. "Research Paper Prompt." Class assignment, WISe 102, Wesleyan College, Macon, GA, January 14, 2015.

———. "WISe 102 2015 Research Paper Instructions." Class handout, WISe 102, Wesleyan College, Macon, GA, January 14, 2015.

Lefebvre, Henri. *The Production of Space*, edited by D. Nicholson-Smith. Oxford: Blackwell, 1991.

———. *Writings on Cities*, edited by E. Kofman and E. Lebas. Oxford: Blackwell, 1996.

Legge, James. "Dao De Jing." Chinese Text Project. Accessed July 1, 2014. http://ctext.org/dao-de-jing.

Libby, Brian. "Bridge to the Future (the Bridge That Bans Cars)." *The Atlantic* 316, no. 3 (2015): 42–43.

Long, Mark C. "Education and Environmental Literacy: Reflections on Teaching Ecocomposition in Keene State's Environmental House." In Weisser and Dobrin, eds., *Ecocomposition*, 131–47.

Macy, Joanna. *World as Lover, World as Self: Courage for Global Justice and Ecological Renewal*. Berkeley, CA: Parallax Press, 2007.

Maran, Timo, and Kalevi Kull. "Ecosemiotics: Main Principles and Current Developments." *Human Geography* 96, no. 1 (2014): 41–50.

Markley, Robert. "Time: Time, History, Sustainability." In *Telemorphosis: Theory in the Era of Climate Change*, vol. 1, edited by Tom Cohen, 43–65. Ann Arbor, MI: Open Humanities Press, 2012.

Marx, Leo. *The Machine in the Garden: Technology and the Pastoral Ideal in America*. New York: Oxford University Press, 1964.

Marx, Steven. "'Think Global, Write Local: Sustainability and English Composition': A Presentation to the UC/CSU/CCC Sustainability Conference." July 31–August 3, 2008. http://digitalcommons.calpoly.edu/cgi/viewcontent.cgi?article=1122&context=susconf.

Massey, Doreen B. *Space, Place, and Gender*. Minneapolis: University of Minnesota Press, 1994.

Mauvieux, Benoit, Alain Reinberg, and Yvan Touitou. "The Yurt: A Mobile Home of Nomadic Populations Dwelling in the Mongolian Steppe Is Still Used Both as a Sun Clock and a Calendar." *Chronobiology International: The Journal of Biological & Medical Rhythm Research* 31, no. 2 (2014): 151–56.

May, John. "Against Sustainability." *I.D.* (January/February 2010): 20–21.

McAdams, Dan P. *The Stories We Live By: Personal Myths and the Making of the Self*. New York: Guilford, 1993.

Mentz, Steve. "After Sustainability." *PMLA* 127, no. 3 (2012): 586–92.

Mezirow, Jack. "Learning to Think Like an Adult: Core Concepts of Transformation Theory." In *The Handbook of Transformational Learning*, edited by Edward W. Taylor, Patricia Cranton et al., 73–95. San Francisco: Jossey-Bass, 2012.

Miller, Richard E., and Ann Jurecic. *Habits of the Creative Mind*. Boston: Bedford/St. Martin's, 2016.

Monsma, Bradley John. "Writing Home: Composition, Campus Ecology, and Webbed Environments." In Weisser and Dobrin, eds., *Ecocomposition*, 281–91.

Moore, Janet. "Is Higher Education Ready for Transformative Learning? A Question Explored in the Study of Sustainability." *Journal of Transformative Education* 3, no. 1 (2005): 76–91.

Morton, Timothy. *Ecology without Nature: Rethinking Environmental Aesthetics*. Cambridge: Harvard University Press, 2007.

Nolet, Victor. *Educating for Sustainability: Principles and Practices for Teachers*. New York: Routledge, 2016.

———. "Preparing Sustainability-Literate Teachers." *Teachers College Record* 111 (2007): 409–42. http://www.gcafh.org/edlab/Nolet.pdf.

O'Grady, John P. "How Sustainable Is the Idea of Sustainability?" *ISLE* 10, no. 1 (February 2003): 1–10.

Orr, David W. *Ecological Literacy: Education and the Transition to a Postmodern World*. Albany: State University of New York Press, 1992.

———. "Four Challenges of Sustainability." *Ecological Economics*. Spring Seminar Series 2003. School of Natural Resources, University of Vermont. https://ratical.org/co-globalize/4CofS.html.

"Our Point of View." Stanford University. Accessed September 10, 2016. https://dschool.stanford.edu/about/#what-we-do-image.

Owens, Derek. *Composition and Sustainability: Teaching for a Threatened Generation*. Urbana, IL: NCTE, 2001.

———. "Sustainable Composition." In Weisser and Dobrin, eds., *Ecocomposition*, 27–39.

Perry, Douglas. "Love Portland's Aerial Tram? It'll Pale Compared to Chicago's Magical 17-Story-High Gondola Network." *The Oregonian*, May 9, 2016. Accessed August 22, 2016. http://www.oregonlive.com/today/index.ssf/2016/05/love_portlands_aerial_tram_itl.html.

Peterson, Tarla Rai and Cristi Choat Horton. "Rooted in the Soil: How Understanding the Perspectives of Landowners Can Enhance the Management of Environmental Disputes." *Quarterly Journal of Speech* 81.2 (1995): 139–66. https://doi.org/10.1080/00335639509384106.

Philippon, Daniel J. *Conserving Words: How American Nature Writers Shaped the Environmental Movement*. Athens: University of Georgia Press, 2005.

Pickle, Linda S. "Written and Spoken Chinese: Expression of Culture and Heritage." In *An Introduction to Chinese Culture through the Family*, edited by H. Giskin and B. Walsh, 9. Asian Studies Development. Albany: SUNY, 2001.

Pinkus, Karen. "The Risk of Sustainability." In *Criticism, Crisis, and Contemporary Narrative: Textual Horizons in an Age of Global Risk*, edited by Paul Crosthwaite, 62–80. London: Routledge, 2011.

Plumwood, Val. "Decolonizing Relationships with Nature." In *Decolonizing Nature: Strategies for Conservation in a Post-Colonial Era*, edited by William M. Adams and Martin Mulligan, 51–78. London: Earthscan, 2003.

———. "Nature in the Active Voice." *Australian Humanities Review* 46 (May 2009): 113–29. http://australianhumanitiesreview.org/2009/05/01/nature-in-the-active-voice/.

Pope, Alexander. "Epistles to Several Persons: Epistle IV." *The Poetry Foundation*. Accessed August 30, 2016. https://www.poetryfoundation.org/poems-and-poets/poems/detail/44894.

Popova, Maria. "20-Year-Old Hunter S. Thompson's Surprisingly Sage Advice on How to Find Your Purpose and Live a Meaningful Life." BrainPickings.org. Accessed August 5, 2014. https://www.brainpickings.org/index.php/2013/11/04/hunter-s-thomspon-letters-of-note-advice/.

Purdy, Jedediah. "In the Shit with Thoreau: A Walden for the Anthropocene." *The Huffington Post*, June 6, 2013. http://www.huffingtonpost.com/jedediah-purdy/in-the-shit-with-thoreau_b_3526416.html.

Rabinowitz, Kate. "DC #1 in Farmer's Markets Per Capita." *Data Lens DC*, August 31, 2015. http://www.datalensdc.com/farmers-mkt-per-capita.html.

Rankine, Craig, Diana Smith, and Joyce Mercuri. "Cleaning Up: How Dredging Is Cleaning Up Ridgefield's Lake River." Department of Ecology, State of Washington, December 30, 2014. http://ecologywa.blogspot.com/2014/12/cleaning-up-how-dredging-is-cleaning-up.html.

Rasula, Jed. *This Compost: Ecological Imperatives in American Poetry*. Athens: University of Georgia Press, 2002.

"Resources." Stanford University. Accessed September 10, 2016. https://dschool.stanford.edu/resources.

Rhetoric @reno, "Western States Rhetoric and Literacy Conference: Literacies and Rhetorics of Crisis." University of Nevada at Reno, October 3, 2013.

Rigby, Kate. "Earth, World, Text: On the (Im)possibility of Ecopoiesis." *New Literary History* 35, no. 3 (2004): 427–42.

Roen, Duane, Veronica Pantoja, Lauren Yena, Susan K. Miller, and Eric Waggoner, eds. *Strategies for Teaching First-Year Composition*. Urbana, IL: NCTE, 2002.

Rollins, Brooke, and Lee Bauknight, eds. *Green*. Southlake, TX: Fountainhead, 2010.

Rose, Joseph. "Portland Traffic Jams Ranked Nation's 10th Worst (If You Can Believe It)." *The Oregonian*, March 31, 2015. http://www.oregonlive.com/commuting/index.ssf/2015/03/portland_traffic_ranked_nation.html.

Rosenlee, Li-Hsiang Lisa. *Confucianism and Women: A Philosophical Interpretation (SUNY Series in Chinese Philosophy and Culture)*. New York: SUNY Press, 2007. E-book.

Sarria, Miguel F. "Medical I Ching 9 Elements." Institute of Integrative Chi Kung, February 2, 2014. http://www.ichikung.com/html/medical_iching.php.

Saunders, Alan. "Philosophy and the Natural World–Val Plumwood." *The Philosopher's Zone*, ABC Radio National, March 15, 2008.

Saunders, Angharad. "Literary Geography: Reforging the Connections." *Progress in Human Geography* 34, no. 4 (2009): 436–52. http://phg.sagepub.com/content/34/4/436.full.pdf+html.

Saussy, Haun. "Sustainability." In *Impasses of the Post-Global: Theory in the Era of Climate Change*, vol. 2., edited by Henry Sussman, 212–16. Ann Arbor, MI: Open Humanities Press, 2012.

Schneider, Richard. "'An Emblem of All Progress': Ecological Succession in Thoreau's *A Week on the Concord and Merrimack River*." *The Concord Saunterer* 19, no. 20 (2011–2012): 78–104.

Schor, Juliet B. *The Overspent American: Upscaling, Downshifting, and the New Consumer*. New York; Basic, 1998.

Schumacher, E. F. *A Guide for the Perplexed*. New York: Harper & Row, 1977.

Scull, John. "Chief Seattle, er, Professor Perry Speaks: Inventing Indigenous Solutions to the Environmental Problem." Accessed February 2, 2014. http://www.ecopsychology.org/journal/gatherings2/scull.htm.

Shi, Aiwei. "Causes of Failure in Translation and Strategies." *Translation Directory*. http://www.translationdirectory.com/article129.htm.

Siewers, Alfred K. "Ecocriticism." In *A Dictionary of Cultural and Critical Theory*, 2nd ed., edited by Michael Payne and Jessica Rae Barbera, 205–10. Malden and Oxford: Wiley-Blackwell, 2010.

Small, Deborah A., and George Loewenstein. "Helping *a* Victim or Helping *the* Victim: Altruism and Identifiability," *Journal of Risk and Uncertainty* 26, no. 1 (January 2003): 5–16. https://doi.org/10.1023/A:1022299422219.

Snyder, Gary. *Turtle Island*. New York: New Directions, 1974.

———. *Turtle Island*. New York: New Directions, 1975.

Soja, Edward W. *Thirdspace: Journeys to Los Angeles and Other Real-and-Imagined Places*. Cambridge: Blackwell, 1996.

Soper, Kate. *What Is Nature? Culture, Politics and the Nonhuman*. Malden, MA: Wiley-Blackwell, 1995.

"Statement of Vision, Mission, and Values." Wesleyan College. Accessed August 27, 2016. http://www.wesleyancollege.edu/about/missionstatement.cfm.

Steiner, Wendy. *Literature as Meaning*. New York: Penguin, 2005.

Stephens, John. "From Eden to Suburbia: perspectives on the Natural World in Children's Literature." *Papers: Explorations into Children's Literature* 19, no. 1 (2006): 40–50.

Stoekl, Allan. "'After the Sublime,' after the Apocalypse: Two Versions of Sustainability in Light of Climate Change." *diacritics* 40, no. 3 (2013): 40–57.

Sumner, David Thomas. "Don't Forget to Argue: Problems, Possibilities, and Ecocomposition." In Weisser and Dobrin, eds., *Ecocomposition*, 265–81.

"Sustainability." Wesleyan College. Accessed August 28, 2016. http://www.wesleyancollege.edu/about/Sustainability.cfm.

"Sustainability Curriculum in Higher Education: A Call to Action." *Association for the Advancement of Sustainability in Higher Education*, 2010. http://wwwp.oakland.edu/Assets/upload/docs/AIS/Conference/2010_Documents_A_Call_to_Action.pdf.

Tate, Gary, and Amy Rupiper Taggart, Kurt Schick, and H. Brooke Hessler, eds. *A Guide to Composition Pedagogies*. 2nd ed. New York/Oxford: Oxford University Press, 2014.

Taylor, Hill. "Articulating Reform and the Hegemony Game." *Workplace: A Journal for Academic Labor* 10 (2003): 115–22.

Taylor, L. Hill Jr., and Robert J. Helfenbein. "Mapping Everyday: Gender, Blackness, and Discourse in Urban Contexts." *Educational Studies: Journal of the American Educational Studies Association* 45, no. 3 (2009): 319–29.

Thomashow, Mitchell. *Ecological Identity: Becoming a Reflective Environmentalist*. Cambridge, MA: MIT, 1995.

Thoreau, Henry David. *Walden*. The Thoreau Reader. http://thoreau.eserver.org/walden00.html.

———, and Bradley P. Dean. *Faith in a Seed: The Dispersion of Seeds and Other Late Natural History Writings*. Washington, D.C.: Island Press/Shearwater Books, 1993.

Timberg, Scott. "The Novel That Predicted Portland." *New York Times*, December 12, 2008. Accessed August 22, 2016. http://www.nytimes.com/2008/12/14/fashion/14ecotopia.html?_r=0.

Trimbur, John, Robert G. Wood, Ron Strickland, William H. Thelin, William J. Rouster, Toni Mester, and Maxine Hairston. "Responses to Maxine Hairston: 'Diversity, Ideology, and Teaching Writing.'" *College Composition and Communication* 44, no. 2 (May 1993): 248–56.

Tuan, Yi-Fu. *Topophilia: A Study of Environmental Perception, Attitudes and Values*. 1972. A facsimile of the first edition with a new preface by the author. New York: Columbia University Press, 2013.

UNESCO. *Educating for a Sustainable Future: A Transdisciplinary Vision for Concerted Action*. November 1997. http://www.unesco.org/education/tlsf/mods/theme_a/popups/mod01t05s01.html.

"Use Our Methods." Stanford University. Accessed September 10, 2016. https://d.school.stanford.edu/use-our-methods/.
Van Norden, Bryan W. *Introduction to Classical Chinese Philosophy*. Indianapolis: Hackett Pub., 2011.
Västfjäll, Daniel, Paul Slovic, Marcus Mayorga, and Ellen Peters. "Compassion Fade: Affect and Charity Are Greatest for a Single Child in Need." *PLoS One* 9, no. 6 (June 2014): e100115, 1–10. https://doi.org/10.1371/journal.pone.0100115.
Waage, Frederick, ed. *Teaching Environmental Literature: Materials, Methods, Resources*. New York: MLA, 1985.
Waddell, Craig, ed. *Landmark Essays on Rhetoric and the Environment*. Mahwah, NJ: Lawrence Erlbaum Associates, Inc., 1998.
Wallace, David Foster. "Consider the Lobster." *Gourmet*, August 2004. Scan available at http://www.columbia.edu/~col8/lobsterarticle.pdf.
Wals, Arjen E. J., and Bob Jickling. "'Sustainability' in Higher Education: From Doublethink and Newspeak to Critical Thinking and Meaningful Learning." *International Journal of Sustainability in Higher Education* 3, no. 3 (2002): 221–32.
Warburton, Kevin. "Deep Learning and Education for Sustainability." *International Journal of Sustainability in Higher Education* 4, no. 1 (2003): 44–56.
Watkins, Matthew. "Law Allows More College Credits for High Schoolers." *The Texas Tribune*, June 19, 2015.
Watson, Burton, translator. *Chuang Tzu Basic Writings*. New York: Columbia University, 1964.
Watson, Kenneth Greg. "Chief Seattle." *History Link*, January 18, 2003. http://www.historylink.org/index.cfm?DisplayPage=output.cfm&file_id=5071&PlayID=34.
Wei, Henry. *The Authentic I-ching: A New Translation with Commentary*. North Hollywood, CA: Newcastle Pub., 1987.
Weisser, Christian R. and Sidney I. Dobrin. "Breaking New Ground in Ecocomposition: An Introduction." In Weisser and Dobrin, eds., *Ecocomposition*, 1–9.
———, eds. *Ecocomposition: Theoretical and Pedagogical Approaches*. Albany: State University Press of New York, 2001.
Weissman, Neil B. "Sustainability and Liberal Education: Partners by Nature." *Liberal Education*, 98, no. 4 (2012). https://www.aacu.org/publications-research/periodicals/sustainability-liberal-education-partners-nature.
Welty, Eudora. "Place in Fiction." In *On Writing*, 39–60. 1978; repr., London: Random House, 2011.
Whitman, Walt. "This Compost!" In *The Walt Whitman Archive*, edited by Ed Folsom and Kenneth M. Price, *accessed August 29, 2016*. http://whitmanarchive.org/published/LG/1871/poems/170.
Williams, Raymond. *Marxism and Literature. Marxist Introductions*. Oxford, England: Oxford University Press, 1977.
Wilson, Edward O. *Biophilia*. 1984; repr., Cambridge, MA: Harvard University Press, 2003.
———. "Biophilia and the Conservation Ethic." In *The Biophilia Hypothesis*, edited by Stephen R Kellert and Edward O Wilson. Washington, D.C.: Island Press, 1993.
———. *The Future of Life*. New York: Alfred A. Knopf, 2002.

Wolf, William J. *Thoreau: Mystic, Prophet, Ecologist*. Philadelphia: United Church Press, 1974.
Wolfe, Cary. *What Is Posthumanism?* Minneapolis: University of Minnesota Press, 2009.
Wood, Nigel, and David Lodge. *Modern Criticism and Theory: A Reader*. 3rd ed. New York: Pearson Education Limited, 2008.
World Commission on Environment and Development (WCED). *Our Common Future*. Oxford: Oxford University Press, 1987.
Wright, Alexis. *Plains of Promise*. St. Lucia, Brisbane: University of Queensland Press, 1997.
Wu, John C. H. *Lao Tzu: Tao Teh Ching*. New York: St. John's University Press, 1961.
Yagelski, Robert P. *Writing as a Way of Being: Writing Instruction, Nonduality, and the Crisis of Sustainability*. New York: Hampton Press, 2011.
Yancy, Kathleen B. "Cultures, Contexts, Images, and Texts: Materials for a New Age of Meaning-Making." *South Atlantic Review* 33 (Winter 2013): 1–12.
Yona, Sipos, Bryce Battisti, and Kurt Grimm. "Achieving Transformative Sustainability Learning: Engaging Head, Hands and Heart." *International Journal of Sustainability in Higher Education* 9, no. 1 (2008): 68–86.
Yu, Kam-por, Julia Lai Po-Wah Tao, and P. J. Ivanhoe. *Taking Confucian Ethics Seriously: Contemporary Theories and Applications*. Albany: State University of New York Press, 2010.
Zapf, Hubert. "Literary Ecology and the Ethics of Texts." *New Literary History* 39, no. 4 (2009): 847–68.
———. "The State of Ecocriticism and the Function of Literature as Cultural Ecology." In *Nature in Literary and Cultural Studies: Transatlantic Conversations in Ecocriticism*, edited by Catrin Gersdorf and Sylvia Mayer, 49–70. Amsterdam: Rodolpi, 2006.
Zencey, Eric. "The Rootless Professors." In *Rooted in The Land: Essays on Community and Place,* edited by Wes Jackson and William Vitek, 15–19. New Haven: Yale University Press, 1996.
"Zhuangzi." BrainyQuote.com. Xplore Inc, 2014. http://www.brainyquote.com/quotes/authors/z/zhuangzi.html.
Zhuangzi Says. Wise Men Talking Series. Beijing: Sinolingua, 2006.

Index

AASHE. *See* Association for the Advancement of Sustainability in Higher Education
American Indian, 151, 153, 160, 163, 166, 167
Anderson, Benedict, 33
Association for the Advancement of Sustainability in Higher Education (AASHE), 21, 179

Beavan, Colin, 59, 89, 90, 100, 109, 110, 112–13
Berry, Wendell, 61, 66, 72, 83, 161
binaries, 133, 134, 137, 139, 144
The Brundtland Report, 175, 178, 179, 184, 185, 186

Callenbach, Ernest, 32–36, 40, 42, 43–45
climate change, 1, 29, 56, 60, 69, 102, 151, 166, 175, 177
compassion fade, 116
consumerism, 78, 95, 97, 98, 101, 108, 112, 130, 176, 179
creative writing, 67, 129, 131–32, 135–37, 144, 146–47
critical geography, 41

The Dao De Jing, 151–52, 154–60, 162–68, 170
dialogue, 132, 135, 142
design thinking (DT), 116–25, 126–28
Dillard, Annie, 21, 24, 25–26, 61, 68
Dobrin, Sidney, 1, 29, 30, 60, 61, 115, 129, 141, 176, 179–80, 182, 183, 192–93, 194n13

ecocomposition: concept and usage of, 29–30, 60–61, 176, 177, 179–84, 190–91, 193; and curriculum, 30, 179–84, 194n13
Ecocomposition: Theoretical and Pedagogical Approaches, 1, 29, 176
ecocriticism, 45, 129–33, 135, 140, 142, 145–46, 147–49, 194n9
eco-identity. *See* identity
Ecotopia. See Callenbach, Ernest
empathy, 44, 116–20, 122, 126
experiential learning, 89, 90, 94, 111–12. *See also* sustainability and First-year Composition, and experiential learning

First Peoples. *See* American Indian
Freire, Paulo, 181

high-impact pedagogy, 89, 90, 93, 100, 102, 109–10, 111–13
human, 7, 10–11, 16–19, 21, 24, 47, 66, 78, 85, 99, 101, 103, 111–12, 118, 127, 131–39, 142, 143, 144, 145, 146, 147, 151–54, 156, 163, 165, 168, 178–79

identity, 18, 30, 33–34, 41–42, 89, 94–96, 98–100, 102, 103, 111, 112, 134, 137
imagination, 45–46, 133, 143
interconnectedness, 58, 101, 133, 151–53, 155, 164, 167, 171, 173, 178, 183, 190
interdisciplinary, 21, 62, 68, 90, 117, 170, 177, 184, 192

language, 10, 18, 31, 34, 46, 51, 56, 70, 76, 90, 94, 111–12, 124, 131, 134, 142, 144, 145, 146, 147, 156–58, 164, 170, 179–81, 185
local food, 91, 94–96, 97, 105, 108, 109, 110
local knowledge, 181–83, 189–90, 191

Mezirow, Jack, 92–93, 94, 95–96, 99, 100, 101, 102, 104, 107, 108, 109–11

nonhuman, 131–39, 142, 144, 145–46, 176, 179

open pedagogy, 181, 190, 195n30
Orr, David, 85, 178, 183, 187, 193n4
Owens, Derek, 61–62, 115, 176, 178, 179, 180, 181, 182, 183, 184, 185

pastoral, 139, 140, 170
place-based writing, 22, 29, 31, 63–64, 69–73, 130, 142–46, 191
places, 36, 38, 40–42, 46, 63, 67–68, 71–73, 83–84, 139, 141, 143, 144, 180
Plumwood, Val, 133–34
Portland, Oregon, 31–42, 44–45

post-process theory, 180, 182, 184
project-based learning, 177, 192

Rasula, Jed, 10–11, 12
reflective writing, 35, 89–93, 96, 109–13, 124–25

service learning, 176, 181, 182
setting, 64, 66, 84, 135, 137, 139, 141–44, 153
shared rubrics, 57, 63, 125–27
shared writing assignments, 117, 120, 124–25
Soper, Kate, 137, 138, 141
The Stanford d.school, 117
STEAM courses, 152
strategies, 29, 35, 55, 58, 61, 68, 71–72, 118, 133, 134, 135, 137, 138, 139, 144, 146
sustainability: in American literature, 10–21, 184, 185, 188; campus office for, 19, 55, 74, 78, 81, 82; campus support for, 55–56, 61, 74–75, 78, 81; campus tour for, 51, 67, 74, 78–80, 83; critiques of, 175, 176, 177, 178, 179, 180, 184, 186, 187, 188, 189; and curriculum, 22, 61–62, 113, 129, 178, 183, 193n4; defined, 17–21, 53, 66; economic, 17, 20, 53, 94–103, 112, 113, 118; in higher education, 20, 21, 90, 178, 179, 183, 186, 193n4; initiatives, 10, 69, 73, 177, 183, 184, 185, 186, 188, 189–90, 191, 192; and narrative, 51, 62, 63–64, 77, 83–85, 132–33, 137, 141, 143; pillars of, 89, 91, 93, 94, 101, 111, 112; social/cultural, 17, 20, 22, 42–43, 53, 69, 89, 97, 98, 101, 103–9, 111–13
sustainability education, 90, 93–94, 99–101, 109, 112, 115, 161
sustainability and First-year Composition (FYC), 8, 58–59, 77, 115; as course topic, 53, 54, 115–17; ePortfolios with, 66, 72;

and experiential learning, 74, 76, 80, 82, 89–90, 112, 120; goals and standards of, 57, 58, 66; multimodal assignments with, 35, 41, 72, 78, 80; reading assignments with, 33, 71, 72, 76–77, 80, 82, 137, 153, 188–89; syllabus development for, 56, 61–63, 68, 69, 75, 85, 170; student comments about, 54, 65, 66, 70, 71–73, 78, 82, 91, 96, 108; student writing samples from, 80, 81, 82; teacher training for, 67, 69, 83, 85, 116; textbooks for, 59–61; writing assignments with, 47, 63–66, 69–70, 71–72, 77, 78, 79–80, 120–27; writing program administration for, 52, 56–58, 85

Thomashow, Mitchell, 94, 99, 111
Thoreau, Henry David, 10–12, 16–21, 22, 59, 61, 161, 188
Tiffin, Helen, 132, 134, 143
transformative learning, 90, 92, 93, 100, 102, 105, 107, 109–13
translation, 56, 154, 156–57, 158, 162–63, 165, 168
transportation, 35–36, 38–39, 91, 103–6, 110

urbanization, 39
utopia(n), 29, 30, 31, 40, 44–45, 46–47

wanwu, 151, 162, 165, 170
Weisser, Christian, 1, 29, 59–60, 61, 129, 160, 176, 179–81, 183, 192, 194n13
Whitman, Walt, 12–14, 17, 20, 24
writing across the curriculum, 30, 61, 113
writing intensive pedagogy, 61, 90, 93, 109, 111, 112, 113, 152, 176–78, 180
Wu, John C. H., 162, 166, 168–69

Yagelski, Robert, 176, 179, 180, 181, 183
The Yijing, 151, 155–56, 163, 165

About the Contributors

Ron Balthazor, PhD, is an academic professional at the University of Georgia. He teaches composition and environmental literature and is the lead developer of the Emma project, a web application for writing. His scholarship has appeared in *Portal*, *The Journal of General Education*, *Readerly/Writerly Texts*, *Literary and Linguistic Computing*, *Kairos*, and *ATQ*. His continuing interests include environmental literature, Thoreau, PHP, Symfony (a web application development platform), honey bees, chickens, worms, and the rich ecosystem of the backyard garden. He serves on the Office of Sustainability's committee for the integration of sustainability in the curriculum at UGA and is the director of UGA's Sustainability Certificate.

Joanne Chu, PhD, director of EcoEthos Solutions, works with leaders and teams to solve their most intractable problems using human-centered approaches. Her practice helps mission-driven organizations achieve greater real-world impact. She has helped several higher education institutions and K–12 schools deepen their ability to deliver their sustainability commitments. She is a graduate of the Institute for Georgia Environmental Leadership and received her PhD in behavioral neuroscience from the University of Texas.

Deborah Church Miller, PhD, is the associate director of First-year Composition (FYC) at the University of Georgia. She earned a BS in wildlife biology from Purdue University and later an MA and PhD in medieval literature and rhetoric/composition from the University of Georgia. Miller oversees day-to-day administration and management of a large First-Year Composition program at the University of Georgia—including ninety or more instructors, lecturers, and graduate teaching assistants and approximately six thousand students each year. She also develops curricula for FYC and upper-division writing courses and regularly teaches first-year composition, advanced composition, composition theory and pedagogy, and the graduate teaching practicum.

Abby L. Goode, PhD, is an assistant professor of English at Plymouth State University. Currently, she is writing a book about the history of sustainability, agriculture, and population control in American literature. Her research appears in venues such as *Early American Literature*, *Studies in American Fiction*, *ESQ: A Journal of Nineteenth-Century American Literature and Culture*, and *American Studies in Scandinavia*. She teaches courses in American literature, critical theory, wilderness literature, writing and sustainability, and American food issues.

Lesley Hawkes, PhD, is an associate professor in creative writing and literary studies at Queensland University of Technology, Brisbane, Qld, Australia. She teaches across a range of units ranging from literary theory to Shakespeare. Her teaching focuses on practical application of theoretical concerns and she uses creative writing to build awareness of key concepts. Her main areas of research are environmental studies and literature, spatial understanding as it relates to literature, and Australian literature.

Pamela Herron is a poet, writer, and educator. Her areas of research include Confucianism and Daoism and how they apply in the modern world; China and Chinese immigration, particularly in the El Paso/Ciudad Juarez area; the importance and diversity of cultural identity; sustainability; and writing and teaching literature for young readers. She regularly presents in both the United States and China, particularly on Confucianism and gender along with multicultural issues. She is committed to a multicultural approach in all aspects of learning. She coordinated the Chinese Language Program for UTEP Languages and Linguistics through the Confucius Institute under the International and Border Programs at New Mexico State University in Las Cruces, New Mexico. Her book of poetry is *En l'air: A collection of poems created in the air*. Her poems and flash fiction have appeared in various journals as have her reviews of poetry and films. *Border Passage: Growing up in Chinatown of El Paso, Texas at the turn of the Twentieth Century* was her first historic fiction, and she recently published *Exploring Ancient China* for young readers. She is currently working on a new collection of poetry written while traveling in China. When she isn't writing, you may find her reading, gardening, or tending chickens in her North Bay California home.

Joseph R. Lease, PhD, is an associate professor and department chair of English at Wesleyan College in Macon, Georgia. He was awarded a Presidential Fellowship and received his PhD from the University of Georgia, and he also earned an MAT from Duke University with a concentration in secondary English. His research interests include twentieth-century American and British literature, action theory and hero studies, and sustainability and pedagogy. Among his sustainability-themed efforts, Dr. Lease co-presented "Design Thinking & Sustainability Problem Solving: Reconceptualizing the First-Year Curriculum" at AASHE in Portland, Oregon, and he organized and chaired the panel "Sustainability in/and Writing Intensive Courses" at SAMLA in Atlanta, Georgia.

Matthew R. Martin, PhD, is the director of Academic Programs at the South Carolina Governor's School for Science and Mathematics. He received his PhD from the University of Virginia after attending Oxford University on a Rhodes Scholarship. He has been a Governor's Teaching Fellow and taught in Lithuania as a Fulbright Fellow. His research interests include southern literature and African American literature.

Justin Rademaekers, PhD, is an associate professor of English at West Chester University of Pennsylvania. Dr. Rademaekers specializes in rhetoric and composition, writing across the curriculum, the rhetoric of science, and environmental rhetoric. He holds a bachelor's degree in environmental science and spent some years working as a biologist aide and environmental compliance technician before earning his master's degree in writing studies from Saint Joseph's University and a PhD in English from Purdue University. Dr. Rademaekers has published work on environmental rhetoric in venues such as the *Journal of Technical Writing and Communication*, *Across the Disciplines*, and *The WAC Journal*. He speaks regularly about environmental education in the English classroom at national and international conferences including the Association for the Study of Literature and the Environment, the National Council for Teachers of English, the Rhetoric Society of America, and the Conference on Communication and the Environment.

Hill Taylor, Ph.D., is academic dean and chief academic officer at the American College of Healthcare Sciences in Portland, Oregon. Previously, Dr. Taylor was an assistant professor at Oregon Health & Science University, where he taught health humanities courses and directed the Office of Learning Support in the OHSU School of Nursing. Dr. Taylor has also taught composition courses at Portland Community College. Dr. Taylor's research focuses on uses and applications of multimodal reflective journaling. Dr. Taylor uses tenets of ecopsychology as a means for student reflection and impetus for composition in the writing process.

Lindsay Tigue, MFA, is a doctoral student in English and creative writing at the University of Georgia and a graduate of the master of fine arts program in creative writing and environment at Iowa State University. She is the author of the poetry collection *System of Ghosts*, winner of the 2015 Iowa Poetry Prize and published by the University of Iowa Press in 2016. She specializes in twentieth-century American Literature, ecofeminism, and the literature of place. She also writes poetry and fiction and her work appears in *Prairie Schooner*, *Hollins Critic,* and *Hayden's Ferry Review,* among other journals. She has taught sustainability-centered writing courses at both Iowa State University and the University of Georgia.

Cheryl Wanko, PhD, is a professor of English at West Chester University of Pennsylvania. Dr. Wanko specializes in the history of theatrical culture and drama in the long eighteenth century and is the author of *Roles of Authority: Thespian Biography and Celebrity in 18th-Century Britain* (2003). Following a midlife career reassessment, she has begun studying environmental rhetoric and ecocriticism, and she presented on efforts to promote sustainability via student advising at the Association for the Study of Literature and the Environment conference in 2015. She is also actively involved in campus service and administration in efforts related to sustainability.

Kim Waters, MA, MBA, MHA, is a doctoral candidate in linguistics at the University of Georgia in Athens. Her dissertation focuses on listener attitudes about "southernness" in both African American and European American speech. Other research interests include endangered languages and creoles, especially two native to her home state of Georgia, Cherokee and Gullah-Geechee, both cultures profoundly rooted in place. Financial support for her research has come from several UGA entities, including: Willson Center for Humanities and Arts (research grant); The Graduate School (Innovative and Interdisciplinary research grant); R. Baxter Miller Graduate Award for excellence in the study and scholarship of African American and Multicultural literature. Kim was also a member of the inaugural cohort of Diversity and Inclusion Graduate Fellows. As a teaching assistant in the English department, Kim taught in the first year composition program under Dr. Deborah Church Miller. Incorporating sustainability as a topic for student research seemed a natural transition from her grassroots approach to linguistic inquiry. She has taken great satisfaction from outcomes related to personal growth in her students as they come to understand that a good planet *is* hard to find and there is no Planet B. The lesson is: *we must all do what we can to protect and preserve the planet we have.*

www.ingramcontent.com/pod-product-compliance
Lightning Source LLC
Chambersburg PA
CBHW070829300426
44111CB00014B/2500